"Kevin's story was no secret to me. Reading it made my heart bleed. This memoir is memorable; it is a gripping narrative, a detective novel told with a congenial and deceptive simplicity. The description of addiction—the cravings, bad decisions, withdrawal, and the endless drug seeking and general life chaos, the desperation and despair—tore through me, reminded me, terrified me. The search for family, the need for connection, for finding faces that mirror your own, was deeply familiar to me. And Oh the places one can go that Dr. Seuss could not begin to imagine, and yet to begin to imagine that one could, ever-so-slowly, climb out from the pit of shame and revulsion. It is not simply a story of redemption; it is a vivid tale of the fall."

—Arlene Lev, author, clinical social worker, family therapist, and educator

DEAR STEPHEN MICHAEL'S MOTHER

A MEMOIR

KEVIN BARHYDT

S.M. WAGUESPACK PUBLISHING

DEAR STEPHEN MICHAEL'S MOTHER

Published in the United States by S.M. Waguespack Publishing, Schenectady, NY, 2020.
ISBN: 978-1-7357600-0-1

Cover Design by Doug Bartow

Printed in the USA

First Edition

To My Mothers
Betty and Virginia

CONTENTS

AUTHOR'S NOTE

My goal has been to be clear and honest about my life, except when doing so might injure others. In that spirit I have changed names while working to preserve my original objectives, and a commitment to quality and integrity. I am proud that you as a reader will experience my truths, however, the story, the experiences, and the words are the author's alone.

PROLOGUE

LEARNING

DEEP BREATH IN.

*B*etty Ann's oldest brother, Francis, died in a hospital in New Orleans, his liver completely pickled, shortly after Hurricane Katrina ripped through the coast in 2005. The second oldest, Steve, a heroin addict, lives in Yuma, Arizona. Steve recently got out of a halfway house. The only drugs he takes now are prescribed for bipolar disorder and depression. The youngest brother, Bob, is a happy-go-lucky beer drinker, still living in New Orleans.

Betty Ann was okay for the most part, as long as she took her medications. Without them, she might be found in the garage, lining up hundreds of empty milk cartons for tomato plants. She lived on a horse ranch, and they didn't grow tomatoes.

Betty Ann was my mother.

I have never met any of these people.

EXHALE.

JUNE 1962

They drive to Canada early in the morning along the Northway, leaving Schenectady, New York, with a letter, a prayer, their plea for grace, all that they have left to try. Even after doctors tell them it isn't their fault they can't conceive a child, they hold on to their grief.

Abused by an overbearing, cold, and deeply unhappy German mother, my father struggles against the broken youth now reflected in an impotency beyond his endurance. The years of undiagnosed depression, made tolerable by beer, cigarettes, and sheer will, now have a home, where all the voices claiming him as weak are waiting to drag him down into a comforting despair.

Almost a year and a half earlier, he had fainted on the job in Manhattan. They said it was his nerves. Telling a man in 1960 that he fainted because of his nerves was like hanging a sign around his neck declaring that he wasn't a man at all. Without knowing about his depression, and years before the real cause of his malady would be revealed, the doctors treated him with little white, yellow, and blue pills. Valium was a hell of a way to settle your nerves.

After six months, my mother got a dog so my father would leave the house to walk him. Major became my father's therapy dog, and my mother went back to work. The stress of having to work on top of caring for him was both frustrating and frightening for her, but how she did love my father. She had married him—Herbert John Barhydt Jr., this blond-haired, blue-eyed James Dean look-alike, high school baseball and football star, World War II and Korean War veteran, General Electric manager who was first in his family to graduate from college—with every intention of being the good Polish wife she found so perfectly displayed in her own mother and grandmother, the ideal blend of strength and joy and warmth and heart. Mostly heart.

My mother and father were blessed by family roots in New York. Virginia was a Sendzicki, and her father had been forced to serve in the army under the Russian Cossacks. After escaping the terrorists on horseback, he made his way to the New World. Processed at Ellis Island with nothing but the clothes on his back, he had the deep belief that he could master this new language and serve loyally in his new community.

When my mother took on the Barhydt name, she knew those roots went deep. The Dutch-German Barhydts had made their mark on the local community as farmers, pharmacists, and a mayor. One Barhydt had even married an Indian princess, or so the story goes.

As Roman Catholics, my parents believe that God holds the strings to their lives, and the key to their happiness. They also know that God listens to His saints, and no local saint is more adored and trusted than the mother of Mary, Jesus' grandmother, Saint Anne.

The Basilica of Sainte-Anne-de-Beaupré in Québec, Canada, is a complete tourist trap, the inside architecture as overwhelming and blunt as its outer layer, but the immense structure holds one small anointed worth. At the front of the main sanctuary, off to the side, an artifact said to be part of the wrist bone of the blessed grandmother sits under glass, where the ill and infirm, the hated and those full of self-hatred, cluster with the families of those who need healing, begging for intervention with a God they fear.

Every year since 1954 my parents have joined the pilgrimage, pleading for the key to their future happiness, the salvation of their marriage.

JULY 2005

"Nice ink," David said, pulling long on his smoke.

"Thanks." I meant it, too. A cool tattoo is always a good conversation starter.

"Where'd ya get it?"

"Tommy Spaulding in Albany." I pulled up my sleeve to show the whole design, a snake coiled around a dagger with a bright red rose in the middle.

David poked a finger at my skin. "Looks fresh still."

I nodded, smiling. "Tommy's colors are amazing."

David took another long drag on the smoke, stubbed out the glowing cherry tip, and flicked it into the street. "When?"

"Early 20s."

"Military?"

"No. Well, yeah, was in the Navy, but got this after I got out."

"How long were you in for?"

"Signed up for three. Lasted eighteen months."

"Really . . ."

"Uh huh. Not a good fit."

"Where were you stationed?"

"Maine. Deployed to Okinawa and Spain."

David looked at me for a long, few seconds. "Not a good fit. Huh."

The truck was packed. The guys lounged, sweating and smoking, glad for the respite, the same men who'd moved us from Prospect Heights to Sunset Park just a year ago. David, the leader and driver, counted the three-hundred-dollar tip I gave him and passed it out. Everyone was happy.

David lit up another and offered me and the others a cigarette. A few of the guys grabbed one. If I'd ever start smoking again, thinking about returning to Schenectady would be the catalyst.

"No thanks."

David inhaled deeply, smiled, tilted his head back to blow the smoke out slow and easy. "Why move to Schenectady?"

"Born there. Been living in Brooklyn for fifteen years."

"So, you're going back home. That's cool."

"Not going back," I said. He probed my eyes, and I returned the stare. Something inside twitched my lips into a small, stupid grin. "Can't go back to what's not there."

"Gonna make some new memories?"

I backed up a step and nodded.

He sized me up now: a five-foot-eight, 170-pound, forty-two-year-old white boy from upstate New York. My smile broadened and he cocked his head as if to say, "Don't give me no shit, boy."

"You don't want to know, Dave." I laughed out loud. "You really don't even want to know."

David nodded, turned away, and headed to the truck. "No shit."

I laughed again. "No shit."

JUNE 1962

In Schenectady, Betty Ann writes her own plea. Every tear she refused to cry for nine months pours out of her. Two pages long, addressed to strangers she will never meet, unsigned.

To Stephen Michael's Mother...

1

LEAVING

JULY 2005

*T*here is only one way to leave Brooklyn, but Eri and I found two.

We both had our own cars, and as would fit our personalities, we also had our own favorite way to leave the true heart of New York City. On this sunny blue-sky day, leaving the place we had never thought to leave, Eri took the Brooklyn Bridge to the FDR, and I rolled up the BQE to the Tri-Borough Bridge. I was cruising at fifty-five when my cell phone rang. Eri never made it out of Brooklyn. She had a flat tire and was stopped in traffic on the Manhattan side of the Brooklyn Bridge. I made it to her car in ten minutes, by which time a tow truck driver had pulled over, set up flares, unloaded the back of Eri's Subaru Forester including our television, changed the flat, and was loading the last of the boxes back into the car. We stood there, looking back at Brooklyn and laughing. Even her car didn't want to leave. That's the power of the borough. That's the power of home and family ties.

Family is forged in Brooklyn by will. Extended sisters and brothers, uncles and aunts and cousins, found in church and daycare, at the Food

Co-op and in Prospect Park. Eating dim-sum in Chinatown and sharing coffee on Seventh Avenue. Saturday family breakfast of banana-walnut pancakes at Tom's Diner. We molded our hearts to the cracks of the broken sidewalks, and Brooklyn made us her own.

We had a lot of favorites when it comes to Brooklyn. "Believe the hype" was my favorite slogan. The Williamsburg Savings Bank building was our family favorite, and very personal, landmark. We had all walked over the Brooklyn Bridge, where pictures of the kids and the city set the tempo for our smiles. Some families measured time as their children grew by making hash marks on the doorframe. We had the Manhattan skyline. Some pictures focused on the bridge, some on the skyline. Many included the Twin Towers. All of them will always mean the world to us.

Leaving Brooklyn knocked the wind out of us all, each in our own way kicked in the gut. The boys were so different. Ever since he was born, it was obvious that Tyler was a lot like his dad. Reaching for the highest highs and crashing hard when the bottom fell out, he grabbed life with wild-eyed optimism. It's easy to imagine Tyler tumbling and screaming and laughing in the wind of a Pamplona-style bull run, and if the bulls got him, oh well, that's life. But when he left Brooklyn, there were no bulls chasing him, only some big house on a new street to look forward to. Tyler didn't know how to adjust to the unknown, so naturally he fell into the warm embrace of denial, just like his dad. "We're only three hours away." "We'll go back every month." "All our friends will come up to visit." His eyes lit up just like mine as we echoed each other's hopes and dreams.

Kentaro, our "Healthy Intelligent (ken) First Son (taro)," is more of a realist. Kentaro had always been the easy kid, rolling with the waves. When Kentaro was a toddler, Eri and the other Japanese moms would get together to teach the kids the language with simple games from their own childhood. Little words mean so much when you are little. Nai-Nai-Bah was the equivalent of Peek-a-Boo. Oh-ee-de is important to know if you want your friends to hurry. Su-wa-te instructs your audience to sit down and pay close attention. But when the lessons were over and the mothers sat at the kitchen table, happily drinking tea and eating gently sweetened pastry, the kids found their own way in the living room. As long as they played well together, the moms enjoyed their break from speaking in monosyllables. But eventually, the children's attention would wear thin and the moms' fragile shell of childlessness cracked as the living room devolved into screams and shouts and fists of fury. The mothers would rise as one, each scanning the playing field first for injuries, then for her own child, and Eri always found Kentaro on the sidelines, quietly holding on to some toy, his own eyes on the scene as if watching a snake pit from above. He gained his first of many nicknames in that group: Owji Sama, the Prince. As we settled into Brooklyn, he lived up to that name, and then some. On leaving Brooklyn, he hoped to keep in touch with his friends, but also knew enough to say proper goodbyes.

I made the short trip out of Manhattan over the George Washington Bridge, on the Palisades Parkway through New Jersey, and headed upstate on the long stretch of the New York State Thruway. My mind was spinning, remembering the conversation at lunch that had sucker-punched me.

In my last week at the Fashion Institute of Technology, my boss and friend Roz Pier told me with a sense of urgency and foreboding seriousness, "We have to talk. We have something in common. Kevin . . . I'm a birth mother."

I felt the wires in my brain crossing, short-circuiting my ability to hide my emotions.

She looked straight across the table at me, her eyes sad and intense but unwavering. "I had twins."

"I understand," was all I could muster.

"I gave them up at birth."

I mentally rewound through the two years we worked together.

"I remember. You asked if I had brothers or sisters, and I said I didn't know."

"Yes." She knew she'd hit a nerve, waited while I processed what was happening.

I had a hard time looking her in the eye. My breath came fast and shallow, and I felt my heart begin to race.

"Okay."

Everything was distinctly not okay.

"Are you sure?"

A strange anger I'd never allowed myself to feel before swept through me, mixed with a sadness that I knew all too well.

"Yes."

I tried not to let the hurt show in my eyes.

"I searched for my children. I found them both."

As I listened, I pushed the pain and sadness to the side, reminded myself that this was Roz, someone I know and trust. The same person who'd cared enough to help me find the new job upstate, and she was trying to help me again.

I saw heartache in her eyes, the heaviness of guilt and pain stooping her shoulders, her head drooping.

"It wasn't easy to find them, and it's still not easy."

"I'm sorry."

"My daughter is open to talking, but my son, Noah, doesn't want to hurt his adoptive parents."

She knew the words reflected my own fears. I didn't—don't—want to hurt my parents. They're not perfect, but they do love me.

"Kevin, this is my story, but it doesn't have to turn out that way for you."

I twisted my fingers in a knot, trying to hold myself together.

"Roz, I don't know what to say. I never felt like this."

"Felt what?"

"I don't know. I feel like . . . I think I know how Noah feels."

"You hate me."

"I don't think he hates you. I know I don't."

As I watched her, something in me shifted. The feelings didn't go away, didn't dissipate, but instead spread into dark recesses of my mind, touching raw nerves and bringing old memories to life.

"I think Noah loves you. You're his mother."

Tears slid down her cheeks, but her hands sat in her lap, frozen. We had changed now, became surrogates. It had happened too fast for either of us, but once here we couldn't go back.

I raised my eyes to her tear-filled ones, to speak the words she longed to hear from her own son.

"I love you." The thought came from Noah, but the words were from deep within own my past.

"But you're afraid."

"I'm afraid I'll hurt my parents. That you won't love me. I'm afraid if I love you, you'll leave me. Again."

Roz blinked through the tears. "Thank you."

A smile stole over my face, as new, unnamed feelings melted through the old fears. "I do love you. I've always loved you."

"I think about you all the time. Every day of my life, I've thought about my children."

"Then why . . . ?"

"My family made it impossible to keep you."

Behind her eyes, I began to see my own mother's grief, poised to explode, to shatter the tension between us. She straightened in her chair, hefting an almost visible weight.

"Every year I relive that decision."

Roz saw the trembling of my body, but I wasn't afraid, just overwhelmed.

"Kevin, have you ever searched for your mother?"

I shook my head, trying to calm my mind. "I tried once, but I never heard anything."

"She may feel guilt and shame. A lot of us do."

Before I met Roz, I had never spoken to another birth mother. She had opened a door.

"Kevin, you have enough on your mind right now, with the job and the move. But if you ever want to search for your mother, I'm here if you want my help. I'll support you."

"Thank you."

"You don't have to rush. Part of the process of searching is becoming ready to search."

The door was open, waiting for me to walk through it.

"Kevin, I don't know why she gave you up, but I know how she felt that day. I don't believe that she doesn't want you. I want you to know, your mother loved you."

I wasn't ready to walk through the door yet, but I was willing to leave it open.

JULY 1962

Herbert and Virginia return from their pilgrimage and receive the call that they have waited and prayed for, the call that will forever change their lives. A lawyer and a judge are involved, and papers have to be signed, but everything is in order.

A few weeks later, along with a one-page note describing his sleeping habits, bottle formula, quiet disposition, and bodily functions, a baby boy is handed over to his new, and very proud, parents.

As chance would have it, that same day the local newspaper interviews the adoption agency's director for a feature story. A baby boy just processed for adoption makes a fine picture, so my first day with my new parents is also my introduction to the news media. It won't be the last time I make the papers.

Born in Schenectady, I'm taken home to Rotterdam, New York. My mother was the only girl of four children, and after many years of watching her brothers start families, she finally has a son of her own. It's a time of great joy, of holding a boy who bears no resemblance to anyone they will ever know and pouring more love into him than they imagine possible.

For my father, it's a time beyond all other times. He was always a boy among boys, a southpaw baseball pitcher and a star football player. Now he is more than a boy and more than a man. He is a father. But not like his father. His child will never see a belt as a weapon; his child will be loved and hugged and will hear music and song and voices of joy. Herbert had married a woman the opposite of his mother, and he would be a man the opposite of his own father.

Baptism is a priority. After a year, the judge signs the final paperwork, which puts the question of my renaming front and center. As a good Catholic entity, the agency had me baptized at birth, but now that

I'm a permanent part of my new family I will be known as Kevin. It's imperative that my new name also be recorded into the holy books.

I had almost been named Herbert John Barhydt III. My father liked his name, but everyone called him John to differentiate him from his father. I'm forever grateful to my parents for choosing Kevin as an acceptable substitute, although I sometimes wondered if they ended the lineage of Herbert because of the broken bloodline.

And so I'm rebaptized, and my name transcribed, documented, and sealed on official church parchment: Kevin John Barhydt.

JULY 2005

We closed on our house on June 13, and the contractor began renovations on our new eighty-five-year-old home. Eri took the boys to Japan for the summer to stay with her mom. While they were gone, I stayed at my parents' house, worked each day at my new job at Empire State College, and spent nights picking out new cabinets and appliances at Lowe's, or painting bedrooms at the house.

The best part of my day was driving to and from work. The peace and solitude of the forty-five-minute one-way trip offered relief from the tension and exhaustion that dominated the rest of my existence. Alan Chartock became my new best friend, his grating but familiar voice on NPR keeping me company every morning from Rotterdam to Saratoga Springs, and again to Niskayuna as the sun set.

I was back where I'd been born, where I had spent my childhood. The daily commute gave me time to think about that childhood, and about my lunch with Roz. Something had begun to tug at me, real and unmistakable. The door that Roz had pried open now manifested itself in my physical world. The door opened into a house I could see. And the house had a name I remembered.

Every evening when I left work, I walked past a row of old Saratoga houses, simple homes, Victorian homes, each with its own color scheme: sunny yellows, lime greens, ocean blues. Many of the houses were rentals for the horse-racing season, but one was a year-round business, a not-for-profit with over a century of historical ties to the community. I read the shingle every day as I left the office and walked to my car: Catholic Services.

The sign burned into my soul. I felt the insistent pull, heard a screaming in my heart and mind that I could not silence, and was no longer afraid. Now I wanted to know. To know who I was. To know who she was, this person who came here forty-three years ago to give me life. In 1962, it was called Catholic Family Charities. Now I crossed the street to stare at the sign, knowing that I wouldn't walk up to the door, not today, not yet. I had to get home, back to my life now. I had work to do, walls to paint and cabinets to measure and rugs to pick out.

Driving home every night, I thought of who I am, of who she is, of how amazing it would be to see her. What I would ask her, what I would tell her. What *will* I tell her? How could I tell her what happened to me since she held me so briefly and touched my face, since the last and only time she heard my voice?

Will it hurt her too much to hear my voice again? Will I tell her that all did not go as well as I must believe she hoped my life would? Can I risk hurting her like that? Will she hate me? Will she reject me . . . again? Can I take that risk? What will I say?

AGE TWO

Except for one frightening hour when I'm two, the first nine years of my life are by the book, unmarred by any trauma. Dad works while Mom stays at home, and their little gift from God grows into the quiet, gentle, happy little boy of their dreams. Dad's job takes him to Manhattan almost every other week, so Mom and I spend our days together, and weekends when Dad comes home are all about family. One summer weekend, General Electric has its annual company picnic at the Great Sacandaga Lake, a rustic and mostly blue-collar landscape dotted with campsites and boat launches. After lunch, the men hang around playing cards and drinking beer, while the women go off to share stories. After a half hour the wives wander back, smiling and laughing.

Mom looks around and back to my father. "Where's Kevin?"

"What do you mean, where's Kevin? He's with you."

"No, he went with you!"

Everything stops, pure panic ensues. The party is over. Everyone spreads out to search. Major, the family dog, loves the water, maybe Kevin went into the water. After thirty seconds, my mom and dad panic. After thirty minutes, they lose hope.

Halfway down to the lake, a woman finds a little boy walking alone, no more than two years old, and carries me to the local rangers. As the ranger rides up on his horse to hand down their gift from St. Anne, my parents' tears of joy mingle with self-doubt. How could they ever have let this happen? They should never have asked God for a gift they couldn't care for. That perhaps they did not deserve. That they were never meant to have.

Never again can they let me out of their sight. They want to protect me, to keep me safe from all harm, but protecting me will not be easy. After eight years of normal childhood, in my ninth year, normal takes a turn. I wander off to new and darker places, and less often am I found and returned safely.

AGE NINE

You don't remember how days like this begin, or what the weather is like. Lots of things blur through the lens of time and distance, even the season. It's funny not being able to remember any other days, though there must have been other days, other activities, other things the leader said and did. Some details stay sharp and clear for a long time, longer than you expect. Longer than you want.

It's during the school year, because 4-H isn't a summer thing. Not a daily event, or even weekly, but maybe several times in a house that belongs to our leader's parents. Sometimes his sister is there, mostly just hanging around in the living room.

The leader talks about cool things, answering even our personal questions. He tells us his number was so high that he missed the draft to Vietnam, but that he wouldn't have gone, would have moved to Canada.

This day, food is a big part of the memory. The smell and taste of brownies are entrenched deep in my memory. The leader's sister is there, at least at first, and gives us enough brownies to put nine-year-old boys on a sugar high for a week. Maybe the sugar creates these snapshots. Memories of being happy, of the taste and texture of brownies washed down with cold milk. A warm feeling inside, the joy so real, so alive even in the remembering.

Somehow, though, the sister is unsure, uncomfortable, and then she isn't a part of the memory anymore. And our 4-H leader asks, "Do you want to see something cool?" Or maybe one of us kids asks, "Hey, is that your room?" Maybe our curiosity sets everything in motion—the blending of the day, the blurring of the brownies into something else, a different kind of happiness.

A man's room, with adult things—big hairbrush, shelves full of books, clothes on the floor. Us kids roaming around with our eyes, our feet, our hands. Taking it all in, asking what's this, and can I touch that, and is that real. Him smiling, answering our questions, closing the door.

The memory is peaceful, comfortable like a room in my own home. I can smell the plaster walls, see the carpet dirty under my feet, feel the scratchy wool blanket on the bunk bed when I jump up on the mattress. There are more things to see, so I climb up top, look at the stuff, touch things that are not mine. I sit on the edge, so high up on the top bunk.

An old bullet. A battery-operated man's razor. The batteries are still good, and it turns on. He says, "It tickles, put it on your leg." He's right, it does tickle, and he tickles us, and then we tickle back, and the razor has no blades so he says to tickle him because it feels good . . . and the memory blurs again, until the penis is so tall, standing straight and perfect and hot and hard and long and soft, and the razor makes him feel good and he wants everyone to try it, and the penis is only inches away, and it's a perfect plaything.

Some kids stay far away, on the other side of the room. Most of us are interested and try.

A few of us, we few, sit on the bed for a very long time and quietly, secretly, play in our new world. His face is moist, he smiles, he moans. We few know we are a part of something we never knew existed, and we are special now, so good at understanding this new world, and we learn fast. We see what most of our friends will never see, never know. We now have that hidden treasure, a perfect awareness of our own childish world, and of our own penises. Somehow 4-H ends; the day grays out, leaving nothing of note, and no one talks about it again. And we never return, never see that leader again.

2

LONGING

SEPTEMBER 2005

*C*oming to Niskayuna seemed easier than leaving Brooklyn—putting the past behind and hoping for a better future while holding on to our best memories. In time, the past faded into the background, as we woke each day in our new home, and a better life began to materialize, in the same way that a dream seems real when the details become more intimate. Remembering a favorite new song, a ceiling that we painted together, the way the kids made places for themselves, first in their bedrooms, then taking over unattended spaces.

Just another workday morning, NPR keeping me company as usual, and as I hit I-87, the Northway was brilliant with sunshine and the green of the trees. I was on cruise control at seventy-five miles per hour, soaking up the colors, when StoryCorps came on the radio. Moments in people's lives, what mattered most to them on a given day, intimate conversations between parent and child, brother and sister, friends.

Mary Lou Maher was talking to her son, Brad Skow, whom she had given up for adoption twenty-eight years earlier. I forgot the colors and the sunshine as the road ahead blurred through my tears. When Brad asked the questions I wanted to ask, Mary Lou became the voice I longed to hear.

"Do you remember the day I was born?"

"They asked me if I wanted to hold you, and I said no, because I was afraid if I held you, I wouldn't be able to give you up."

With each word, my tears thickened. I thanked God that the segment only lasted two minutes, even as Mary Lou's last words pounded in my ears.

"I missed twenty years. And you can't ever get that back."

It's all gone now.

I couldn't go to work. At the next off ramp, I stopped in Yaddo Gardens, sitting and shaking and crying and thinking about how much I missed her, my mother who had no name or face or voice. How it killed me to miss her and not even know her at all. Yet somehow, I did know her. Through the loss and the emptiness and the missing her, I knew her as part of my own lost sense of self, of how not belonging in this world, never fitting in, had become my identity.

I knew her because I missed her and longed for her and waited for her to find me, and because I wanted Mary Lou to be her, and I wanted to be Brad. I cried for her as if crying for God to be with me, to know someone who can never be known, someone who is known by their absolute absence.

I arrived at work to a full morning and afternoon of training, complete with a sit-down lunch for all the attendees. Relaxing into the casual camaraderie of lunch, as chit-chat about news, weather, and sports waned, to fill the void I mentioned the radio broadcast with Mary Lou and Brad's story.

Laure-Jeanne had heard the same show. She mentioned her former boss, who had found his birth family. As she relayed how he reunited with his mother, I was frozen in the moment. I couldn't speak, and she could see the memory of the morning in my eyes. She looked at me and said without question, "You're adopted, aren't you?"

The rest of the room politely drifted away as she and I turned all of our energy to my story, to my wish and need to find my mother. She promised to reach out to her old boss, David Luck, and introduce us.

In the days and weeks that followed, David told me of his search, his family, and their reunions. I told him my history, what I knew and didn't know, and what I wanted—needed—to know. Laure-Jeanne, Roz, and David guided and consoled, and shared their experience, strength, and hope with me. With their help, my focus sharpened, and my objectives narrowed.

I needed to know my real name.

AGE TEN

Major is a beautiful dog, even at fourteen years old. A springer spaniel, Dad's long-time companion. Despite the cold and wind, Mom tells me to take him outside. With the backyard all ice, we head around the side of the house.

Major sniffs around, looking for just the right spot. Neither of us can see the thick sheet of ice hidden under the light coating of snow, treachery in wait from what we both see only as frozen ground. One step too far, and his hind legs slip apart, slamming him onto the ice. Muscles rip, and tendons tear away from bone.

Gingerly I tread over the ice. I try to grab his hind end and lift it off the ice, but for the first time ever he lashes out, snapping at my helping hands. I plead, "Come on boy, come on Major," but without a foothold, he can't pull his back paws together.

Desperate, I lie down on my side, shoving one booted foot against a paw to hold it and hooking my second boot around his other paw. As he yowls in pain, I squeeze his legs together. He stands, shaking but upright. He still hasn't peed but can barely move. When I call him to me, he turns and like an old, old man with a walker, takes one tiny, cautious step, waits, then another, and another, trembling and terrified.

We eventually make it to solid ground on the patio, and barely navigate the small step up into the garage. I run gasping into the house, but by the time we come back out Major has crawled under the steps.

Dad kneels by the steps and tries to help, but each time my father's dog of fourteen years snarls and bites at his hand. At last, leaving him in his dark place, we go into the house to eat dinner.

We put food and water next to the stairs to coax him out, but by bedtime he hasn't moved. We keep busy—eating meals, watching TV, doing chores. In the house, things seem almost normal, although we feel his absence.

After two days Major crawls out to lap at the water. Mom puts some cardboard down for him to lie on and blocks the crawlspace under the stairs with a board. He only growls when I pet him. Dad spends most of his time in the garage, just sitting with him.

The next morning Mom tells me to sit in the back seat. I wait in the car until Dad carries Major out and settles him on a blanket next to me.

"He's old, Kev," Dad says. "He lived a good life." His voice sounds strange.

"Do I hold him?"

"Just pet him, talk to him."

I want the ride to last forever. It only takes minutes.

We park at the far end of the lot, so far from the brick building, a hundred yards that seems a hundred miles. A man comes and talks to Dad, while Mom sits on the other side of Major in the back seat.

My hands can't stop caressing him, tangling in his long hair still so soft and feathery. Dad opens my door, and the man takes Major's collar off and gives it to Dad, who hands it to me, the tags jangling, clinking in my hands.

Dad pats Major on the head and turns away as Mom puts her arms around him. Major sits next to me, unmoving and indifferent. My knees feel weak, and my stomach churns with guilt and sorrow. Why couldn't I have seen the ice? Why wasn't there a way to fix Major's legs? Who is that guy, and why doesn't Dad do something, and what is in that building? I know I don't really want to know, as tears stream down my face.

I crouch down and look at Major, face to face, and I feel his warm breath. Mom puts her hands on my shoulders and moves me out of the way so the man can take Major, and as he walks, we see how every step hurts him, and it hurts us, too. I watch as he totters away, wavering and unsteady, and he can't hold his pee and it makes a zigzag on the asphalt that reminds me how Eddie and I pee in the snow sometimes, and I smile and my face feels as though it's breaking. Like my heart.

We huddle in the parking lot, Dad holding me and Mom holding him, and I cry and cry and cry. I need Dad, his strength and comfort, and he's there, stronger than I am, as strong as I need him to be.

JANUARY 2006

That first winter in Niskayuna, Eri insisted that the boys do some outside activity besides making snowmen and sledding, and we signed them up for skiing lessons at Maple Ski Ridge. After strapping the boys into their rental equipment, I made my way to the lodge. Hot decaf, a warm fire, a good book, and two hours to myself. That was the first week.

By the end of the second week, the boys bubbled over.

"We got to ride the lift. We went to the top!"

The top was about one hundred feet from the bottom, but it might have been Mount Everest.

"That's great! You guys will really love it again next week!"

Their faces morphed from joy to disappointment, then to longing.

"But Papa, we want to go again now."

"Now? Well, okay, but hurry up and be careful."

Now their faces were confused.

"But we can't go by ourselves. You have to come with us."

So began my new mission. I rented a pair of skies (only after being told that, no, I could not ride the lift in my sneakers). I rode the lift to the top, turned, and promptly fell, bringing both the boys down with me. Their laughter caught me off guard, and I grumbled and cursed under my breath as I struggled to find my snow legs.

Together, the three of us assumed the "pizza" stance, riding up and sliding down the hill we now laughingly call Maple Ski Bump. We learned to ski together, and before long I had to admit that skiing wasn't half as bad as I had expected. Seeing my boys watching me be a father made me want to be a better dad. Made me want to remember my own father differently. Made me think about my brother-less childhood, and how my friends were my whole world. Made me remember.

AGE TEN

The good times are hardest to remember in full. Memory is like when you're outside in the dark and someone lights a match, and the flash fills the air and spots of colors dance in your vision and then fade. Some good times are easier to remember, and the colors glow brighter longer.

We drive up at dusk, a big night out with the family and my mom's mom is along for the ride. The thirty-minute trip takes us three miles above the town of Altamont, high up near the hiking trails and cliffs of Indian Ladder in the gentle hills of Thacher State Park.

Highland Farms Restaurant is one of our favorite family dining spots, not our typical Chinese buffet or Italian night out at Canali's. Even at ten years old, I know this is a special night, with Dad in his jacket and tie and Mom in her Sunday best—a mini vacation for the family.

No other children are there, which keeps me on my best behavior. In the winter, Dad likes to eat in the bar, with the huge fireplace and slate floor, but on a summer evening like tonight, we sit in the more intimate and elegant dining room.

My grandmother, my *babcia*, orders things from the menu that no one else will, and ever since his time in the Navy, Dad eats just about anything. He still loves his meat and potatoes, and I love to emulate him, but he also dares us to try new things. My cheeseburger and fries contrast with their exotic foods, but it's the best cheeseburger and fries I've ever had.

Knowing that I only like salt on my salad, Dad tells me pickles are just salty cucumbers, then roars with laughter when my face puckers up on the first bite. I spit the mushy chunks into my napkin while Mom smiles, wipes the juice from my chin, and hands me my Shirley Temple to wash down the sour vinegar taste. Dad doesn't lie, he just helps me wrap my mind around something different.

Dad doesn't drink much, but there are exceptions. Tonight after a few too many beers, he's on a roll, teasing every waitress. My mom yells at him to stop, me giggling and ashamed at the same time. He's my dad, and in my ten-year-old eyes, he can do no wrong.

It doesn't matter if the waitress is three tables away, he just shouts across the room that the Shirley Temple for his son is perfect. The hostess brings our check and politely asks if we want any dessert to go. Dad waves goodnight to everyone, his face glowing with a smile that makes them all smile and wave in return.

Driving home, while mom dozes in the front passenger seat, Dad gradually lets the car pick up speed. As we round each curve, I pretend to fly from one side of the car to the other, playfully slamming against the car door or sprawling across Babcia's lap. Mom sits up in her seat, done dozing and getting nervous now. I poke my head between the two of them, smiling and laughing.

"Faster! Faster!"

Dad smiles at me in the rear-view mirror, shifts the car into neutral, and straightens in his seat, his hands gripping the steering wheel. We barrel down the mountain, the wheels squealing around the turns as our speed increases, and I scream in ecstasy.

Mom holds on to the door handle, and Babcia tries to hold on to me, as I bounce back and forth. Dad laughs and hunches over the steering wheel like a race driver, holding on for dear life yet unwilling to brake.

Flying down the dark road feels like riding a roller coaster in the night. Headlights glare and a horn blares as Dad yanks the car back into our lane. He overcorrects, and the tires on the passenger side scatter gravel. No guard rail, only a ditch and the blackness beyond.

Dad grips the wheel, fear showing in his eyes as the rest of us scream, Mom and Babcia with terror and me with joy. The bravest man alive pumps the brakes and shifts the transmission back into drive, easing the car to the bottom of the hill where the now-quiet town's one stoplight makes us wait for the train to pass. The car is silent now, but my world has expanded. Dad is sober, and I'm drunk with happiness.

3

STUMBLING

MARCH 2006

*W*here were you adopted, Kevin?"

This search could take years. That truth felt debilitating. Roz knew it, but also knew it was part of the process, that this damned slog of logistical preparation also would serve me well emotionally and spiritually.

"Catholic Family Charities. They're called Catholic Services now. The paperwork I found points to an office in Schenectady, but all the records are in Albany."

"You need to call them again."

I reached out to the Albany Catholic Family Charities office more than fifteen years ago, and all it got me was basic nonidentifiable information. Mother was French, Irish, German. No health problems. One of her brothers might have been cross-eyed; I have an uncle. Father was English. That's it. Nothing more.

"I'll call them. I just know it will be the same as last time."

"You don't know that, Kevin. Have faith."

I wanted to be willing to follow the process, but I was focused on what my mother's face would look like. How it will feel to touch her cheek, to hear her voice.

"I'm trying."

"I know you are."

I told Roz about David Luck, and she was thrilled, or at least as thrilled as her stoic demeanor would allow.

David was kind and generous. His willingness to correspond with me about being an adoptee uplifted and refreshed me, in contrast to the heavy ache I felt with Roz.

I gave David my background: adopted in 1962 in Schenectady through Catholic Family Charities; the records are sealed; I requested and received nonidentifiable information from them; I have two wonderful parents; I registered with the New York State adoption registry.

"I want to extend the search. I don't know how to move forward from here."

"I think I can find some information that may be helpful."

"Thank you, David. That would be great."

"You should follow through with Catholic Services. Adoption record secrecy has been greatly reduced in the past decade. You may have better luck now."

"David, how long ago did you find your family?"

"It's been years now."

"How?"

"I wrote back and forth with my birth father for a few years before actually arranging to meet him and talk."

"You met him first?"

"No. My mother first. It took longer for my father. He had no idea I existed. I was respectful of the fact that my existence was a big shock for my father. My birth mother was thrilled." David was the only child she had ever had. "After I found her, she told me she cried tears of joy every day for a year. Now she has three grandchildren and two great grand-children." His reality was my dream.

Roz and I continued our talks almost daily, mostly about how to research local newspapers for old birth announcements. It took commitment to spend days pouring over microfiche at the Schenectady County Library, but I promised to make the time.

I also made another plan as well. The risk seemed to outweigh the gain, but the idea kept poking me, telling me to pay attention and listen to the voice in my head.

Ending my daily phone call with Roz, I willed myself to walk out of work and into the parking lot, breathing deliberately, letting my eyes shift in and out of focus, not ready to look at the thing I knew I needed to do.

I stopped and took a deep breath of the fresh Adirondack air, letting my eyes take in the trees and colors and sounds, and took a few slow steps toward the street. Standing on the sidewalk, I stared at the sky and let my eyes drift down to the roof, the second floor, the small porch, the front door, and finally to the sign: Catholic Services, Saratoga County.

All I wanted was to run back across the street into my office and slam the door. Instead I steeled myself to cross the street, clear my mind, and open my heart as I opened the door. Smiling, I asked the receptionist if I could talk to the director.

"Sister Charla Commins is not in," the receptionist said pleasantly, "but is there something you need?"

I was afraid if I didn't speak now, I'd never come back. Yes, there was.

"I was adopted in 1962 in Schenectady. I'm hoping to find out as much as possible about my birth family, and I wanted to ask for some advice. I work across the street at Empire State College. I never had such a strong desire to know about my birth, but every day as I walk through the parking lot, I see the Catholic Services sign, and it calls to me. Sometimes I think about it all day, I can't help but wonder if God is telling me to cross the street like I did just now and open this door and ask these questions. I don't know why, I don't know how she can help, but I feel strongly that I need to meet with your director."

When I finally ran out of words, the receptionist smiled and took my name.

I returned to my office and waited for a call from Sister Charla Commins. After several days, I called over to make sure that Sister

Charla had gotten my name and number, and was told that yes, she had, but she was busy at least for the rest of the week and would likely call early the next week when her schedule allowed. This was not what I wanted to hear, but I'd made a pact with myself that I would let this process unfold as it must, not as I would have it. Not in my time, but in God's time.

When the call finally came from Sister Charla, she was open and kind and strong. I could meet with her today if I liked, later this afternoon or in an hour at 11:00 a.m. if I was available. I left my office at 10:45, stood outside in the parking lot for ten minutes, and walked in the front door of the office at 10:55.

Sister Charla was both a spiritually and physically prominent woman. It was clear that Jesus was alive and well in her measured approach as she welcomed me into her office. I felt simultaneously safe and challenged, knowing that my one mandate was to be completely honest. I told Sister Charla my story: a story that normally softened people's temperament and brought them to high alert. Yet my words of brokenness and healing had little outward effect on Sister Charla. She listened with her God-given stillness and intensity, and a pure and efficient bullshit detector. As a recovering bullshitter, I was grateful to intuitively recognize someone whom I could trust.

She expressed true sympathy for my plight but made it clear that there might be little she could do beyond reach out to those who had access to my adoption files. We could meet again soon. I believed her. I trusted her. She understood why I was there, and never once questioned the validity or necessity of my journey. She saw me both as a man on a quest and as a boy without a mother.

Leaving her office, I breathed normally again for the first time in a long while. My lung capacity was the same, the Saratoga air had not changed, but as I crossed the street, I inhaled deeply and felt a new strength and confidence, mingled with apprehension and joy.

After a week, an email from Sister Charla appeared in my inbox. I almost cried with anticipation.

Hi, Kevin. It was so nice to meet you last week. I called the Catholic Charities Adoption Office to see if there were any new ways to "search." The answer was not really. Said there were probably sites on the net that you could research. They asked if you had gotten unidentifiable info and I said that you had. However, if you want to make sure that you have all that is available, you could call the agency archivist, Mary Decotis, at—. Mary has been with the agency forever. I think she only works part time now. She and I worked on several cases early on. She is a gem. Also the site my staff person used quite successfully is Bighugs.com. Good luck. I'm hoping you will find peace of mind. If I learn anything else that might be helpful, I'll be in touch. Sister Charla

AGAIN I HAD HIT A WALL, stuck and without recourse. But I at least had some hope in the archivist, Mary Decotis.

After speaking with Roz, I made a list of everything I knew so far: hospital where I was born, day I was discharged, attending doctor's name, agency I was adopted through, placement date, where I was baptized, court where the adoption was finalized, when the adoption was finalized.

Roz helped me compile a list of what I needed and possible paths and resources.

Progress was now real. I had no idea how long this ride would last, or where the road would take me, but I felt deep inside that I was approaching the point of no return. I wasn't sure I felt any closer to finding my mother, but at least I felt a little less far away.

AGE TEN

When the rains come right before a deep freeze, our backyard, the neighbor's, and the next neighbor's ice over and turn into a skating rink almost as long as a football field. We congregate here, skating until long past dark. When it snows, we shovel paths through the ice and chase each other through the maze.

Hockey is our game. My best friend, Eddie, is low and fast, like a water bug skimming on the surface, darting away to keep from being checked. He's a perpetual motion skater: body compact, legs powerful and dense. Slamming into Eddie feels like bouncing off an old truck tire full of cement.

Chuckie's the strongest, but not as fast. His dad built their new house, Chuckie helping him until well past dinner. Twins Ronald, whom we call Bubby, and Donald don't have skates. Still they run and slide with us, happiest when they're not thinking about going home.

Hockey is less a sport and more a game of chase the guy with the puck. The greatest challenge is avoiding the trees. The space is open from end to end, but on our corner lot the lawn ends at the street, with an oak tree on one side and a sprawling old weeping willow at the other. At the far end are three maple trees that serve as both goal and backstop.

Eddie has the puck, but it gets caught in a tangle of tree roots that bulge above the ice. I come after it, and Eddie is so focused on that puck, he seems to want to keep me from wanting it. Sandwiching me between himself and the tree, he slams me into the trunk, again and again, crushing my back and shoulders, knocking the wind out of me. Like any ten-year-old boy, I don't like being cornered, and being pounded in front of the other kids confuses even the best of friends.

Somehow, I dodge out of the way, so he hits the tree instead of me, landing on his face. The puck slides away, but I no longer care about it. He's down on the ice, and my skates are free. I jump on him, my skates pounding his legs and arms, my knees driving into his back, his side, his stomach. Jumping up and dropping down again, over and over, and now he's crying, and my friends stand watching without a sound and my mother runs out of the house calling *stop, stop, stop.*

We're happiest when the sky is gray, so the sun doesn't melt our skating rink. Nothing is worse than hitting a wet spot and stumbling, digging my blades into soggy grass. Except when we fight, which isn't often. Not often at all.

4

SHIFTING

MARCH 2006

Subject: your birth parents

Dear Kevin

You are a lucky guy . . . I finally tracked down the lady who will find your birth parents.

Her name is Beth. She lives in Kingston, New Hampshire. She is expecting your phone call.

Her home phone is ———.

Her work phone is ———.

Good luck and warmest regards

david luck

*I*t felt quite unprecedented for me to be told I was a lucky guy, but to be told I was a lucky guy by Mr. Luck himself? It was a new day for me.

Beth was a birth mother who, like Roz, had found her child. Like Roz, she also had a profound desire to help other mothers reunite with their children. Beth asked questions that I didn't think would help me find my mother. She wanted to help me walk, not run, and to discover as much about myself as I could before my hoped-for reunion with my mother.

Beth sensed my fear, but she never held back in her passion for results. She knew what the stakes were for me.

Kevin,

Your parents must have had your adoption papers. Maybe they have them in a file or safe.

They were given them the day that they adopted you. Please understand that I'm not saying that they are hiding it from you. This is very hard on them also, even if they say they want you to do this. You are their son and to have you find someone that is blood, they may think they are going to lose you. They will always be your parents, and we are like an extended family member who also is blood. Your birth mother cannot take you away from them and I am sure she does not want to do that. Yes, she would like to be part of your life if and when you find her. Just make sure you tell your parents that you love them and that you will always be their son no matter where this search ends up.

We didn't get much snow, just enough to let us know that winter is not over yet. I'm hoping that this weather is good for our maple sugarier. Take care, have to start supper for my husband. Good to talk to you.

Beth

BETH ALWAYS ENDED our talks with more casual conversation, which helped me feel normal, that somehow searching for my mother didn't make me a freak, but instead awakened in me links that had always existed, creating a new sense of who I am. I began to trust her as a mentor for my preparation, a surrogate mother.

WITH EACH SMALL CLUE GATHERED, I felt momentum building. My parents dug through their files, old documents and random pieces of paper with lawyers' names, dates, judges, and courts.

Most of the people were dead. The lawyer that handled my adoption had been gone for years. After a few days of calling, I tracked down the law firm that took over his practice, but the secretary told me most of his old cases went in the trash. With every dead end, Beth propped me up, and with every blind alley I walked down, I found new hope that I would soon discover some new piece of the puzzle of who I am.

As a search angel, Beth helped me with logistics and guided me through the emotional process, through high hopes and darkest fears. Sometimes she prompted me to imagine finding a mother who would welcome me with open arms. Other days, she asked me to anticipate the worst and talked me through the best way to keep my support system by my side. Her son found her, and they had an indescribable love for each other, a story I heard again and again. But Beth warned me that anything could happen in this search, and that each day that I came closer to resolution, I also had to prepare for any eventual outcome.

"Will your family support you if you find her?"

"Yes." I'm sure in my reply.

Beth coaxed me along. "Do you think they would withhold any information from you if they had it?"

Again, I'm confident. "No, I trust them."

She was heading somewhere, and I knew it, but I trusted her.

"What is your relationship with them now?"

"Really good with both my mom and dad." I knew what was coming next.

"Was it always good?"

Silence. Beth let the phone hang in silence as long as I needed.

I took a slow, deep breath. "No."

AGE ELEVEN

My dad is still alive, still breathing, but to me, he's dead. How can I grieve when he is still here? Yet I feel him gone already, beyond health and joy and laughter. Beyond hope.

Small flashes of memory seem normal enough. Dad playing with me, throwing the ball in the backyard. "Follow through on your throw." "Two hands, Kev. Use two hands." Then time hiccups, memories shift and echo in silence, like blips on a radar, no warnings, nothing out of order, but not quite right.

When Dad comes home from work, I run with my ball and glove, jumping up and down, "Come on Dad, come on," but he pats my head with a pained, wincing smile. Mom takes his jacket and briefcase, and he walks away, shoulders hunched and head down, to stretch out on the couch while Mom cooks dinner.

Instead I play catch alone, the hardball making a bone-jarring THWAT-thump THWAT-thump as it pops off the pine clapboard wall and bounces from the concrete patio into my glove. With dinner cooking, Mom takes pity and comes out to throw with me, tossing the ball underhand, but the look of disappointment on my face is too much to bear. She goes back inside, sets out the plates and silverware and paper napkins in just the right place, making the table look so neat, so happy, so normal.

This day is different.

Early October in Rotterdam is warm and dry enough that I spend whole days outside with my friends. We're in somebody's backyard, near enough that I hear my mother calling.

"Kevin! Come on home."

I run into the house, out of breath, standing in the doorway, impatient at the interruption.

"What? We're playing, Mom."

The look on her face stops me in my tracks.

She closes the door, and I see Dad lying on the couch, his face ashen. He gasps for breath, rolling his head back and forth in terror, and his eyes bulge. Pain, fear, horror twist in his throat. My mother sits me next to him and tries to hold a cold washcloth to his forehead, struggling against his thrashing.

She looks at me, and though her voice shakes, her words are calm, even soothing.

"I need you to stay in now."

"Okay," is all my mind can come up with.

"Uncle Clev will come and get you. The ambulance is coming, and Dad has to go to the hospital."

I nod as her face ages a hundred years in a minute. She turns back to the washcloth, and a single tear trembles on her chin, then falls.

My friends cluster on the corner, waiting for me to come back out. I sit, frozen, staring at nothing, forgetting about my father until he calls my name, telling me it's going to be all right. He grabs my hand, his fingers fumbling.

He's crying now, panicked. His once-athletic body is failing him— pummeled by two wars, by marriage consummated without child. And as he stares at me, my only thought is to wonder why my eyes can't seem to see him now.

Why, as his heart gives out, does mine shut down?

Dad is sent from Ellis Hospital in Schenectady to Boston for surgery and I go to stay with Aunt Lola and Uncle Clev. My nature as an only child is to get my needs filled before others, and Uncle Clev and Aunt Lola are not built that way. To them I am less a third child to care for than a strange entity to endure. For my cousin Carmel, I serve only as an intensifier for her brother's teasing.

Cleveland Beau and I share a room, talking late into the night. Lacking any siblings, I spent the first eleven years of my life in my bed alone with my thoughts and fantasies. Now as my mind churns with anxiety, Cleveland Beau hears whatever questions pop out. "Did you ever see a naked girl?" "Do you ever get a hard-on?" "Will my dad ever come home?" "Why are there hairs around your dick?" "Do you like to touch yourself?" "Will you touch me?" "Do you like me?" "Will you tell anyone?" Soon, though, he just turns out the light and goes to sleep, or pretends to, leaving me alone again, unable to quiet the voices in my head.

Without my parents to console me, uncertainty takes hold like a fever. Every day feels sadder and darker, the loneliness swelling up inside me. My inability to sleep turns into quiet crying, then all-out sobbing, sending Cleveland Beau to his parents. Sitting on my bed, Uncle Clev just lets me cry. He has no words, no comfort to offer.

The house is dark, the walls covered with cheap wood paneling, every piece of furniture full of dog hair, smelling of old smoke and beer, frayed at every edge, matching my fraying nerves. I've always had a nervous stomach, which now degenerates into chronic diarrhea. I sit on the toilet, lost and crying, shitting until my body is dehydrated.

When no one is around, in my brokenness I kick Ralph, their old basset hound. As mean as he is, he only snarls and walks away. The more lost and forgotten I feel, the faster my self-hatred grows.

Mom doesn't call much, and when she calls, she doesn't talk to me. Afterwards Uncle Cleveland says little. My dad is fine. Everything will be better soon.

Cleveland Beau, Carmel, and I are having dinner, just the three of us. The pizza slices are huge, hard to hold even with two hands, with a thin, soft crust dripping with grease. I hold the pizza flat in the palm of my hand, as if handing it to someone.

I'm so intent on not dropping it in my lap, I don't see Cleveland Beau reaching out until suddenly he shoves the pizza into my face, into my eyes and nose and hair.

I wipe the sauce out of my eyes to see Cleveland's twisted smile, and Carmel snickering, then giggling, and finally laughing out loud.

Unknown feelings punch my gut, rise up in my chest, and pound in my skull.

My instinct is to kill him, to smash his head in and shove pizza down his throat. I chase him all over the house, sauce and cheese and mushrooms still clinging to my face and hair and shirt, Cleveland Beau laughing so hard he can hardly keep away from me. My mind is white-hot, rage indistinguishable from my fears. *How could you be so mean? Why did you take my father away from me? When will he come home? Why isn't he here to help me? Why did he get sick? What do you people want from me? What? What? What?*

Cleveland and Carmel can't stop laughing; my spirit is broken and my rage unstoppable. Uncle Cleveland holds me and lets me cry. Later he whispers on the phone with my mother, and when he finally hands the phone to me I can't speak, only sit and listen to her voice, until Uncle Clev takes the phone back and again speaks in whispers.

My mother comes back the next day, first talking with Uncle Clev and Aunt Lola in low, urgent tones. She doesn't spend much time with me.

"Uncle Clev will drive us up to Boston tomorrow."

"To pick up Daddy?"

"Yes."

"They fixed him?"

"They did an operation on his heart."

"He's all better?"

"No, but he's going to get better."

"They fixed him?"

"Yes, Kevin, they fixed him."

It's a nearly four-hour drive in weekday traffic, but Uncle Clev makes it in less than three. Mom sits up front in his old station wagon. The back seat folds down, they tell me, so Dad can lie down for the ride home. My job is to keep him comfortable, to sit with him and talk to him. It'll be fun!

At the hospital, through endless hallways, Mom finally stops outside an open door.

Two men are in the room, neither of them my father. One of the men lies unmoving, eyes closed. The other man is gaunt, his hair uncombed, his face stricken, his whole body shaking. His eyes bulge as tears stream down his cheeks, over his slack jaw, and down his neck onto his pillow.

I turn to Mom, wondering. "Where's Daddy?"

She points at the crying man and tries to smile. When I turn to face him again, his arms reach out like the dead trying to escape the grave.

He sobs, "I never thought I'd see you again."

His gown is like tissue, his beard rough, his body wasted. So much of him gone, lost forever.

"It's okay, Kevin, sit with your father."

I can't move my feet. Uncle Clev picks me up and sets me on the bed next to Dad, where I can feel his body quivering under the sheet. His hands stroke my back and my arm. He shows me his scars, tells me he almost died, that he might not live out the year, but he's so glad to see me, he loves me. His son, such a good little soldier, he says.

My body shakes and my underpants are wet. I'm eleven years old.

AFTER DAD COMES HOME, something begins to unravel in me, as if my sense of self is being depleted. I feel even more afraid now, watching my dad cry in his bed, lacking the strength or will to do more than walk to the bathroom.

Again, I cry at night. Mom runs into my room telling me to hush, I'll upset my father. I teach myself to keep the pain inside, until the confusion turns into despair and the hurt consumes me. My recourse is to kick and wail, "Please let me die. Please let me die."

My father cries in his bed, shaking and sobbing because he can't help. My mother begs, "Don't get your blood pressure up. Don't strain your heart. Don't have a heart attack. Don't get upset. Please calm down."

I howl until she comes to me. I'm on the couch, kicking and biting the cushions, punching and scratching at her even as her strong arms hold me while the pain slowly ebbs, tears and snot and coughing dwindling to an occasional tremor. Mom puts a pillow under my head and strokes my hair. My will is gone, and I float on the couch, the same couch on which my father almost died, her words soothing me.

When my breathing steadies, she tucks the afghan over me, under my chin, still stroking my hair. Eventually my mind goes, and my eyes shut.

No one ever speaks of these nights. Morning never comes, and the nights never happened. But one night is different.

My plan is simple: Start a small fire in the log barrel by the fireplace. My parents have some fire-starter logs—an easy and even burn that lasts an hour or so. The smoke will wake up my parents, and then . . . After that, my plan is vague, but my jumbled mind insists it will work. This will make them notice.

I light the long stick match, touch it to the corner of the paper wrapping on the fake log, wait until the flame takes hold, and lie back down on the couch. In my mind's eye I see it happen: My mother wakes up, smells the smoke, bundles me out of the room as she yells, "Fire, fire!" My father douses the flames and opens the windows to let the smoke out. We huddle together, grateful for not having died together, happy to be alive together.

But their bedroom is too far away; the smoke doesn't go where it's supposed to. I put out the fire and restart it, hoping the smoke will accumulate. I keep trying, again and again, but my body wants to sleep, and even in my distraction, I know they can't save me if they don't smell the smoke. Finally, I make the obvious decision. I long to yell "Fire!" as I'm shaking my mother's shoulders, but the best I can manage is a weak, "Mom, there's a fire in the living room."

She lets my father sleep as she puts the log, the paper wrapper barely singed, in the fireplace. Her tears flow, her face a mask of desperate helplessness, as she looks around the living room, then at me, and back around the room.

"Are you trying to kill us?"

"No," I plead. "I didn't do it."

"I don't know what to do. Why?"

"It just started."

"Why did you do that?"

"No, no, it wasn't me! The fire just started. It just started."

Left alone on the couch, I curl up and fall asleep alone. My mother has nothing left to give me. No blanket over me, no soft pillow, no moment of warm, comfortable togetherness. Nothing but empty, sad relief. I have all I deserve.

5

BECOMING

MARCH 2006

$\mathcal{I}$ was becoming ready to meet my mother and more capable of knowing myself. The intense wondering about who my mother was merged with the desire to tell my mother who I am. Beth asked me to write a letter to my mother, and though I had no idea what to say, Beth assured me it wasn't the words that I wrote but the action of writing them that had the most impact. The willingness itself brings strength. I trusted her, so I wrote a letter to an unknown recipient.

Subject: adopt (letter to birth mother)

Hello.

My name is Kevin. I am writing with the hope that we might know each other.

If you do not wish to respond I completely understand. However, I would be grateful if you would reflect on the possibility of corresponding. If you are willing to continue reading this note, I thank you.

I was born in Schenectady at St. Clare's Hospital on June 27, 1962. I am living a wondrous and full life. I'm happy for every moment, and I try to pass that on in any way I can throughout each day. There are many people that bring me unexplainable joy, and I am blessed to be included in their lives. I am content. I have found it hard to put my thoughts into words. More than anything I want to say: "Hi. How are you?"

That beginning would be more than I could ask for, and more than I could expect.

I will be honest that I do have hope that you will be willing to include me in your life, in any way that might feel right.

Please know that you are in my thoughts and in my prayers.

Kevin

BETH and I sent innumerable emails back and forth. She helped me research, and I sent her everything I'd gathered over the years. The older the documentation, she reminded me, the more helpful it might be, especially any paperwork that was redacted. Many times, these came to a dead end, but Beth never allowed hope to diminish, encouraged me at every setback.

Hi! Kevin,

Just me returning with my answer to your question. It is your Adoption Decree that you want. As I said before your parents should have this. If they do please send it to me, do not send a copy. Make one for yourself and after I see it I will return it back to you. I just sent back the other paper to you today.

Not much in the information that you sent me. We do know that your mother was not from NY.

Address for NEW YORK DEPT OF SOCIAL SERVICE

40 N PEARL STREET

ALBANY, NY 12243

Talk to you soon,

Beth

Hi, Beth.

Hope all is well.

I've sent the request for my non-ID info to Social Services (I had it notarized). I will let you know when I get a response.

I also have been trying to find the old files from the lawyer my parents used. Unfortunately, he has long since died, there is no record of what firm he worked for and I can't find his old records. Since they don't tend to hang on to things for more than 7 years (unless it's a will), there is a good chance that the old files are gone. I could go down to the county courthouse and request the decree, but from what I understand that would go nowhere. I have a feeling that my parents are being truthful, that they never got a copy of a decree. It seems in NY that those documents are sealed and in the court files. Either way, my parents don't have any files that I can find. I've gone through all of their filing cabinets and only found an old birth certificate and an old amended baptism certificate.

Please let me know if you have any other thoughts since I seem to be hitting a wall here.

Again, hope all is well.

Kevin

THE FIRST PAGE of the report from Catholic Services came in the form of a chart, with items listed for both mother and father.

Item: Age at separation
    Mother: 20
    Father: Not recorded

Item: Ethnic Background:
    Mother: German, French, Dutch, Irish, English
    Father: English

Item: Education (year completed)
 Mother: 12th
 Father: 12th

Item: Religion
 Mother: Roman Catholic
 Father: Not recorded

MY MOTHER'S eyes were brown, my father's blue. My mother was five foot three and a half inches, 115 pounds, with blond hair and fair skin. She was attractive and worked as a secretary. My father was five foot seven, had brown hair with a medium complexion. He was a salesman.

Along with the chart was a narrative, prepared for the courts originally, and perhaps for my adoptive parents.

Talents, hobbies, and special interests of birth mother: She enjoyed doing handwork and she played the accordion. She had taken a college preparatory course in high school.

Talents, hobbies and special interests of the birth father: Nothing is recorded.

Health history of birth mother: She was in good health. Her mother had asthma and had rather severe attacks since the age of 18. Birth mother's three siblings were all in good health though one had polio when he was young. All three had a problem with one eye. The condition corrected itself in two of the children but the third was scheduled for eye surgery. (Though the condition is not specifically identified it sounds like it may have been strabismus or crossed eye.)

Health history of birth father: There is nothing recorded except that he was in good health at that time.

Facts and circumstances related to the adoption: The birth mother came to live in this area from a distant state to stay with friends until she delivered. She talked of adoption as the best plan for her child. She felt she could not raise the child by herself and away from her family, who apparently offered no support to her as far as returning home with the child. It was a difficult time for her because she felt close to her family. The birth mother looked forward to being with them again and did return there.

At birth Kevin weighed 6 lbs 11 oz and was 52 cm in length. Delivery was normal after a full-term pregnancy. No birth abnormalities were noted.

On 7/2/62 the infant was discharged from the hospital and on that date he was placed in a foster boarding home where he remained until 8/9/62, when he was placed with Herbert and Virginia Barhydt. The adoption was finalized on 8/14/63 in Schenectady County Surrogate Court.

Prepared by Helen T. Dunigan, CSW Adoption Archivist

THE DETAILS MADE my heart leap. My imagination brought her to life—a young, twenty-year-old woman, five inches shorter than me, looking up into my eyes, her blond hair shoulder length, straight and soft. Together we walked in an open field and sat under the blue sky, smiling while she played guitar and sang softly and I listened, smiling back at her.

Still the dry and static descriptions, the gaps between the details, overwhelmed my fantasy and shadowed my hopes. But they also fueled my sense of mission, gave me the courage to move beyond my fears. If I had any hope of finding my mother, I needed to have a name.

"DAD, DO YOU REMEMBER when I was baptized, was there another name listed?"

"I'm not sure," he said, "but your name might have been Stephen or Michael."

"Stephen or Michael." Had my mother given me those names? Or did

Catholic Charities do the job for her? "Do you remember if there was a last name?"

"No, I don't know the last name. I'm not sure if one had been given to you."

"That's okay. Thanks, Dad."

"I hope this helped a little."

I never loved my father more than I did at that moment. His was an act of genuine sacrifice, knowing that I might find my birth parents, that I could bond with them in a way he and I never could. In a moment of confusion and uncertainty, his utter selflessness realized our love for each other in a way neither of us had ever imagined it could.

Along with that hope resided shared fear. If I knew my first name, perhaps I could know my last name. I had powerful information: the church where I was baptized, when I was baptized, when I was re-baptized, and most importantly, my name. Knowing my name gave me hope, a starting point. Now I could begin the search in earnest.

But before I could reach out to the church that had my baptismal records, St. Madeleine Sophie, I needed to practice my skills. I wrote a script so I'd remember what questions to ask, in what order, keeping in mind the number-one advice: ask for help, and then shut up. Let my contacts process their feelings and work out their own way to help me.

I found two practice churches—one small, in a rural area, and another larger one in downtown Albany. I started with the rural church first.

"Hi, my name is Kevin Barhydt. I'm conducting a genealogy study, and I'm hoping you can help me, or at least direct me to someone who can."

The woman on the phone sounded kind. "I can try to help you. What were you looking for?"

"I know that my father had a brother and a sister. My Aunt Lola is younger, and she's still alive, but I think he had a brother who was born but didn't survive." These were truths—my aunt was alive, and my father did have a brother that died—but then I began to bend and shape the truths I told.

"Are you looking for your father's brother's information?"

"Yes." I waited and let her take the lead.

"Do you happen to know when your father's brother was born?"

"I think it was in 1962." Let her help, I told myself. Let her drive.

"Okay." Her mind was already at work. "We have those files here, I think." I heard shoes click on the floor, a metal cabinet drawer opening. "Do you have any idea when? What month or day?"

Again, I squeeze the truth, blending myself into my father's brother. Telling stories with truths makes it imminently more possible to keep the story straight, especially a story that is bent and shaped for effect.

"I think it was June or early July," I said, then threw out a solid truth. "It might have been the end of June, I think June 27 might have been the date, but I'm not one hundred percent sure." The word *might* kept the mystery in her hands, asking her to help find that missing information that would give me surety.

"Let me put the phone down, and I'll look in our files." Metal drawers opened and closed, paper shuffled, as she worked to find something I knew didn't exist. I listened with a sense of guilt, but no remorse. I knew she wouldn't find the files, that she would tell me how sorry she is. We would chat a bit, and I would thank her for her help. I knew that this time was too easy, and I needed to take the next step: the church in Albany, where I used the same shaping techniques, looked for the same kindness and generosity.

From the moment I explained my quest, I sensed that the gatekeeper at the large church knew I wasn't conducting a genealogy study, but fishing for information I should not have access to. Polite but very professional, she told me those records were not available via phone, but I could send a request in writing if I liked. I stayed positive and friendly as she dictated the address of the Catholic Diocese, and I wrote it down so I could read it back to her. I knew I would never send the request, but I wanted to at least give her the opportunity to feel that I am an honest person, and that this was a legitimate conversation.

I knew if the next call didn't go well, I was up against a brick wall. I had to trust myself, trust that the process and my ability to create the narrative I'd shaped would not fail me. Whoever answered the phone at

St. Madeleine Sophie would meet me at my most desperate, and my most determined.

The conversation was almost identical to the one at the rural church. The woman offered more than mere kindness. In her voice I heard a real softness, caring and open. It might take a little while to get to the files, she said, but if I gave her my name and number she would call me back. I hung up the phone determined not to let desperation turn dark. If this was a brick wall, it wasn't because I lost hope and believed that old story that I was unworthy. Not this time.

After an hour I heard the kind voice from St. Madeleine Sophie again.

"Hi, is this Kevin?"

"Yes, this is Kevin."

"Your name is Kevin Barhydt, correct?" she asked gently.

"Yes." It was time to be very quiet now.

"Well, I found a baptismal record for Kevin Barhydt from 1963." She paused.

"Oh," I replied. Be still.

"But it points back to another baptismal record from 1962."

I inhaled slowly, not wanting her to hear my breath quicken. "Oh?"

"Yes," she said. "The name is Stephen Michael."

I wondered how my voice would sound. I wondered what she would hear in me. Breathing in and out carefully, I looked out my office window at the treetops of Congress Park, measuring the next moment by the weight of my own will. In a few seconds this would be over. I would thank the nice lady, and she would tell me to have a nice day, but in the moment, I needed to ask one more question.

"Is there a surname?" I waited and listened.

"Yes," she said in her singsong voice, "but I can't pronounce it, so I'll have to spell it." I thanked God for the pen and paper in front of me, my notes from all the churches, and with all my strength held my breath and waited and wrote with great care as she spelled out the letters:

"W-A-G-U-E-S-P-A-C-K."

My name is Stephen Michael Waguespack.

AGE ELEVEN

All I want is a sense of normalcy. Sixth grade was a big enough transition by itself, but now Dad's incapacity and depression set the tone for Mom and me every day.

School offers freedom, a chance to remake myself. I want to laugh and bounce around the hallways like the big kids, knowing where the hallways lead, how to navigate the giggling girls with fake smiles as distracting as their burgeoning breasts.

Everyone cool in middle school has something that they own: a cool brother or sister, a special place. I need a cool thing, too.

"I know where I can get pills."

"No you don't." The bigger kids laugh and walk away.

"Is it true?" A kid I know sidles up to me. I don't remember his name. I nod. He stands close.

"Show me."

"They're at home."

"Cool." He smiles, leaning back against the lockers. "Bring them in tomorrow."

I ride the bus and wait for my mother to come home. She's tired all the time now and can't be bothered with my neediness. Dad's needs take all her energy.

At dinner, I play the good little soldier, watching Dad's tears mix with his food. My parents are too focused on Dad's inability to eat to notice that I seem to have forgotten how to speak. My nerves tingle in time with my rapid breathing.

Something's broken inside. I can't hear them, can't look at him, can't stand her coddling voice. My soul sinks into a mist, a daydream, Mom's pork chops and perfectly mashed potatoes and canned peas disappearing into the jumble of frayed nerves, confused thoughts, and broken heart.

I feel like I'm floating, light-headed from too much oxygen. The daydream solidifies into a plan. I imagine each detail, fantasize every moment.

As they watch TV in the next room, I tiptoe the five feet from my room to their bedroom. I remember the laminated chart the Rotterdam police officer showed us in fifth grade, like the menu at our favorite Chinese restaurant. Marijuana cigarettes and neat white lines of cocaine, hypodermic needles for shooting drugs into your veins, and pipes for sucking smoke into your lungs. Two from every pill bottle neatly arranged on my father's dresser. My heart beats slowly, my pupils fully dilated in the dark room.

I pocket ones that seem like fun. "Yellow jackets" will give you a rush; "blue devils" will mellow you out. I'm only half right. They're barbiturates. The little blue aspirin are ten milligram Valium.

The next morning, I wake up even before I'm called to breakfast, downstairs with my shoes on ready to go, my eyes wide open as I climb on the bus. Half the stolen pills are in a baggie stuffed down my underwear. I pretend to sleep, my head bouncing against the window, but once the bus fills up, I pull the baggie out to sneak a look, then quickly shove it back into my Fruit of the Looms.

We meet up right outside of homeroom and duck into the bathroom and crowd into one of the three open stalls, but he doesn't latch the door.

"You got the stuff?" I smile and pull the bag out of my pants. "No, man, take 'em out and show me."

I reach into the baggie, choosing one of each, immersed in my coolness.

The door flies open, knocking him aside, and a man I've never seen before shoulders into the stall. I drop the baggie into the toilet, but his hands lock around my arms and pin me to the wall before I can flush. He fishes the bag of pills out without letting go of me. The boy smiles up at him and leaves without a word.

Everything moves in slow motion, like watching trees bend in the wind on a fall day after a long rain, leaves scattering in chaos. My physical presence seems to float as I'm escorted down the hallway, students staring. The gossip of the day, of the week even.

I drift through the chaos, my brokenness exposed and on full display, the elation of yesterday now deflated to some emotion I can't describe. I don't know that my brokenness has a name, that without meaning to

I've assumed a new identity. It starts out as simple survival, but eventually becomes my way of negotiating every breath I take. Eventually I will understand: my name is Shame.

At home my father goes to his room to lie down. My mother pronounces sentence in the kitchen.

"You're grounded for a month."

"Okay."

I stare blankly as my brain rewires itself. She hasn't changed, but somehow I don't recognize her as my mother. Her voice, like everything around me, is distant, receding, and I can't tell which one of us is leaving. I only know I want to be alone.

The words come through a wall. "Go to your room. I'll call you for dinner."

She's trying to be stern. I'm unable to move.

Will she open the kitchen drawer that holds the strap, the leather belt with the buckle removed? The belt that she—never my father— takes out only when I refuse to obey, slapping it loudly on the counter and asking, "Do you want the strap?"

Today she seems unable, or perhaps unwilling, to contemplate the strap. Both of us stand quietly until tears well up in her eyes. She turns away, leaving me alone, and goes to the bedroom where my father is already crying, and closes the door.

6

<h1 style="text-align:center">SEARCHING</h1>

APRIL 2006

*T*wenty-Seven North Main Avenue in Albany was built in 1917, and the house showed its age. The wooden porch creaked under my weight. Inside smelled like my grandparents' house in Schenectady, and I half expected to see my *babcia* cleaning the hallway, stooped and sweeping with a smile full of kindness.

The part-time archivist for adoptions came out to greet me in the foyer, and I immediately felt at home. In fifty-nine years of service to Catholic Charities, Mary DeCotis had been caseworker for hundreds of adoptions. Delicate as a bird, she exuded motherly compassion.

In her office I told my story, but not the one I had told Beth, not the story of abandonment, loss, and pain. Instead I told the story I knew people like Mary want to hear. Beth had coached me, as had David Luck, and now I shared this adapted version, blending the facts much as I had when I called St. Madeleine Sophie.

"I was adopted and raised by wonderful parents, but always had an ache in my heart, an emptiness that I knew could never be filled." It wasn't a false story, just tailored to an audience of one. I looked into

Mary's eyes and spoke softly, gently. "I find myself praying at night, wanting to include my mother in my prayers by name. I don't need the last name." I smiled and dropped my eyes. "I only wish I knew her first name."

"I want to help you, Kevin, but those records are sealed." I heard nothing but deep compassion in her voice.

I kept talking for over an hour, as I was tutored, circling back again and again to my request. Mary continued to share her sympathy, and her regretful inability to acquiesce. The conversation was on the verge of an interrogation as I breathed in slowly, near tears, and asked one last time.

"I know it's not possible for you to give me the last name, but it's so hard not to know who I'm praying for. All I want is some small sense of who my mother is, so in my prayers I can ask God for His blessings on her." If I thought it would help, I would drop to my knees and pray with Mary right then and there. "Is there any way you could just tell me her first name? Please?"

I was instructed, over and over, to ask the question, then stop talking. Let the person grapple with the request, strong in the knowledge that they want so badly to help.

Mary looked at me, and with finality said, "I'm sorry, Kevin, I can't give you your real first name."

My brain froze. She didn't realize I was asking for my mother's first name? For over an hour, Mary had misheard my request. All this time she thought I was asking for my own first name!

Maybe it was her age, or her hearing, but none of that mattered. My heart seemed to stop beating, and my lungs couldn't take in air. Through sheer will, I forced my involuntary muscles to respond. My awareness sharpened. A flush spread through my neck and shoulders and face; the top of my head began to sweat; my hairs stood on end. I had only seconds to decide how to reply, and no idea what the right thing to do was, but somehow I found the ability to speak.

"Oh." I smiled, a spark of peace and joy lighting my eyes. "My name is Stephen Michael."

She stared at me as if I'd executed a death-defying act. Out of nowhere I found the right words.

"My name is Stephen Michael. I've always known that."

I saw in her eyes: Mary experienced the same jolt I felt. More than ever, we connected in mind, body, and spirit.

"I've known my name all my life. My father told me."

Again, as trained, I stopped talking. *Breathe in. Exhale. Wait for the next moment to simply happen.*

Abruptly Mary stood up and politely, but with great haste, ushered me to the door. "You have to leave my office. I need to make a phone call and you can't be here."

She closed the door, leaving me standing alone in the hallway. The old house was suddenly my friend; as Mary returned to her desk, I clearly heard her footsteps. Cautiously I leaned in and pressed my ear to the door as Mary dialed the phone. From the tenor of the conversation, I gathered she was talking to the Catholic Services attorney.

"I have a young man here who was adopted in 1962. He met with me today, and I told him that the records are sealed, but he knows his first and middle name."

Silence.

"No, he isn't asking for his last name. I know we can't give that to him. But there's a letter in the file. I need to know if I can give him the letter."

Silence.

"The letter says, 'Dear Stephen Michael.'" Mary's words carried through the door like the voice of an angel. "He knows his name is Stephen Michael."

Silence.

Mary grew more insistent. "I have the letter here in the file. Can I give him the letter?"

Silence. I couldn't breathe. Mary was quiet for a long time, too long. Finally I heard her say, *thank you* and hang up the phone. I nearly forgot to move as she walked to the door, but just in time I stepped back to the middle of the hallway. My mind told my body not to move, to stay standing, don't wobble now.

Even before the door opened, my hope soared . . . until I saw the look on her face.

"I'm sorry, Kevin, there's nothing else I can do for you."

I heard her words, clear and crisp. Every syllable followed the neural pathways from my ears to my brain, yet my mind refused to accept them as valid, the way the needle catches on a scratch in a vinyl record. *There is a letter*, my mind insisted. *It's a letter to me. Why can't I have the letter? I have to have the letter.*

I wanted to fight, to scream, to argue and demand. All my old instincts tried to kick in. But the essence of who I am has changed from what I used to be. The comforting words and unconditional support of Beth and David and Roz calmed me in the face of refusal. The search for my mother was what mattered. I needed to honor the search. To honor my mother. To remember who I am and honor myself.

I thanked Mary, shook her hand and then, after a moment, asked if I could please hug her. Our embrace was peaceful and quiet, but it revived me, and as I turned to leave I smiled, and she smiled back at me.

AGE TWELVE

I stand outside with Tony Rotundo. He's two years older, but new to the school.

"Hey, Tone, can I have one?" I ask, trying to sound cool and casual.

Tony grins, enjoying his status as my mentor. "Sure," he says, shuffling a cig from his pack. "Here. Need a light?"

I know if I inhale, I'll choke and make a fool of myself. The harsh Winston smoke burns my throat, so I suck just enough to make the tip glow, holding the smoke in my mouth and letting it out a puff at a time, mimicking Tony's smoke rings.

"What are you doing?"

I try to look innocent and cool at the same time. "What?"

Tony yells, "You're not even taking it in, are you?"

When I don't answer, staring at the ground, his anger cools to disgust. "Just don't waste my cigarettes."

I'd rather he stayed mad. That night, I swear I'll never let Tony down again. I want—no, I need a friend. And if smoking is what lets me stand next to Tony and have even that briefest of connections, it's a small price to pay.

At home I feign cheerfulness, even greeting my father who sits slumped in his chair, then sneak to the cabinet by the refrigerator that holds his final packs of Lark cigarettes. They're old and stale, the pack untouched since his surgery. I hope he's forgotten about them; more likely he's just waiting to feel like his old self again.

A pack and a book of matches, safely stashed between my mattress and box spring. After dinner, my parents well into their evening TV and the volume turned up, I begin practicing.

I light one after another, choking down the urge to quit along with the smoke, feeling dizzy and queasy. I'm determined to show Tony I can hack it the next day.

I learn to let the smoke sit in my mouth then open my lips and inhale gently, not too fast. My body relaxes as the smoke fills my lungs, then dissipates into the air of my bedroom.

I make it through half the pack before throwing up in the wastebasket and have to lie down until the room stops spinning. Sneaking down to the bathroom to dump the puke and rinse out the basket, I brush my teeth and say goodnight to my parents, buoyed by success and new prospects.

Tony is the big brother I look up to, a strong kid, charming, not quite handsome. His eyes are dull even when the rest of his face is laughing over my stupid comments. Tony has all the cool ideas, me his perfect apprentice. When he asks what I'm doing on Friday, I don't think twice.

Tony makes everything seem effortless. After dinner, I meet him in my front yard and head out down my street for the main road and a straight shot to the Little Super Market.

Bouck's Grocery is our favorite local store, a mom-and-pop shop, but they aren't open at night and don't carry beer anyway. Willard Bouck knows the neighborhood, and if you're ten cents short, he'll give you credit, and sure as hell remember it the next time you come in. Maybe Willard assumes we're buying smokes for our parents, or more likely thinks if we're brazen enough to walk in and put our own money on the counter, then we're old enough to smoke.

Tony walks tall and with purpose, me trying to match his stride and not falter trying to keep up with him. We talk important nonsense about school, how much we hate our teachers. We smoke, inhaling deeply, the butts cupped discreetly in our hands in case an adult sees us. We pass Ferris Tavern, where Tony tells me he can get in, but I can't, not yet, maybe next year after I grow a few more inches.

Our voices drop as we get closer, then evaporate to silence when Little Super comes into view across the road. Tony whispers for me to keep walking, looking straight ahead as if the store is the last thing on our mind. Once out of the light from the windows, we dart across the road for some bushes. I pull out my money, but Tony laughs and says my first time is on him, his treat.

Tony comes out of the store and walks back down the street as if I'm not there. I scurry to the other side and follow at a distance, keeping to the shadows. I watch Tony duck down a side street, not so much as a glance my way, taking back roads.

These streets are different from what I'm used to—mostly small, one-story houses with gravel driveways, if they have one at all. Unkempt yards with overgrown flower beds, scrubby weeds, and unattended grass that gives way to sandy dirt. The shadows are deeper here without streetlights and few porch lights lit. Safer but not home free yet. We keep our voices low, Tony cradling the paper bag to make sure the two six packs don't rip through and smash on the road, until we reach the freight train tracks.

My first beer is barely cool as I swallow ever-bigger sips, watching Tony to mirror every move, every puff, every laugh and hoot and holler. The Schlitz tastes to my uninitiated tongue like room-temperature piss. Every new can sends our conversation in a new direction, from girls to school to how we can get some of my dad's pills next time. My every cell knows something is happening. I'm altered, different, new, and there's no part of me that says *stop*. Not one of my senses wants this to stop.

After my third or fourth Schlitz, I feel like I've just stepped off Chipper's Magical Mystery Ride at Storytown USA in Lake George. It's my favorite scrambler ride, housed in a dome that even looks like my middle-school image of a brain, painted a dark and menacing organic green.

Once inside and seated, we're plunged into absolute darkness, the ride begins to spin, and as we pick up speed, the darkness is pierced by a dozen strobe lights synced to *Sergeant Pepper's Lonely Hearts Club Band* blaring from the speakers. When it's over, everyone else stumbles out of the ride, ready to throw up, but for me it's the only time I feel what I think is normal.

As far back as I can remember, my mind has felt as if there's a gyro spinning inside. I never seem able to collect my thoughts for more than a few seconds at a time. The Magical Mystery Ride gives me a specific kind of calm, slows my mind to conventional speed. Getting drunk with Tony achieves the same tranquility, the first time in my life I feel like an ordinary kid.

By the time we finish our sixth beer, conversation has devolved to slurred nonsense, my philosophical questions on par with a three-year-old's.

"Tony." I'm all seriousness. "Did you ever feel like you had to fart, but then it's just diarrhea?"

Tony doesn't shame me, doesn't even laugh, just smiles and shakes his head.

We wander home, and somehow I make it to my room without saying goodnight to my parents. I wake the next morning with a slight hangover, but at eleven-going-on-twelve, I bounce back easily. My only thought that day is confidence that I've found what I've been searching for, what was missing. I know what I'm going to do for the rest of my life.

Every day after school, I swipe a few sips from each bottle in my parents' liquor cabinet. The gin gives the biggest burn but the greatest kick, the sweet vermouth makes me want to puke but delivers a nice, mellow buzz.

Every day after school, Tony and I smoke in the woods and make our plans. Tony finds a new place to drink under the stars, a small mountain of dirt at the new housing development. This time, instead of the piss-tasting Schlitz, we splurge on the cold mountain air of Coors Tall Boys.

I make it through five cans, then violently throw up, feeling like my guts are splattered on the dirt in front of me. I sit back, take a deep breath, wipe the puke from my chin, pop the sixth tall boy, and drink it down without stopping.

I promise my parents I'll never touch Dad's meds again. I'm sorry. I've learned my lesson. I'll change. I made a mistake and won't ever do it again.

On the way to school, I give Tony one of each pill, and I take two of each. Two blue capsules, two yellow capsules, two small blue tabs, two small yellow tabs. Tony looks at me like I'm crazy, which only makes me feel more alive.

As we arrive at school my memory of being busted creeps in. My heart starts to race and sweat trickles down my spine.

"Hey, Tone, do you want the rest?" He looks straight ahead and shakes his head. "What should I do with them?"

"I don't know, man," he replies. "Toss 'em."

Stealing the pills is an achievement. I had worked at it, driven myself to adrenaline overload. No way am I throwing that away.

I pull the baggie out of my shorts, counting. Eight pills left, all capsules, mostly blue. My heart is still racing as my mind calculates— this will only double what I've already taken. I'm not even feeling anything yet, it'll be fun. This way I can enjoy school without worrying about getting busted again. I swallow them dry, dropping the empty baggie on the floor as we shuffle off the bus.

Today is the most highly anticipated event of my so-far bland academic experience. Sex education. Yesterday the boys learned about the boys and the girls learned about the girls, but today we switch. We're all giddy.

The boys cluster in one classroom for second period. No one notices how I slur my words, or maybe in all the excitement they just don't care.

The high hits fast and hard. Everything goes dull, sounds blurring and fading as my mind numbs to the point of stupor. I sit at my desk, only vaguely aware as the projector plays the video we've waited our entire school careers to see. My head drops down and consciousness dims in sync with the lights in the room.

My eyes open, but I can't make them focus. Someone has shoved balls of wax in my ears. My surroundings seem distant, sights and sounds coming in bursts that make my head spin.

I'm in the hospital. I can't stand up, can't keep my eyes open, can't make my tongue form words. I'm in a wheelchair. No one knows what's wrong with me, but they say I'm not drunk; there's no smell of alcohol. They think maybe pills. They pump my stomach.

I slouch in the wheelchair and watch them draw blood as if from someone else. The orderly takes my blood pressure, pulse, respiration, all low. He helps me stand and holds me up to step on the scale. As he tries to measure my height, I turn toward him and puke what's left of my guts out, hosing his pants and shoes. I hear him cursing as I fall to the ground, and then there's nothing.

I've ODd, been in and out of consciousness for more than thirty hours. At some point I am coherent enough for the hospital to discharge me, and my parents take me home and put me on the couch. Someone sits next to me day and night. I'm breathing, and they are grateful for that.

7

FALLING

APRIL 2006

I knew the most important choice I made every day of my search was to be patient.

Fuck patience.

I wanted my letter. I wanted my mother. I wanted answers. What is my mother's first name? Who is my father? Where is my mother now? Why did she leave me? Why didn't she want me?

Through Beth I connected with Judy, another search angel who seemed to be willing to invest an infinite reservoir of time and energy in my search. David and Judy bore the brunt of my anxiety as I rambled on about my experience with Mary, the frustration of not knowing what secrets the letter held. They encouraged me to keep charging ahead, to leave no stone unturned. To be patient.

Dear Kevin

It sounds like you are progressing very nicely in your search. First, as I indicated to you in my last e-mail, one of tricks is to suggest there is a

"HEALTH" issue that must be resolved by finding one or both of your biological parents. This plea will sometimes get someone's attention.

Second, the best tactic is to find a "mole" like your friend at the hospital who can go find the records. As I told you that's how my birth mother was first located . . . i.e. a sympathetic heart at the hospital. If your friend can't get to the "archives room" surely she knows someone who can . . . keep working that angle . . . maybe you have other good friends who know someone at the hospital.

all the best

David

Subject: Re: support group info

Hi Kevin,

I know from past experience with those searching in NY that it is a very tough state in which to obtain information, but not impossible. I don't have any experience with searches in NY so will have to find others who can assist you.

Have you written to the hospital for a copy of your records? Have you contacted the doctor and lawyer to see if they would provide anything at all to you? Would the lawyer perhaps be willing to contact your bmother and ask if she'd agree to contact from you? At least 90% or more of birthmothers want to be found so it would be a good assumption that your bmother is one of them.

Judy

I WAS SO focused on getting my hands on the letter, I told them I had to wait to approach the hospital. That was only half true, and even I wasn't fully aware of my hesitation.

"You need to be patient in the process, Kevin." Judy's voice calmed me. "But more than anything, be patient with yourself. Let your own emotions guide you." I knew she could hear my sigh over the phone line. Her voice sharpened, cutting through the moment like a knife. "Okay, Kevin. Are you ready to take the next steps and reach out again for the letter?"

"I am."

"Are you open and willing to accept whatever the letter might bring?"

"Yes."

"You need to really ask yourself this, Kevin. Is there a dream or wish or want that you think the letter will fulfill? And if it doesn't, what will happen to you? Who will you be?"

The letter was mine. It was addressed to me, from my mother, and I was going to get it, no matter what it took. I would get my letter. Judy held my hand, coaxed and prodded until I was ready to take the plunge.

I called Mary's direct line and left a voice message for her to please call me. I knew Mary only worked part time, so when she didn't return my call, I made myself wait another two days.

When I got her voicemail the second time, I hung up and dialed the main office number. The receptionist put me on hold to forward my call to the director, Mary's supervisor.

"Hello, you wanted to speak with Mary? What is it that you need to speak to her about?"

The supervisor listened carefully as I explained how I had already met with Mary about my adoption, and she was expecting my call. I expected them to stonewall me. I expected to argue. I expected every scenario I could imagine. But I didn't expect what I got.

"I'm sorry. She's not with us anymore. Mary died."

I took a breath to take a damn-the-torpedoes attitude, to not take no for an answer. The letter was mine. I meant to be clear that I insisted on getting it. Instead, something shifted in me.

"I'm so sorry."

"Thank you. Is there something I can help you with?"

"I'll call back another time."

I hung up the phone and cried. I didn't expect to feel sad, and broken, and cheated, didn't want to feel this way, but I did.

I needed to take a break. It was time to stop, to breathe, to make sure I should have made this call, should have even started this search, should have ever wanted to know. Was it right to even want to know?

AGE TWELVE

"The money sucks, but the tips are good."

Tony has a paper route seven days a week. Most of our drinking's on his tab while I supply the pills, but he has a plan to help us both out.

"The daily delivery isn't worth it," he says. "If you want, you can have the daily route and I'll keep Sundays."

"It's not worth it?"

"I mean, don't get me wrong. You can make money at it. I just don't want to do both."

"What if I do Sundays?"

"Fuck no." Tony takes a long pull on his cigarette, tips his head back and blows smoke toward the sky. "I earned Sundays, man. You gotta earn it."

"Cool. Okay, I'll take the daily route."

"Cool." He passes me a cigarette and gives me a light. "I ain't gonna deliver papers forever. When I get a better job, I'll give you Sundays."

"Thanks, man."

"Just don't fuck it up."

He's right; the money isn't great. A lot of assholes think they can avoid paying and get the paper for free, but it doesn't take me long to figure out the deadbeat houses. I sneak up on them around dinner time and in front of their family shame them into paying.

The cash helps keep the alcohol flowing, and now that I have a reputation for being able to get good drugs, I get a new mix of friends. Tony and I still hang out, but I'm accepted back into my old friend Eddie's circle, including Frankie and Paul.

Paul lives right behind our house, but he's older, and we never really connected before now. Paul's older brother, Lenny, is known for two things—he's an expert boxer, and he deals drugs. Frankie's a new kid at school. I don't even know where he lives, because he spends every night with us.

Paul sneaks us down into the finished basement of his house where, as long as Lenny doesn't chase us out, we can enjoy his parents' wet bar and smoke dope to our hearts' content. Eddie's house is off limits. One time, Eddie's parents are out, and we think we're safe to party in his room, but his parents come home early and catch us. His mother screams that we're all bums, and his father, drunk as usual, punches Eddie and shouts threats as the rest of us run out through the garage.

Up 'til now, I've had a small bedroom on the first floor, right next to my parents' room and the bathroom. My mother has the upstairs room over the garage, where she sews, irons clothes, and creates crafts like furry tissue box covers, complete with two eyes and a button nose.

I make the case that I'm getting older, and the larger room will give me some privacy, and my parents acquiesce. The stairs are right off the kitchen, perfect for sneaking my new friends in and out at any hour.

Paul pretty much keeps to himself, mostly from fear of his brother, but Eddie, Frankie, and I are inseparable. It doesn't take my parents long to figure out that my friends come in the house smiling and polite but stumble out after midnight loud and obnoxious. My father ignores us, avoiding confrontation to keep from raising his blood pressure and stressing his weak heart.

My mother is the bouncer, but we quickly learn how to circumvent her security check at the kitchen door. One of us, usually Eddie, waits outside while Frankie and I pass muster. We come in and hang our jackets in the kitchen so she can see we're not carrying anything. Once upstairs, I open the window and drop down a bag tied to a rope, big enough for a quart bottle of whatever we're drinking that night.

As the winter sets in we turn to Mad Dog 20/20, or if we have the cash, Yukon Jack. The best nights are when Frankie shoves a pint of 190-proof Everclear down his pants. Two shots each is all it takes.

MY OLD FRIEND Donald starts going along on my paper route. He doesn't have a bike, so he jogs alongside as I ride, slow enough so he can keep up, giving him papers to run up on one side of the street while I ride up on the other, throwing them on the front steps or in front of the garage door.

We're almost done, on our way back, and I stop in the middle of the street to light a cigarette. Donald doesn't smoke, so he grabs a few papers and strolls over to the last few houses. I sit on my bike as the nicotine clears my senses. The September air tastes fresh and crisp, the blue sky and puffy white clouds are mesmerizing.

I look up and see someone watching me from in front of a low-built brick house.

The boy walks up. Face to face he's exactly my height, but somehow seems much younger than me. A cute doxie puppy hovers around his ankles. The boy smiles.

"Hi," he says, not putting out his hand to shake, just standing so straight and still that I only stare at him without answering.

His eyes dart up and down the street, then back to me.

"I'm Davey."

I'm still gawking. He bends over and scoops up his dog.

"Want to pet my dog?" he asks, his smile at full volume. I've forgotten to pull on my cigarette, and I flick it away. I let the dog sniff my hand and lick my fingers. I smile and pet the top of his head, scratch his neck and behind his ears.

Donald's back and stands next to me. It's getting late, and he wants to finish up the route, but I don't move, still petting the dog, Davey holding him.

Donald is rigid, not smiling, his eyes cold and remote. He knows something, knows that Davey is not like us. He steps back and turns away, rejecting Davey's overture.

"It's a cute dog," I say, trying to prompt Donald.

"It's getting late." He looks at me, concerned now. We've been friends a long time, and I don't want him to be mad at me.

I scratch the puppy's ears one last time. "Take it easy." As I put my foot on the pedal and roll away, Donald jogging alongside, I hear Davey calling.

"I'll be here. Both of us will be here tomorrow." His high-pitched voice is hopeful, wistful.

The next day on the bus home, Donald says he doesn't have time to help me anymore. I really like having a friend to hang with on the route, but I act like it's cool. "Whatever."

On my bike I try to pace the route but keep getting ahead of myself. Maybe it's because Donald isn't with me.

I see Davey long before I get to his house, his dog at his side. He waves and I pull my bike to the side of the road.

"Where's your friend?" he asks, not smiling.

"He doesn't want to help me anymore."

"He didn't like me." Davey looks right into my eyes. It's a statement, not a question, but a prompt for my response.

I put my bike down on the grass and drop to my knees, and the dog comes to me. Davey kneels next to me, laughing, almost giggling.

"He likes you." He smiles and rolls back on the grass. We sit for a while, playing with the dog. The puppy loves when we call him back and forth, running the few steps to our laps and rolling over for belly rubs, his sharp baby teeth needling our hands and fingers but not hurting, only pricking our skin gently.

"How many papers do you have to deliver?" he asks, looking at the bag of newspapers on the grass by my bike.

I know the exact amount is lower, but I want to impress him. "Over one hundred."

"You must be strong to carry them all." He nods toward the bag.

I laugh and rough up the dog playfully. "It's even more on Sunday. On Sunday, you have to split the route, or carry two bags. I used to carry both bags before I gave it up to my buddy Tony. He likes doing the Sunday route, but I make more money doing the weekly, so I gave it to him." I mix the half-truths, knowing I can keep track. Davey's already impressed enough.

"Stand up back to back."

Even though we're about the same height, he insists I'm taller.

"I'll prove it," he says, grabbing me by the shoulders. "Turn around."

We stand forehead to forehead and he crouches down and laughs as I stand on my toes.

Davey invites me in for a bottle of Coke. His house is smaller than mine, older and cramped. We head downstairs, where his father has a workbench and tools, much like my own father's and grandfather's workbench, old desk drawers brimming with gadgets, cabinets with jars of mixed bolts and screws and nuts. Davey's basement has the same kind of magic, except his father works for the railroad, so all the tools and nuts and bolts seem bigger, more exotic.

Davey shows me a box of toys from when he was little, pulls out a bag of old hats, mostly knit snow caps.

"Try this one on."

He steps toward me and pulls the cap onto my head, steps back and laughs, reaches up to pull it off, puts another one on, and I let him pull it down over my ears. His hands linger on the hat, holding it down over my ears, moving closer to me, his feet toe to toe with mine, our knees barely touching.

"What are you doing?" I look past him, back to his intense gaze, then away again.

"Do you like the hat?" He drops his hands on my shoulders.

"Yeah. I guess." I'm warm all over.

"Do you want me to take it off?" His eyes bore into mine.

I stare back, calm, at home. "Yes."

He pulls the hat off, giggles and rubs it across my face, pretending to tickle me. Then his hands are on me, pulling me against him. Our mouths open and close as we kiss, open and close. He steps away, just far enough to unbutton my shirt, and rubs his hands over my chest and belly.

He strips, first me, then himself, and pulls me down on the frayed rug that's barely a cushion on the concrete basement floor. Laying himself down on top of me, rubbing and kissing, he moves up and down the length of my body, rubbing, humping, moving, kissing, back and forth, until with a great shudder, he cums on me, our bodies now wet, sticky, soaked.

I can't cum that way, so we clean up and get dressed. I finish my Coke in silence.

"I have to finish my route."

"Will you come back tomorrow?"

We kiss awhile longer, then I stand to leave, wondering if he sees my trembling.

"It's better if you go upstairs and leave alone," he says. "Just in case."

NIGHTS ARE FILLED with smoking pot, hash if we have it, and drinking. Weeknights blend into weekends, and weekends become three-day binges.

What kicks us into high gear are the acid trips, which become weekly celebratory events. We drop windowpane during school just to see what happens, and when we aren't tripping, we're popping brown and yellow tabs of PCP.

All winter Frankie, Eddie, and I sneak dope up to my room in our underwear and hoist bottles of whisky and wine up from the window. During the day, I wash out the bottles with hot water, scrape off the labels, and line them up around my room. My mother challenges me, but I tell her they're just decoration, old bottles I found in the woods.

Cold weather also provides an excuse to stop at Davey's house. Other than his daily ritual of dry-humping me, Davey is straight as an arrow, with zero interest in smoking, drinking, or getting high. Me, I'm willing to try anything that involves sex, drugs, or drink. But our connection is a fundamental one—we're both looking for an escape, a way to mask the confusion of life.

Davey has no other friends, and his mother thinks I'm a nice boy. I'm the proof that her family is normal, and that makes me feel almost normal. But for his father, more than anyone else, I'm the veil between desire and reality. I'm a surrogate son for Lori, but the epitome of what Gene envisions a son should be. If I'm everything he wants in a son, he's everything my father has ceased to be, and when we talk, we feel a mutual sense of relief and comfort in our alternate universe.

With me in the house, Davey feels a new sense of freedom, the weight of the chains around his neck lifted, if only for a few hours. He loves watching me play chameleon for whatever he, his mother, or his father need me to be, as changeable as a sunset's last few seconds.

As seventh grade winds down, I've been suspended twenty-two times, mostly for skipping classes, which usually leads to skipping whole days of school. My parents refuse to pick me up anymore, leaving me to walk home, which suits me better anyway.

I fail science and, with one exception, get straight Ds on my final exams, just enough to push me on to eighth grade. I pass English with a B. In standard aptitude tests, I score at first-year college level for reading, and second-year college for writing. The results surprise my teachers, give my parents hope, and make no difference to me whatsoever.

The first day of summer school, some of the other kids make fun of a new kid, slapping the back of his neck and yelling "Redneck!" before running back to their chairs. He literally has a red neck from sunburn below his military haircut.

The other boys soon tire of the game, but I keep it up every time the teacher turns his back or leaves the room. I revel in the way he glares at us with equal parts shame, anger, and humiliation, his face turning as red as his neck, and I want to see how far I can push him.

Eventually he jumps out of his seat, tears running down his cheeks, and faces me. "Keep it up! Keep it up," he says, almost sobbing the words.

"Or what?" I jeer. "What the hell are you going to do?"

With the other kids taunting, "Redneck, redneck, redneck," I laugh and spit in his face. Everyone else is howling behind me. I spit at him again, and he turns, defeated, and slumps back into his seat.

I think I'm a hero, but suddenly the mood shifts. The kids in the back start throwing paper wads and shouting insults at me.

"Barhydt, you're an asshole. What the fuck did you do that for? Fucking creep."

I realize I've been ambushed. Now the redneck kid hates me, and I'm outcast from the rest of the crowd. It's nothing new to me, but at least I've had some fun first. I've already learned enough to know that every friend will eventually either leave me or stab me in the back. I know how to enjoy the ride of fake friendships as long as they last.

After class, I expect somebody to jump me. I have a reputation as a wild kid, but I'm not known for my ability to fight. I'm ready for a beat down. Oddly, nothing happens. Everyone shuffles out of the room. But when the redneck turns to leave, he stops and looks at me.

"You didn't have to do that. Those kids all hate me. You don't even know me." When I don't say anything, he starts to turn away, then stops and asks, "I'm Bruce. Do you want to come over to my house?"

"Yeah, okay. Sure." Why not enjoy the ride?

Bruce lives with his mother, off the main road, a ten-minute walk from school. His mother is at work. The house is a rental, unpainted fading cedar siding. Inside, there's no food, nothing in the refrigerator, nothing at all to eat or drink. Bruce's room has a mattress on the floor, his clothes stuffed in some boxes. I ask if he has any dope, but he says no, he doesn't do that.

"I'm gonna get going. I'm hungry."

"Wanna get some money?"

"For what?"

"Then we can go get some food," he says. At least he's paying attention to me.

"Where do we get the money?"

I follow Bruce to the back of the house. From a window, he points across a long field of weeds and high grass, to a house standing alone, just as threadbare and dilapidated as Bruce's.

"That guy lives there all alone. He's gone during the day."

"You sure he's got money?"

"Yup."

"How do you know?"

"I've been in the house before."

To get up my nerve, I smoke a cigarette, then we head across the field. The weeds grow almost up to the house, and there's no yard to speak of, just rock-hard dirt with a few scraggly plants sticking out here and there.

Bruce goes right up to the side window and pushes on the ripped screen and jiggles the window open.

He gives me a dopey half smile. "Let's do it!"

I give him a boost, and he slips into the house, reaching back through to give me a hand up. The house is dim and dank, smelling of old food and musty air. As my eyes adjust to the light, I see piles of dirty magazines everywhere.

"Where's the money?" I ask.

"Over there. Go ahead."

He jerks his head toward a shabby dresser and starts rummaging through the magazines, sorting them into piles. It's obvious they're what he really wants.

I come back over. "There's not a lot of money. I only got a few bucks. Just coins, no bills." I jingle the change in my pocket.

"You want to eat?" he asks.

My mind is racing, spiked with fight-or-flight chemicals. I'm no longer thinking about food, but I nod anyway. The refrigerator is empty except for some beer, which I grab, and Bruce finds a box of Kraft mac and cheese. He stacks up the magazines and the mac and cheese, puts the screen back, closes the window, and we head out the back door.

"Act cool, man. Just walk naturally."

I dump the change out, and we split it down the middle. Not much, but it's something. Flavored by adrenaline, the mac and cheese is the best I've ever tasted, and we sort through the magazines as we eat.

Bruce says he's done this before, and the guy won't call the cops, and now I see why. The magazines I grabbed are Penthouse and Hustler. Bruce is pickier; his have heavier bond paper, more like a fancy book than a magazine. They're not typical porn with men fucking women, but instead show little girls naked, staring at the camera, or walking in the woods, or sitting on a swing.

Bruce sees the look on my face and mistakes it for desire. "I'm gonna keep these. You can have the rest."

"That's cool with me. I have a bunch at home," I lie.

He digs his half of the change out of his pocket and hands it to me. "Okay, you take the money then."

I finish my mac and cheese and pocket the money. "Cool. Thanks. See you tomorrow."

The first time is always amazing. The first beer, the first pill, the first time Eddie and I smoke weed out of an apple pipe. I love that feeling—

preparing, imagining, visualizing, getting ready to drink, pop, smoke, snort. In that moment I feel most alive, completely focused.

Stealing is the same.

Once I start stealing, I never want to stop. More than anything, I love the deep wanting, that moment when it's about to happen, the bitter taste in my mouth like licking tinfoil. Adrenaline pumps through my skull, and my sinuses clear the way they do after orgasm.

Every time I steal, I feel unstoppable, even as my whole being screams at me to stop. When I get drunk and high, people shun me, as if they're afraid I'll give them a disease. When I steal, I know I am the disease.

Stealing feels like ripping out my own heart and kicking my mother in the stomach hard enough to break her spine all at once without taking a second breath, without even exhaling. Breathe in. Now destroy all I love and learned and know and care and hope and dream. Puke on myself and the ones who cared for me when I had a cough and fever. Drop my eyes to the floor and bathe myself in a shame shower of filth and black water hot enough to steam my skin into gelatin lumps of fat. Now exhale. Repeat.

Little by little, the last pieces of who I am fade, and then I'm gone. I walk and talk and eat and mow the lawn, but I live in complete obsession for my next robbery. So I can steal cash. So I can have money to buy drugs and alcohol. So I can plan my next robbery. Breathe in. Exhale. Repeat.

When you fall riding a bike you get back on and learn, eventually, how not to fall again. When you steal, that is the falling.

8

SHATTERING

APRIL 2006

S era is my youngest daughter from my first marriage."

Judy kept trying to email me, but because I didn't reply, she called me on the phone.

"How many children do you have?"

"Two girls and two boys. Kentaro and Tyler are from my second marriage. They have two older sisters, Sera and Dawn. Sera is short for Seraphina. It was her great grandmother's name. Hated it as a kid, but she loves it now. The girls are a few days shy of one year apart."

Judy waited. I couldn't say the words yet.

"Dawn is doing great. She's a nurse, married, and has a little one."

I trailed off, could feel Judy holding back her impulse to ask more.

"Sera is a lot like me. She's been struggling since she was sixteen. She's twenty-five now. She and Dawn both live in Ohio."

"You said you got a call from your daughter?" Judy prompted.

"From Dawn. I was on the road," I said, trying to impose order on what's happened. It helps to ground myself in the details. "It was a few days ago, and I was on the road, doing some training for work. My first stop was in Syracuse."

I knew I was avoiding the question. Just like I always did. Judy brought me back.

"I didn't know you're a grandfather."

"I have two sons, two daughters, and a grandson."

I imagined Judy trying to do the math and smiled inside. I'd seen the look on people's faces so often.

"My grandson is three months older than my oldest son."

After a brief moment, Judy said, "Wait. What? Your *grandson* is older than your sons?"

"Hard for even me to wrap my head around it sometimes." Usually I was up to explaining, but not today. "It's a long story."

"So you got a call from your daughter?"

"I was in the hotel. Dawn called. 'I've got some bad news, Dad.' I know it's either her mother got beat up and is in the hospital, or Sera is in jail. I'm used to getting those calls, I'm just not ready to have the conversation, so I say to her 'Sweetie, can I call you back in an hour?'"

Judy was just listening. I'd almost forgotten she was even on the line.

"I take a shower, call Eri and say goodnight to the boys. Finally, I sit down and close my eyes for a minute, just breathing in and out, and call Dawn back."

"Hi sweetie. Sorry to take so long. I just wanted to get showered. It's been a long day."

"That's fine, Dad. Did you want to talk tomorrow?"

"No, now is fine. Is it about Sera?"

"Yes, Dad."

"I figured it might be."

"Dad, I don't know how to say this so I'm just going to say it."

"Okay, sweetie."

"Dad, Sera has AIDS."

Judy didn't make a sound as the words poured out. Sera's boyfriend had tested positive for HIV and never told her. She found the results hidden in his dresser drawer, confronted him, they fought, and he hit her. He beat her. She left him, and Dawn took her to get tested. Her viral load was off the charts, around sixty thousand, so the virus was reproducing exponentially. Her CD4, or T-cell count was 198. A healthy person would have five hundred to sixteen hundred. Anything below two hundred is considered AIDS.

"Dawn has been really strong. We both cried a lot, but I'm really proud of her. She's a good big sister. And a wonderful daughter." I added quickly, "They both are."

Judy asked gently, "Is she sick?"

"We don't know."

I'm so grateful for Judy's unwavering support.

"Sera's had a lot of medical problems, but she wasn't seeing a doctor, so we just don't know. She has a high viral load, so she's more likely to develop symptoms quickly, but we won't know for a while. Right now, she's having a mental breakdown, and we're trying to get her some help."

"Are you okay, Kevin?"

"I don't want my baby girl to die." I wept, as my whole world shattered.

AGE THIRTEEN

Every day after summer school, Bruce and I roam the neighborhoods, pick a house, find an open window, or break a small window on the back door and let ourselves in.

Once in, we take no more than five minutes, moving fast, upstairs to the master bedroom, then to look for piggy banks in kids' rooms, quickly filling our pockets with all the bills and change we can find. On our way out, Bruce skims through the basement while I check drawers in the kitchen and rip through the living room. We check the street out front before slipping out the back door and walking casually down the driveway.

Even with my wad of money growing, I add solo night trips to my routine. Instead of walking the streets, I cut through the woods by the power lines that run parallel to the New York State Thruway, looking for paths to the backs of houses.

Without Bruce, I scrounge for cigarettes and booze as well as cash, bringing a canvas bag along with me to carry my take. I stash everything in the woods behind my house, in a hole under a plank of wood covered with leaves and branches.

I tease Bruce that my count is higher than his, even though he got me started in the first place, but as summer school ends, the numbers don't matter much anymore. We guess as a team we're up to fifty or sixty houses.

In the top dresser drawer of the master bedroom, I hit the jackpot— six one-hundred-dollar bills.

"Holy shit, let's get out of here!"

I've never seen Bruce afraid like this. I'm calm as ever as I stuff the money into my pocket and keep digging through the drawer.

"Let's go, let's go," he begs.

I smile and pull two two-dollar bills out of the drawer. He stands at the bedroom door as I find and pocket two handfuls of silver dollars. By the time we leave, he's practically jogging.

I'm ready for more action, but Bruce is almost in tears. He heads straight for the bike path that runs along the railroad tracks, then veers off down the hill toward Normans Kill Creek. He loses control, and I ram into him, and we fall on the slate rocks.

He isn't hurt, but I cut my palm by my pinky finger, and it won't stop bleeding.

"Stick your hand in the creek and let it soak."

The cool water calms us both, and I watch as a little trickle of red ribbons through the clear water and dissipates on its way to the Hudson River. We lay out the six hundreds, more money than we've ever held before, each of us pocketing three hundred. Bruce wants to go home, so I go with him to get a Band-Aid for my hand. I shove the three big bills in my underwear and put the two-dollar bills in the bottom of my sock, then we take off again on our bikes.

We ride toward the other side of town and find a corner store. We buy some sodas with the silver dollars, hanging out at the store. I give

Bruce the rest of the silver dollars to stash by the creek before we both head home.

"See you tomorrow?"

"See you." Bruce pauses. "Maybe we should stop."

"Maybe. See you tomorrow."

Pedaling home gets harder and harder, until I realize the back tire on my bike is completely flat. I start to push along the side of the road, watching for a good place to get on the back streets. Then a car pulls off the road next to me, two men sitting in the front. I don't know either of them.

"Hey, you got a flat tire?"

"Yeah." He's just a guy, but even though it's the middle of the day, the hair on the back of my neck bristles. Something is wrong.

"You want a ride?"

"No." I keep pushing, keep walking.

He leans out the car window. "Do you know Kevin Barhydt?"

I freeze, my heart pounding. "No." I feel the heat in my body rise.

"Where are you coming from?" The man asks, his tone gentle, resting his hands on the steering wheel.

"Don't walk away from us, kid!" the other man barks.

"He's not walking away." The driver turns back to me. "Why don't we give you a ride home?"

"Just put the bike in the back and get in the car," the man says from the passenger side. I can't see his face clearly but can feel his glare.

"Hey, it's okay." The driver opens his door and puts his foot on the road, showing me his badge on his belt. "I'm Officer DeCarlo. You want a ride? That tire looks pretty flat."

"Just put the bike in the trunk and get in the car, kid," the mean cop snaps.

"Okay, okay." DeCarlo steps out of the car but leans back down into it. "The kid's coming, okay?"

He turns back to me, his voice calm and kind.

"Come on, kid, I'll help you out."

He walks over and puts one hand on the left handlebar grip, and together we roll the bike up to the back of the car. With the bike in the trunk, he pulls the lid down as far as it will go and ties it off with a cord, his hands quick and deft. Somehow, without seeming to, he coaxes me forward, and I slip into the back seat. DeCarlo slides back into the driver's seat, his tone calm but serious.

"We can help you, but you've got to tell us the truth." He looks at me in the rearview mirror. "You're Kevin Barhydt, right?"

"Yes." I swallow hard.

"I told you it was him. He's a liar. Let's take him in." The mean cop's harsh voice hurts my ears.

"No, he's not a liar. He just told us the truth. You're not a liar, are you, Kevin?"

I know that they know something, and I've got no choice now but to play it out.

"Empty your pockets." The mean cop doesn't give me an inch.

"Kevin, you have anything in your pockets?" DeCarlo asks.

I turn both my pockets inside out, smiling, laying on the charm, leaning back so they can see.

"Turn around," the mean cop says. "Check his back pockets."

DeCarlo leans over the seat, and I feel hands, first one pocket then the other.

"I just want to go home," I croak through the dryness in my throat. "My bike tire is flat."

I can't think. For a few minutes they argue, whether they should take me home or to the police station. DeCarlo loses the debate.

"Did you check his back pockets good? Turn around again."

The mean cop checks my pockets again, front and back. My hands are sweaty now. His face fills my vision, uncomfortably close. "Take off your shoes."

I give him one shoe, then the other, afraid I'll pass out. The mean cop probes each sneaker with his fingers and, clearly disappointed, hands them back to me. All I have to do is put them back on, but my heart is pounding, the pressure in my head making me dizzy.

"Can . . . can I put my shoes back on?"

The mean cop says, "Yeah, go ahead."

My heart skips a beat, and I lean down to slip my shoes back on.

DeCarlo says, "Did you check his socks?"

The mean cop hangs over the back seat as I pull my left sock off and hand it to him. I fumble with the right one, trying to block his view. He shoves me back and grabs the sock. A look of triumph spreads across his face as he feels the crinkle of bills.

The mean cop smiles. DeCarlo smiles, too.

At the station, I'm arrested. I tell them about the silver dollars I spent in the store and take them to the creek to find the rest of the silver dollars.

I don't say anything about Bruce. I say, I don't know about any hundred-dollar bills. What I don't know, is that Bruce is at the police station too, or that they already have his half of the hundred-dollar bills. That a girl we know from school saw us in the neighborhood and gave the police Bruce's name. That the only reason they know my name is because Bruce told them.

Bruce doesn't come back to school in the fall. I stop counting at one hundred houses.

PROBATION IS INTIMIDATING, until I realize I only have to see the officer once a week. Bernie already has more than a hundred other kids to deal with every week, so as long as I stay out of trouble at school and show up for my meetings, as far as he knows everything is fine. He doesn't have time to call my parents, and the few times they come to probation meetings with me, I'm on my best behavior.

Frankie and Eddie come over every weeknight. My parents are just glad to know where I am. Flush with cash from robbing houses and stealing from my parents, I usually splurge on whatever dope or booze we need for the night.

Frankie's older brother makes monthly drug runs from Texas to New York, and whenever he's in town, Frankie is our man of the hour. He sets us up with a bottle of Everclear, some acid, a mix of crystal meth and heroin, and a clean needle.

We shoot acid just to kick-start the night. After a shot each of Everclear, we spend the rest of the night listening to Hendrix, Zappa, Rundgren, and Buchanan, cranking up the guitar solos as we pass the bong around. We don't really need to smoke weed, but it settles our stomachs and keeps our hands busy.

I've given up the paper route, and sex with Davey trails off. I care less about him and sex than I do about getting high, and on weekends I'm gone most Friday nights, not returning to my parents' house until late Sunday morning or early afternoon.

Most of the time, I'm down in Schenectady. Neil, Tony Rotundo's friend and dealer, lives there and takes me under his wing. I party all weekend, then bring some dope back to sell at school during the week.

On Sundays, I wait in the woods or across the street in Eddie's garage, until I see my parents drive away for church or to go shopping. When they get home, they wake me up to find out where I've been, but I yell and curse and punch walls until they leave me alone, relieved I'm home, not in jail, and alive.

9

FAILING

APRIL 2006

*S*ister Charla?"

Her office was only across the street, but I decided to call first, out of respect.

"Yes, this is Sister Charla. Can I help you?"

"Sister Charla, this is Kevin Barhydt."

"Hello, Kevin. How can I help you?" She was polite and professional.

"Sister Charla, I wanted to say how sorry I am about Mary." The phone went silent for a moment.

"Thank you, Kevin. I miss her very much. She was a very dear friend." Her voice sounded broken and sad.

"I'm so sorry for your loss. She was a wonderful woman." I felt sad, too, for both of us. "I only met her once, but I could tell how much she cared for everyone around her."

"Thank you, Kevin."

Now the hard part.

"Sister Charla, when I met with Mary earlier this month, we talked for a long time. She was as helpful as she could be." I hesitated, not sure I trusted myself to find the right words. "I know there is a letter from my mother to me. Mary knew about the letter. My mother named me Stephen Michael. My father told me that was my name. The letter is to me, Stephen Michael, and I'm hoping you can help me."

"What letter, Kevin?" I'd ambushed her.

"Mary said there is a letter written from my mother to me in the files in Albany. When I called to follow up with her a few weeks ago, that's when I found out she had passed. I didn't want to bother you, but I'm not sure who to talk to about it."

Sister Charla collected herself.

"Kevin, please give me some time to look into this."

"Can you help me? Please?"

"I can't promise you anything, but I will get back to you as soon as I can."

AGE FOURTEEN

For ninth grade, my parents enroll me in Bishop Gibbons Catholic High School. Dad thinks sports will be good for me, so I spend the last days of my summer in football camp.

At first, everyone seems to be as clueless as me about what's expected. The coaches joke around, make us do push-up after sit-up after leg lift, warn us that tomorrow we'll be praying to stop, but in a week, we'll beg for more.

My body isn't limber or snappy, but my muscles, however sore, rise to the challenge. Working out actually feels good, foreign but familiar.

Then the coach catches me off guard, asking what position I want to go out for. No one bothered to tell me that at least a fundamental knowledge of the game is assumed. The coach takes pity on me, sizes me up, and says tight end.

The other tight end hopeful—an extremely handsome six-foot Latino hunk—is a natural. My tryout is nothing short of humiliating. I'm a joke, everyone on the field knows it. My only goal is to disappear as quickly as humanly possible. Back at home, I throw the football at the window and hit the lamp on my desk instead.

Something snaps. I rage, my words unintelligible. I overturn my bed and throw the dresser down the stairs one drawer at a time—clothes flying, wood splintering, holes gouging the walls.

Safely barricaded from the world, I crank up the music and start on a nickel bag, smoking the first joint while rolling the rest.

Deep breath in. Out. In. Out. Another joint, then a cigarette. A third joint. My brain is quiet now, listening to the music, hearing each note, dreaming of playing in front of ten thousand people, everyone smiling and singing along.

A fourth joint. Stomach queasy now. Stub out the joint. Cigarette makes me dizzy. Stub it out, too. Sit and rest, breathe. Light the joint again, take small hits, watch the smoke, music still playing but can't hear it anymore, don't care anymore.

My mind can process again now. The scorn on the coaches' faces makes sense. The other kid is great, so much better. They like him, don't like me, have no reason to like me. I can't play football, don't want to play, don't understand the rules, don't know the positions, don't fit in, don't fit in, don't fit in. It's okay, understandable and reasonable that they have no use for me. A fifth joint. No queasy stomach now, nothing but peace and calm and understanding.

A month into the school year and still no friends. It isn't easy to get high with the Franciscan Brothers monitoring the hallways, almost impossible to get outside. At lunch time, I skulk down to the bathroom farthest from the cafeteria and suck down a joint so I can fade into the rest of the day.

On my walk back into afternoon class, some kid that I hardly know throws a wad of paper at my face, taunting me with friends around laughing, and without thinking I push him, hard, and he falls. It seems I hardly touched him, but I'm stoned and confused and kids are yelling, "Kevin did it. He hit him for no reason."

Faces swirl around me. I hear myself laughing, but my voice is not my own, and my laugh goes in fits and starts as the Brother takes me from the class, and the school is in an uproar, and the boy has to go to the hospital.

The blur continues from school office to home and expulsion, and now my probation officer calls my parents and says, "But Kevin said everything was going well at home." My parents tell him, "He's out of control. He stays out all weekend, and we don't know where he is. He's out with his friend Neil, who is already out of high school, and Tony Rotundo, and he's down in Schenectady on the streets, sleeping in basements."

I sit across from Bernie, and he says he has no choice now. He has to take me out of their home, out of my home.

I cry, pitiful. "Please don't."

"You can't stay at home. It's either foster care, or juvenile detention."

My choice, he says.

The news settles in slowly, and weekends with Neil become a daily lifestyle, living in half-built houses and talking through the night, imagining we can live like this indefinitely. Coming home when the house is empty only to steal anything I can find—nickels, dimes, quarters, Valium, Percocet, gin, vodka.

But the holidays are coming, and after missing Thanksgiving, we decide to go home for December. My parents are glad to see me, but fear of what I know is coming keeps me from hearing them. Whenever they speak, I scream. *You hate me. You don't love me. Please don't let them take me.*

No one else is at home when the social worker calls to tell my parents they have a foster home.

"Your placement has to start within a set time. You're scheduled for next Saturday."

That's December 18, 1976.

My tears flow but she stands firm.

"Please don't make me go before Christmas," I beg.

"I can't control the date, Kevin." Her voice is soothing and kind, but unwavering.

"I've got a knife in my hand."

"Kevin, don't cut yourself."

I lay my arm flat on the counter, and the blade goes back and forth on my left wrist, my right hand forcing the blade down harder and harder, the blood running onto the counter. I talk her through each slice, telling her how my wrist is open now, the skin doesn't hurt any more when the knife pulls across it, and my tears have stopped, only small sobs into the phone.

"You won't take me before Christmas, you won't."

I hang up the phone and stare at the knife in my hand, so much blood already on the blade, but now the feeling of cutting feels necessary, so I go on and on. Even as I close my eyes, my hand knows how to move the blade, my wrist knows how to lie still, being sawed into pieces.

PROBATION OFFICER, social worker, mother, father, judge, court clerk, and me—all alone, confused and stoned, my wrist bandaged. I can't sleep the night before, so I smoke bowl after bowl of weed, trying to forget what's happening tomorrow.

I keep thinking the judge will ask my parents if they have any objections, and my father will bellow, *NO! You can't take our son away, we want him with us, you can't have him.* But he doesn't.

The next morning is nothing but procedure. My parents somehow turn my life over to Bernie's judgment. Social Services tells me to say goodbye to my parents, Mom not able to hold it together, Dad making a good show of it, saying it will be okay, they will visit me, and we'll be together for Christmas, and every two weeks on the weekend. And then they're gone.

THE HOUSE IS old and smells like Uncle Frank's after Aunt Sophie died, and the house didn't get dusted, and the windows didn't get opened for weeks. The old lady, Marie, seems even older than the house. Her husband, Sam, is weathered, but looks like the one I'll be afraid of. His eyes are old and faded as he smiles and welcomes me to my foster home. Sam seems normal, a regular guy, like my Uncle Clev, and that makes me feel comfortable. The bedroom becomes my new world.

A few days before Christmas, a visitor comes to see Sam and

Marie. Tim is a mirror image of me—skinny, scraggly hair, soft eyes, and a gentle voice. We bond without ever knowing each other's last name.

Tim gets high, and Tim drinks beer, and Tim likes girls. Most importantly, Tim steals. He says he feels bad that he never has money to get presents for Sam and Marie, who fostered him when he was little. He tells them he loves them, how wonderful they are, all the lies they want to hear.

At night, Tim and I go for a long walk, just to talk and get some fresh air. Our eyes are adept at picking out the signs as we roam the neighborhood. Dark windows. No car in the driveway. House set back. Hedges between houses. Large basement windows, or low kitchen windows.

We find three that night. The first two are typical, not well off, and we leave with what we hope are some real diamonds and gold jewelry. The third is different.

A Christmas tree, fully decorated, gifts piled around the base. I stop and stare at the familiar scene, flashing back to my parents' house, snooping to see what presents were mine, not daring to open any, just basking in the riches laid out for me, how much I had to look forward to in the morning. A chill shivers my spine. This isn't my house, and I want to cry, to run home, not to Sam and Marie but to my home, to be with my parents, to cry out loud that all I want is to be with them, to be normal again, to go back before life got so full of hurt and tears, so void of light.

When I turn to tell Tim we should go, I see his tears. Feeling lost, we sit down in the middle of the presents. My heart calms and fear dissipates. He's as lost as I am, and together, in some stranger's house, we find a momentary peace.

We are here to steal, but instead we borrow what we can't have. We fondle each present, careful to put the children's gifts back neatly in their place while setting aside the smaller adult ones that are easy to carry.

Using wrapping paper to guess the intended recipients, we organize the packages between us. Tim wants gifts for Sam and Marie, the closest facsimile he has to adults who love him. I pick several to give to my mom and dad and hoard a few for myself.

On our way back to Sam and Marie's, we talk about how happy they'll be to get our gifts. We laugh at how opening their gifts will be as much a surprise for us as it is for them. But the laughter seems to make us hurt worse inside, and we walk the rest of the way back in silence.

When we steal from a home, we risk arrest and prosecution. Until tonight, it's never felt like I'm stealing someone's life.

The New Year begins, and new routines help me make sense of things. Marie ignoring me and Sam heading out to hang with his friends at the bar down the block. Getting up in the morning, going to my new school, getting high with my new friends, feeling like the kids in the hallway might jump me any minute. Every couple of weeks, I go back home for a weekend, and that throws my routine off. My parents want to spend time with me, to make up in one weekend what they've missed for two weeks, trying to forget how our life has been disrupted, just like the clot in my father's arteries that made his strong body collapse into a heap on the couch. Some brokenness is beyond a doctor's skill to heal.

They try to laugh and act normal, but now the house feels strange to me, and the loss of time with them feels large and heavy in my mind. My heart feels dim and remote while my mind screams for relief, my only goal to hole up in my room and retreat into my numbness.

My parents feel as though they've lost their son, but at least I'm in the house again. At least my body is.

On Sunday, I care for nothing except getting as high as possible before getting in the car. Going back to Sam and Marie's means nothing except the return to my new routine. Just a month ago, I was in agony over leaving my parents. Now, while they weep, I have no use for agony.

"Can you give me some money? Thanks. Okay, see you in two weeks."

I pocket the money, walk into my new home, and close the door.

RUNNING AWAY from Sam and Marie's seems like a bright idea.

Run away, tell my parents and social worker that they tie me up, hold me at gunpoint, drink every day. Tell them that Marie's only job is to hang shopping circulars on doorknobs, buy two bottles of vodka, and pass out in her chair, while Sam makes me breakfast and swears she's under the weather. The courts will admit they've made a mistake and let me come home.

I'm learning to mix. Everything's true, except the gun and tying me up. Weaving fact with fiction gives me a sense of power. Each sharing grounds the story in my heart until I'm no longer lying, because I believe it myself. And my parents believe it. The social worker doesn't defend Sam and Marie, and I envision bending the whole legal system to my storytelling will. I'm confident I'll soon be back in my room with my friends.

Instead I'm dragged, punching, kicking, screaming *fuckyoufuckyoufuckyou nonononono*, my mother and father crying, from their house and deposited with Thelma and Ted Carpinteria in a household of kids ranging from age eleven to eighteen.

Danny Germaine is twenty-three, but he doesn't come home except to drop off another batch of weed and pick up his profits from Ronnie and Paulie. Ronnie Tucci is eighteen and looks like every high school football player wannabe-team-captain douchebag.

Tina and Brandy Carpinteria are Thelma and Ted's biological daughters. At sixteen, Tina is in love with Paulie, her adopted brother. Paulie's fifteen and was adopted after Thelma fell in love with him too. Brandy is fifteen and my dream girl.

Louie DiBraccio is Thelma's nephew, the only kid smaller than me, which at first makes me think I won't be at the bottom of the pecking order. He's a few years younger, only eleven, but with the hardness of an eighteen-year-old street kid. In Schenectady, the name DiBraccio is synonymous with the local mafia. Louie's mother is in rehab, his father in jail.

This is my new home.

After the social worker leaves, I unpack and sit in my room, feeling out my new world. I lie down on the bed and close my eyes, listening for the sounds to tell me how to avoid the future, my future, lurking just outside. Tina, Brandy, and Louie knock and ask if I want some anise, a sickly sweet, colorless liqueur, because Thelma has gone to the store, and Ted isn't home from the post office yet.

The bar is off limits, but if I'm cool, they'll share the booze with me. We smoke a joint and drink the syrupy liqueur, and the buzz comes quickly, that familiar feeling that tells me nothing matters, will never matter again, and it settles me in for the night, settles my mind and my body, and Brandy sits too close to me, and I think I'll never survive here, and who cares if I won't because right now I never want to leave.

THELMA'S BEATINGS ARE HARSH, but that makes me feel normal because she beats all of us. After a few weeks, I don't cry anymore, not because I toughen up, but because I dread the shaming of the other kids. I'm embarrassed when I cry, but Louie takes a beating without a tear. I want to be accepted so I can fit in. When I come back from weekends with my parents, carrying cash, crystal meth, pills, and bags of dope, I feel welcome. I'm a customer for Paulie and Ronnie's dealing, and a supplier for our family party nights.

The first month goes by without anyone at Draper High School paying much attention to me, but slowly my name gets around. I'm skipping class, hiding out under a stairway in the center of the building when a student comes up and speaks in a whisper.

"Are you Kevin Barhydt?"

"Yeah." I think she's cute, wondering what's up.

"You need to stay out of the halls." She looks at me without malice, but with less than kindness in her eyes. I stare at her blankly, confused about whether she's trying to warn me about something. She walks away without another word.

The next morning before school, Ronnie comes into my room, eyes burning with rage, and slams me into the wall again and again. Eventually he lets me drop to the floor and kicks me into the corner.

He looms over me, barely breathing hard, and speaks for the first time. "Did you rob a fucking teacher's house?"

I have no idea who lived in any of the houses I broke into. "No. When? I don't think so," I stammer.

He kicks me again. "You got busted for robbing a house, right? That's why you're here, asshole."

"No." I try to sort through the sequence that led me here. "I got probation for robbing a house," I grunt between kicks. "I was sent here because I got in a fight at Bishop Gibbons. They took me out of my home."

He picks me up again and pins both my arms with his left hand. "That was a fucking teacher's house." He punches the side of my head so hard I see stars. "That was a fucking teacher's house." Punch. "That was a fucking teacher's house, a teacher's house at our fucking high school, you fucking asshole." Punch. "He's a fucking teacher at school." Punch. "He knows who you are, and he knows who we are, and he's after your fucking ass." Punch. "You're fucked, and now we're fucked. You're fucked so we're fucked, so fuck you. You're fucking out of here." His spit sprays in my eyes and hair, his knee rams my balls. "Got it? You're fucking out of here." I crumple to the floor, only half conscious.

I hear whispering through the haze, sense everyone walking past my room, my humiliation on full display, but I can't look up, can't respond.

I manage to change my shirt and stumble to school by myself. The sweet girl from yesterday stands at the top of the stairway talking to a man, the gym teacher. He's over six feet tall, black hair cut short so it doesn't need combing. He looks younger than the other teachers at the school, and he smiles as she turns to point at me before walking away.

The man comes down the stairs, still smiling, but I see his fists are clenched. He stands looking around the atrium. It's late; classes have already started, and all the classroom doors are closed, the hallway empty. Still smiling, he looks down at me, and as I look back at him his face turns red.

"I don't ever want to see you again." He looks ready to kill me now. "Do you understand me?"

Even as I look up at him, afraid, my mind shifts, remembering random moments—the shame of the morning beating from Ronnie, Sam and Marie's pale imitation of parenting, my parents crying when I was taken away, the helpless, hopeless look in my father's eyes, how all my childhood friends are gone.

I don't move or make a sound, and he begins to shake with rage, and I know there's nothing he can do to me.

"You're the six-hundred-dollar house." It's a statement, not a question, the only time I was ever caught. How he knows my name, I don't know, and I don't care. The fact of him makes me feel guilty, but it's also freeing, real power.

"That was my house, you little asshole. My bedroom you rooted around in, my wife's clothes you touched. That was money for my mortgage, my family's home." He wants to hit me, to pick me up and throw me across the school, smash me out the front door onto the sidewalk. But because he's a good man, a teacher and a husband and father and son, he can only stand in front of me and shake, his fury nothing more than empty, impotent rage.

Robbing houses never felt foreign, never bad or even unnecessary. Getting and having money for drugs was the natural course, a simple priority.

His hurt and rage make me feel good, justified, connected to him, to his family, to the girl who warned me and then pointed me out to him. I didn't want to hurt them. Nothing about stealing has ever made me want to stop, and neither does this man. I only needed the money to get the drugs to quiet the gyro in my head, slow my mind and numb my heart and my soul.

Understanding dawns. I know that I deserve his hate, that he doesn't deserve the shame I brought on him. I deserve to not live at home. I deserve what that 4-H leader did to me. I deserve to not know my own mother, for her to abandon me and give me away. I deserve to be punished, and this is my role in life, who I was born to be. But today, I can't give him what he needs, I can't be punished in this public place, and I have failed him. I am a failure.

I LIVE ON THE STREETS in downtown Schenectady for a few days. The cops catch me and take me back a few times, Thelma beats me, Ronnie threatens me. I sneak out of the house and never come back.

In the morning I make my way to the railroad tracks, just to sit and stay off the streets. A kid I know is there too, skipping school. I want to save my money for dope, so we head to the convenience store, and I teach him how to distract the cashier while I steal two cartons of Marlboros, some snack food, and a quart of Genesee Cream Ale.

When we climb the path to the tracks, someone is already sitting there smoking, a grown man, but young, early twenties. He ignores us, so we settle down to smoke and drink our beer. Finally, he breaks the silence.

"You guys skipping school today?"

"Yeah," we say, nodding. We're cool.

"You wanna give me a swig of that?" he asks, the cigarette dangling between his fingers.

"Sorry, it's all we got."

He stands and gestures back toward the store. "I know where we can get a case of beer, but I need your help."

I hand him the quart, smiling. "Cool," I say, nudging the other kid with a smile.

"Nah, I'm gonna get going." The boy takes off and disappears around the curve in the tracks.

Jimmy lives on the second floor above a local bar called Fast Eddie's, one room with a bathroom. A truck drops the beer delivery every afternoon, piling the cases at the bottom of the stairs. He and I each lug a case up to his room. No kitchen or refrigerator, so we drink the beer warm.

I rob houses at night, come back with dope, and we get high and drink warm beer. During the day, I walk to one of the local markets to steal bread, baloney, and cheese for us to eat.

Three weeks later, we've run out of dope and money, and it's way too early to start stealing. I keep drinking beer, but Jimmy gets pissed and threatens to throw me out if I don't come up with some money.

"Don't your parents live nearby?" he asks, pacing the room.

"Yeah, they do."

"So just call them and tell them you need some money."

I'm too drunk and tired to argue. I stumble down the stairs to a pay phone on the street. I've known the number for as long as I can remember.

It takes my parents fifteen minutes to get to the bar. My father is driving, and I stand back a few feet, watching, afraid they've called the cops or the social worker or my probation officer.

"Do you have the money?"

"Get in and we'll take you home." He sees I'm ready to run and doesn't try to get out of the car.

"No. If you don't want to give me the money, then why the fuck did you come?"

"We'll give you the money. We just want to make sure you're okay." My father looks to my mother for support and back to me. "Why don't you just get in the car and we'll go for a ride?"

"I don't want to go home."

My father pulls out his wallet, keeps it folded, closed in his hand. "I'll give you the money."

I've held that wallet so many times, taking whatever bills I thought would go unnoticed. I know what's inside, a few twenties and tens, a handful of ones. I don't want to get into the car, but my need for the money is an almost physical pull.

"I'm not going back with you. I don't want to go home, and I'm never going back to any foster home."

Fear is turning to anger, just a few steps away from rage.

"What did they do to you there?" my father asks.

My mother is fighting back tears. "If they hurt you, we can tell some-body." Her voice shakes, grief or anger, I can't tell. My rage rises, and she looks down helplessly, twisting her hands in her lap.

"Nothing," I shout, backing up a step. "They didn't do anything. I'm not going home. I'm fine. I just need some money, just a little bit. If you're not going to give it to me, forget it. Just leave. What difference does it make where I live? You don't care. Nobody cares."

"Here's the money." My father pulls a twenty out of his wallet. "Get in the car and I'll give it to you."

"Why do I have to get in the car?" I'm ready to bolt. Fuck the money.

"We won't take you home. We won't take you back to those foster homes. We just want you to be okay. Maybe take a ride so we can talk. Just down the road. Then you can have the money."

I believe him. My father is weak, but he's incapable of telling a lie.

We drive in silence, turning less than a minute later into the parking lot of my parents' church. My father hands me the twenty as together we get out and walk to the rectory door.

I stand a few steps behind, ready to bolt. A woman answers my father's ring and ushers him in, holding the door and waiting, not saying a word or even smiling, but wearing a patient, gentle look that draws me in.

A disheveled, nearly bald man appears, and under his tattered cardigan, I see the familiar white clerical collar and black shirt.

He jokes and smiles with my father before turning his attention to me, still standing by the door. Lounges in his kitchen chair, smiling up at me, and introduces himself as Father Ralph.

"Do you want a sandwich and soup? I'm about to have lunch."

He gestures for me to sit, relaxed and friendly, so casual and comfortable that I relax too. My response to the white collar is deep, instinctive.

"Herb, can you wait in the car with Virginia?"

My father nods, puts his hand on my shoulder for a brief moment. "I'll be right outside, Kev."

Another instinct takes over, and I shake his hand off, recoiling from his touch. I remember the money, and Jimmy waiting, and I glare.

"Why don't we just eat first? Is that okay?" Father Ralph doesn't touch me, doesn't try to restrain me, but his strong, clear voice cuts through my anger, and I nod. My father closes the door behind him.

"So, you've been having some trouble at home?" Father Ralph asks, lighting a cigarette.

I nod, my eyes focusing on the pack on the table. He offers me one— a non-filter Lark, the same kind my father used to smoke.

I light up, picking a few shreds of tobacco that stick to my lip. We smoke until the food arrives, eat the soup, then the sandwich, all in silence.

"Do you want to come stay with me, Kevin?" I hear the question but have no idea what he's talking about.

He laughs and leans on the table, lights up another cigarette, tossing the pack on the table toward me. I already feel a buzz, but I grab another anyway.

"Not here, Kevin." He laughs again. "You wouldn't want to live here."

He leans back in his chair and blows a cloud of smoke into the room.

"Look, you can't live with your parents, right?" I nod. "And you don't want to live with one of these foster families either? Right? That's what your parents tell me, that you keep running away from there. Right?"

I sit and smoke, wondering where this is going.

"If you keep running away, they'll put you in reform school. I know you don't want to go there. You know what reform school is, right?"

I nod, but put on a tough face, like I don't care. "They have to catch me first."

"And they will," he bellows, leaning forward right in my face. "You're already sitting here with me. You think you won't get fucking caught?"

I've never even heard my parents say *fuck*, much less a priest, and his sudden shout throws me off guard.

"You're a good kid, I can tell, and you've got nice parents, but they don't have any fucking idea how to control you, do they? Do they?"

With every sentence he notches up the volume. I jump when he slaps his palm on the kitchen table.

"Do they?" he screams in my face. "What's your plan? Huh? What's your plan?"

I want to hit him, slam my fist against his nose and run out the door. Fuck the money. Fuck my parents. Fuck everybody. He laughs, looks right through me, and I hate him all the more.

"Have another cigarette, Kevin. You want one before you go? You're going to go now, right?"

"Right." I take the cigarette and light it, but something keeps me in my chair.

Father Ralph leans forward again, puts his hand on my arm. "You don't have a plan. Let me tell you what's going to happen. Do it your way, and you'll get caught. You won't make it if you get caught, and you're gonna get caught. You're a good kid, but you're just a punk. That's Plan A." He leans back in his chair and gives me an appraising look. "Your parents are good people. They can't handle you, but they love you."

He sounds like a priest again.

"I run a home right down the street. It's called WAITT House. W-A-I-T-T. You know what WAITT means?" I shake my head. "'We're All in This Together.' That's your Plan B. Those are your choices. A or B."

"You run a house?" I ask, finding my voice again.

"Right now, it's just counseling for kids like you, but we want to have kids live there. A group home where kids can live who can't make it at home, but instead of reform school, they stay in the house and go to school. Does that sound like something you would be willing to do?"

"No." I don't look at him. "I'm okay for now."

"You're okay?"

He's pissed, not raising his voice, not angry like Ronnie got angry, but angry like the teacher at Draper.

"Your parents are sitting out there. They're trying to help you; I'm trying to help you. You won't make it living on the street. Do you want to go to reform school? Do you want to go to jail?"

"No." I want the money, and I want to leave. I wish I'd never come here.

"No? Good. Do you want help? I can help. Plan A or Plan B?" His voice trails off. Like my mother when she asks me why I'm so upset, not judging me, just caring, waiting, hoping. Father Ralph is stronger than both my parents combined, but still soft enough. Neither of us speak for a long minute.

"Plan A or Plan B, Kevin. Your choice. Do you want help, Kevin?"

I want another cigarette. He gives me one, and I take a few drags.

"Where is this place?"

10

CRYING

OCTOBER 2006

K evin, this is Sister Charla. Would you be able to stop over at my office? I have some news for you about the letter, and I'd rather talk to you in person about this."

My heart pounded in my chest. I'd only spoken to Sister Charla a few days earlier and didn't expect to hear back so soon. My thoughts scattered, my senses set on edge, as she welcomed me into her office with a smile.

I watched her smile fade.

"I called Mary's supervisor in Albany. She and I are old friends, and if not for that, I don't think she would have been willing to discuss this. She realizes that somehow Mary told you about this letter. That doesn't sound like something Mary would ever have done, but now that Mary's died, it makes the matter moot."

I wanted to tell her that Mary never said a word, that I listened to her private conversation through a door. Mary was honorable, and I used my well-honed deceptive skills to get the information from her.

I wanted to say all these things, but I sat still, looking straight at Sister Charla, and relaxed my face so as not to give my thoughts away. I was taught well the art of letting others speak.

"There is a letter, Kevin, but we can't give it to you."

My mind snapped into litigation mode, ready to demand this letter that my mother wrote to me. I was ready to tell her that I would sue, that she would hear from my attorney. I'd go to the news media if I had to.

"We can't give you the letter, because it's not addressed to you." She sat back in her chair and let me process this statement.

I knew she was trying to help me. I saw no defensiveness or hostility, no stone-faced looks.

"There is a letter?"

She nodded. Her eyes were resigned, imploring me to understand, to accept.

"There is a letter, but it's not addressed to you. The letter doesn't say, 'To Stephen Michael.' It says, 'To Stephen Michael's Mother.'"

I sat utterly still, looking up at the ceiling, my imagination trying to find the right order to the puzzle pieces. As her words swirled around and finally settled in my soul, I felt an explosion of loss. My mother named me, gave me away, and never wrote a word to me.

Hi, Judy.

I know it has been a while and I wanted to reach out to you.

First, I hope you had a great summer. Mine was busy, and we are now settling into a new school year. All is well at home.

An update on my daughter, Sera. Sera has been taking meds for several months now and her viral load has gone down. By the last test results, however, we also know that her t-cell count is even lower than it had been. That is upsetting, but since she has not shown any opportunistic infections we are waiting to see if over time the t-cell count will return to normal levels. The doctors say it could just take time. We should be getting a new test and results later in October. Hoping and praying.

I have found, through patient questioning, that the letter at Catholic Charities is not addressed to me but is the letter from my birth mother to my adoptive mother. This is good news, since all I need to do now is ask my mom to send a notarized letter requesting the letter and they will send it to her. It is a copy of the original letter, which was to have been given to my adoptive mom. However, I have asked her in the past and she assured me that she never got any letter. It's possible they never offered it to her, or that she denied it, or that she got it and forgot it. I trust her, but I know her memory is not complete, just like most of us, including me.

To sum it all up, I'm very excited. One step at a time has gotten me my first, middle and last name. Now I will have a letter that has been out of my hands for 44 years. That is exciting. And maybe, just maybe, it will have a first name.

I've typed up a letter and will find a place to take it to get it notarized. I will speak with her soon and ask that she send the letter. I will keep you updated.

Many thanks, and please let me know how you are doing.

Kevin

October 2, 2006

Catholic Charities
27 North Main Avenue
Albany, NY 12203

Dear Margaret Ellett:

I am writing to ask that you send me the letter from the birth mother of my son, Kevin John Barhydt, born June 27, 1962.

Please forward this letter to me at:
29 Brentwood Lane
Schenectady, NY 12306

Sincerely,
Virginia Barhydt

THE LETTER ARRIVED ON A TUESDAY, just two days before Thanksgiving. I left work early, drove straight to my parents' house, and found my mother sitting at the table, her face streaked with tears. I sat down to talk with her, letting the letter wait, opening myself to experiencing and remembering every single moment. I felt Mom trembling when I put my hand on her arm. Her tears came again, and she brushed them away quickly.

I said softly, "You read the letter?"

"Yes." Her voice caught. She tried to laugh and cleared her throat.

"I'm sorry you're crying. Are you sad, or are these happy tears?"

"Both."

"I'm so sorry, Mom." I knew that hearing me say *Mom* would both help and hurt. I focus on the moment—caressing her arm, holding her hand, as she clasped mine hard, squeezing my fingers, releasing, squeezing, holding on tight.

"I could never do what she did." She took a deep breath. "I could never be as strong as she is."

She blew her nose and wiped her eyes, taking some deep breaths and exhaling out hard through pursed lips, as if releasing her weakness and pain. She pushed the letter toward me on the table and left the room. As I read the letter, my tears blurred the words so carefully placed on the unlined page, the handwriting I was seeing for the first time. Her words were not written to me, but about me. Because of me.

ERI WAS WAITING for me at home and I fell into her arms. I cried, and my body heaved, every breath a gasp, and she held me without a word. I was overwhelmed, my senses heightened, as if stumbling through fog, fighting to keep myself upright and on my feet, just trying to keep moving.

I handed Eri the envelope, and she sat at our dining table as I stood at the kitchen sink, hand washing some dishes. The water running over my hands, I scrubbed the plates and cereal bowls and spoons from breakfast, staring out the window at the treetops over the neighbor's house, until I realized how much time had passed. English is Eri's second language, but it wouldn't take her that long to read two pages.

I shut off the water, wiped my hands, and turned to see the letter open on the table and Eri sitting in the chair, crying in silent agony, tears dripping off her chin. She imagined the unimaginable, read the letter as if she wrote these words for Kentaro or Tyler, for her sons. I stood, barely able to breathe, seeing the face of my mother as she writes, her hands shaking, unable to stop crying for her son, for her baby boy that she will never see again.

To Stephen Michael's Mother,

As you see I've named your child after St. Stephen, to give him courage, and St. Michael, to protect him. I know that you will probably want to give him another name, along with your surname, but I will always think of him as Stephen Michael.

I want you and your child to know that I am not an evil person. I did something very wrong, but I have and will continue to pay for it. I know that a great deal of good has come from my having Stephen, for I know that he will bring a great deal of happiness into your home.

You will note that I do not refer to him as being my child. God has created him in my body, but you will make him into the kind of man that God wants him to be. Therefore, you are his mother more than I have been. You are accepting a great task, for which you will receive my eternal gratitude and prayers.

I have loved your child very deeply through these past nine months and it hurts me very deeply to give him up. But, I know that you will love him as much as I do and that you will be able to give him a normal and happy life. He will always have my love and my prayers as he has had in these past months. I will pray also for you and your husband, that you will be able to raise your son in the light of God's graces.

May God shed an abundance of his graces on both you and your husband forever.

Thank you.

AGE FIFTEEN

The only other person living at WAITT House is the supervisor, a young, handsome guy from the Bronx named Larry. After a week, I start to feel human again as my mind clears, and my body stops shaking. They let me take my final exams at the house. With a clear head, I pass everything but math, so I need to take that in summer school.

Daily hour-long counseling sessions are required with the WAITT House therapist and nurse, Jayne McCarthy. I feel like I fit here, that I don't have to be alone anymore. I want to believe what I'm feeling—that there's something good here, and something good about me. I'm also desperate to get high.

I make it through the days talking with Jayne and smoking cigarettes with Larry, but after dinner, I'm left alone. All I can think about is how to get wasted. Larry's room is right next to mine, and he never sleeps until I do. I think about smashing things, so they'll have to take me out, but I want to be on the streets, not locked up. So I tell them what they want to hear, and wait.

Philip George is from the Hill, the heart of downtown Schenectady. He's the same age as me, but as tall and broad as a grown man. He settles into his room, making sure I know he's the new king of the house, and asks me if I get high. When I nod, unable to believe my luck, he lights a joint, passes it to me, and smiles.

Billy and Freddy join our group, both from Schenectady. The four of us quickly convince Larry that we can keep ourselves out of trouble, and we take off together to get high on the Hill.

Philip George's only living relative is his Uncle Albert. Al is a huge black man, and Philip George looks just like him. Al always has dope, and always keeps a gun close to hand. I admire and fear Philip George. Al, I worship.

Philip George may be the strongest kid in the house, but I'm the one with the money. With my thieving skills, I'm always able to steal money when I visit my parents. I'd rather be the one with the dope. I want to be like Al, a thief and a dealer.

I tell him, "I know where we can get a stereo. Almost like new."

"A house?"

"Yeah. My parents are going out Saturday night."

"Why you want to steal from your own house?"

"They don't want me. It ain't my house. They're not my real parents anyway."

"Foster home?"

"Adopted."

He looks at Phillip George, and they both shrug.

"What kind of stereo?"

"Brand new Panasonic with cassette tape, turntable, receiver, and two top-of-the-line speakers."

"How much you want?"

"An ounce of dope."

"Not worth it."

"There's a wedding silverware set. It's worth a lot. Take anything else you want."

Al nods, and we're set. After sunset, I sit in the front seat of Al's Cadillac, Philip George in the back seat, and we roll up to my house.

"You've got the key?" Al asks.

I jump out of the car and open the garage door so Al can put the Caddy where my parents' car usually sits. Within ten minutes, we have everything in the trunk and back seat of the car. Al runs up the stairs and breaks the kitchen door in while I smash the back window from the outside.

My new status lasts a week, until I run out of Al's dope. After that, Philip resumes his position as king, and since I don't have another house lined up, I'm shit out of luck.

Billy sticks by me, though, and we come up with a plan—smash the front window of the corner deli, break into the cigarette machine, clean out all the cigarettes and the change in the machine. Our stupidity is in direct proportion to the severity of our withdrawal.

The longer we stand in front of the store, the more we convince ourselves we can do this. We gather rocks for smashing, stones half the size of a brick, piling them up in the corner of the parking lot. Lurking in the darkness by the trash bin, we take the edge off, beyond the street-light where the flicker of our joint won't attract attention. Calm sets in, a trance of confidence, convincing us that our lack of fear is courage and strength.

"Let's do it!"

We heave stones at the window, each one smashing into the glass harder than the last, spidering the safety glass with cracks. When we run out of rocks, we stare stupidly at each other, dumbfounded at the failure of our brilliant plan.

Somehow, at the same instant, we know to run, bolt in opposite directions, then both turn to look back. That's when the fear hits. The sudden solitude, the loss of comfortable companionship, leaves us as cold and empty and afraid as if we're already alone in our jail cell. We run, away from the glass, away from each other, away from whatever happens next.

What happens next, inevitably, is that the police show up at WAITT House. In separate rooms, we tell our stories. I rat out Billy, tell the police he's a bad kid, and it wasn't my fault. Billy tells the cops that we worked together, but that it was all his idea. Billy lies, and afterward never speaks to me again.

The cops talk at me. To block out the sound of their voices, I think about Billy taking me to visit his mother. "That's a really cool picture of Elvis," I say, pointing to the ugly black velvet painting, the one Billy gave to her for her birthday. He smiles, and never says a word, as his mother goes on and on about how wonderful it is. Even my good lies never seem to last very long.

FATHER RALPH TELLS my parents he has one last hope. Everyone is desperate, except for me. The last hope is more terrible than any threat of jail.

The drive only takes five minutes from WAITT House. The outside of Bridge Center is neat, buttoned down, trying hard to look like just another house on the street. Most of them have been converted into multi-unit homes. It reminds me of my *babcia's* house, with its heavy door of dark wood, punctuated by decorative glass as thick as the bottom of a Coke bottle. Even the door handle looks old, comforting. As the door shuts behind me, my mind and soul give up the fight. My next and final stop. Started by some church folk in Albany as a drop-in center, Bridge is now a full-scale drug therapeutic rehab community.

WAITT House is warm, old but comforting, and the people seem to care. Bridge is the opposite of warm, the opposite of comfort, as hard as the streets. The program lasts up to eighteen months, school the only place we're allowed to go outside without supervision. Daily counseling and AA meetings are mandatory.

People here live as a family, but no one here will put up with my shit. Lying, stealing, fighting are punished. People wear signs around their necks: "I stole," "I lied," "I'm a drug addict."

From my parents' house, to foster homes, to WAITT House, nothing has ever seemed so bad. This will crush me, I know. I won't walk out the door for the next year and a half.

Father Ralph looks at me. "So, Kevin, do you think you want to stay here?"

What the fuck is wrong with this picture? They're giving me a choice? This is up to me? Are you fucking kidding me? It's a request, not a life sentence after all! With all of my will, I clamp my mouth shut, sure it's a trick. But it's clear they really want me to decide, and my lips move, and words tumble out.

"No. This isn't for me." Everyone looks away. "I'll go back to WAITT House. I promise I'll change." Father Ralph thanks them for their time. Driving back to WAITT House, no one speaks, but I'm smiling. Back in my room, Philip George and I smoke a bowl.

No one comes to family court with me, not Father Ralph, not Jayne, not my father nor my mother. Just my probation officer and the lawyer. If I admit to my problem with drugs, if I'm honest about the night with Billy, they'll consider sending me back to WAITT House.

They only allow me one lie, and now it's over—Vanderheyden Hall for a thirty-day evaluation, likely ending in the detention center until I turn eighteen. There's nothing left inside me, no tears, no begging, no sobbing for help. This feels like the right thing, the fair thing. Because there's nothing left in me to save.

On the way to Vanderheyden, we drive past the grim residential units of the reform school. Everyone knew that's where I'd end up, and I easily accept the inevitable.

As I walk into the old brick building, the other kids instantly size me up, each one of them standing close enough to nudge me, daring me to react. I resist the urge to look away, to succumb to their intimidation, instead standing up to the ugliest kid in the room, two inches taller than me. Right away I see in his eyes that he won't make the first move. I almost laugh out loud at the sense of power I feel, as inexorable as the rage of my own self-hatred.

This is my moment of truth. My first lesson at Vanderheyden Hall is that power is choosing not to care. About the adults. About the kids. About myself. Self-preservation is only as effective as my own willingness to self-destruct.

A few hours later the boy I faced off with, Donny, makes an overture.

"Fuck you." He looks across the table at me and sticks his hand out for me to shake. "Fuck you."

"Fuck you back."

We both laugh and fall into a banter like we've known each other forever. Maybe we were separated at birth, we think, and the only difference between us is his baby blues and my hazel green eyes. Our birthdays are only four days apart.

The only girl at Vanderheyden for evaluation has short hair, doesn't want to have sex with us, and is a real bitch. We like her right away.

Days are strictly regulated—meeting with the counselors right after breakfast, and the rest of the day being observed. Being watched, just to be watched. If we go off on a rant, they document it. If we say anything they consider insightful or significant, they write it down. They're not there to help us, only to record what they see and hear.

In the morning sessions we discuss sex, other kids in our schools, the friends we thought we could trust who stabbed us in the back. We watch in awe as the girl cries, so overwrought that they have to call her parents, but they don't come through, and she pretty much stops talking. A few days later she's gone. Donny finds out that she tried to kill herself.

That hits Donny hard. For a few days, he rages at everyone, then stops talking altogether. Finally, he opens up with me. He wants to kill himself, too. We talk and talk and talk, because talking is all we have to keep us from going insane. Every day at Vanderheyden is a day without getting high, and every day without getting high is like having our flesh scraped raw.

I tell Donny about my suicide attempt. He doesn't believe me until I show him the scars on my wrist, and suddenly everything changes. He doesn't want to die anymore—he wants to hit somebody. Break somebody. Kill somebody.

Kids, both boys and girls, come and go, but the routine never varies. Then something unusual—one of the counselors asks if we'll help him return some borrowed chairs to the Elks Lodge.

Anything that gets us out of the building for an hour or so is a positive. We help carry the chairs into the lodge while he talks to his friends at the bar, then he treats us to sodas and gives us a few quarters to play the jukebox. As we lounge around the table drinking our sodas, we talk about being outside, where we might end up, how we feel about that. We're all experts at putting up a tough front, and the counselor doesn't even try to puncture our facade.

The next song comes on the jukebox, Jim Croce. A song my parents would crank up the volume on, all three of us singing along. Burned in my memory, the lyrics push to get out past my lips.

"If I had a box just for wishes, and dreams that would never come true . . . "

I bite my lip to stop myself from singing but keeping those words in does more harm than good. Everyone stares in disbelief at the tears streaming down my face.

No one speaks; even Donny backs away. A new girl turns away with a sound of disgust. The counselor asks what's wrong.

"It's just a fucking song," the new girl blurts, squirming in her chair, a superior smirk on her bitch face.

Donny lunges across the table, stabbing his finger in her face. "If he wants to cry let him fucking cry!" The counselor puts his hand on my shoulder, taking it away quickly when my eyes say he's gone too far. My insides are melting, and when the song ends no one says a word.

11

PLEADING

MARCH 2007

*W*ithout my mother's first name, I'd hit a wall. I enlisted my mother and father to dig up any and all paperwork they could find. I searched for more clues, anything that might lead me to my mother's first name. I found a treasure trove of guidance online; *Shea's Search Series: The Definitive Guide to Self-Empowered Adoptee Search* became my template and guide. I made lists and attacked each item with a passion beyond hope or determination, my Adoptee Manifest Destiny.

Documentation piled up in my office at work, at home on my bedroom floor, on our dining room table and living room floor. I cataloged all the non-identifying information and copied it word for word into spreadsheets to share with my search angels. I made copies of both my birth certificates. I tried and failed to retrieve the Petition to Adopt and Final Decree of Adoption from the court.

The folders and lists held more questions than clues, but I pushed on. Shea's Series suggested, "In most cases, a baby born to an unmarried woman or who was scheduled to be adopted after birth, will not have a birth announcement in the papers. Mistakes have been known to happen, however, so it pays to make copies of the birth announcements for babies born on your birth date at the hospital or in the city or town of your birth."

Leads and possibilities cropped up everywhere, but after several months I was no closer to finding my mother's first name. I had one place left to look for my hospital birth records. But the risk of failure was high.

"St. Clare's Hospital, may I help you?"

"Yes, I was wondering if I could speak with Joan Demarco?"

"Where does she work?" The voice was local, familiar, like a teacher I might have liked.

"I think she's in admitting." Ask, listen, reply, keep it simple, and let them do the work for me.

"Please hold."

Just looking at my script on my computer screen, I felt sweat gather on my body.

"Admitting, can I help you?" Another voice, less comforting, but still familiar. I knew these people. I grew up with these people.

"Hi, this is Kevin Barhydt." I state facts, keep my request short. "I'm an old friend of Joan Demarco. Is she working today?"

"Who?" I felt her listening, making sure.

I enunciated carefully, firmly. "Joan Demarco."

"Hold on a second."

The woman set the phone away, but I could still hear the conversation in the background.

Do you know a Joan Demarco?

She's not married anymore. That's Joanie. She's not working today.

"Hello, sir?" Her voice was confident with facts, upbeat.

"Yes."

"Joanie isn't working today." The words were simple, straightforward.

"Oh, okay." Keep breathing, almost done. "Thank you. Can you tell me when I can call back when she might be there?"

"I think she's on tomorrow. Let me check." She was with me now, working as a team. "Yes, tomorrow she's on during the day."

"Thank you very much. Have a great day."

"Thank you, you too. Bye."

THE NEXT DAY JOANIE, surprised to hear my voice, hesitated to talk on the phone, especially at work, but I managed to quiet her fears enough that she gave me her home phone number.

My connection with Joanie went way back, before I ever thought I'd want to know my mother. Joanie was my fantasy, a beautiful, smiling blonde with pale blue eyes and a voice as soft as I imagined my mother's would be. Everything about her made me feel calm.

When I first met Joanie, she was the wife of my girlfriend Michelle's brother, Michael. Joanie and Mike had a house in the country with a horse and a pond and a few acres, Joanie's dream come true, except for Mike. At least, that's how I thought she must feel. Her gentleness made him seem all the more craggy and crude. When he drank beer and smoked pot with me, I laughed and joked, all the while wishing I could be alone with Joanie. She wasn't simply a consolation; she was the only ray of light I can remember through my years of addiction.

I knew I didn't want to open that door again, to let the past come back to haunt me, but this was different. I had to make this call.

"Hi, Joanie. It's Kevin Barhydt." I didn't need a script for this call. She was perfect in my memory, even more perfect now.

"Hi, Kevin." Her sweet voice immediately put me at ease. "I nearly forgot you were going to call. I'm just getting settled after getting the kids off."

It was almost daunting how right and good this call made me feel. I was so glad to know her now that I almost didn't care where it would lead. We talked about her family, her kids, her husband. Her children were adopted, as was her child from her marriage with Mike. Mike won custody of their child, but I didn't mention that, never opened that wound.

The topic of her children left the door wide open for me.

"Joanie, you know I was adopted, and that's why I'm calling. I really appreciate you taking the call."

"Sure."

"I know it's a lot to ask, but here's the deal. I was born on June 27, 1962, at St. Clare's Hospital. I'm hoping you can help me get access to the records."

I heard her voice change. "How? I'm not even sure if they have those records."

"They do, Joanie," I pressed on, "but they're probably in an off-site archive."

"I want to help you, but I'm really afraid."

"Do you know anyone, or can you ask around and see if you know anyone who knows anyone who can help me?"

"If I got caught, I'd be fired." The silence lasted a long time. "I'm sorry, Kevin. I have a family now. I really want to help you, but I can't."

"I don't want you to be afraid, Joanie. I know this is too much to ask. I just don't know how else to find out what I need to know. I want to know who my mother is, Joanie. I know the information is there."

"I can't, Kevin. I wish I could."

"I don't want you to get in trouble, and I understand if you can't do it." Although my own heart ached, I didn't want to hurt her. "I just have to ask you, please think about it."

"If it were in my building, or in the computer, I could try. But I don't even know where to look. I don't know where they keep those records, and I don't feel comfortable asking the people I know about it." Her voice cut through me, slicing my hope. "You know Mike still works there, too, and he already made a lot of people think I'm no good."

Her voice broke. I couldn't hurt her this way.

"It's okay, Joanie." I changed my tone. "Hey, I always loved watching you with your horse. You always seemed so natural with animals."

I heard her breath slow as she calmed down, relieved that it was over.

"I don't ride anymore. Maybe someday."

I might never talk to her again, and I couldn't end our conversation that way. I took a deep breath.

"Joanie, I never told you this, but I think you are so very beautiful. I told Michelle this once, but I don't think she ever told you." I felt awkward but had to make her understand. "I've always wanted to see a picture of my mother around the age she was when she had me. When I met you, you reminded me of what I thought she might look like. When I think of her, I picture you sitting in tall grass, your hair shining in the sun, and you're talking to me, as an adult. I don't say anything, I just listen to you tell me how much you love me, smiling at me and laughing with joy. You've always been that picture for me, Joanie. I really treasure that, and I wanted you to know."

Joanie was quiet for a long time again. "Kevin, that's beautiful. I wish you could find your mother. I wish I could help you. If I can, I will. If there is an easier way, if you find out where the records are kept, I might be able to help."

"No, Joanie, don't worry about it." I needed to let her off the hook. "I'll find another way."

"I know the years you were with Michelle were not the best." Her voice was gentle, soft, but sad. "I knew that wasn't the real you."

"Thanks, Joanie." I didn't know what else to say.

"There's nothing to be ashamed of, Kevin." I almost saw her reaching through the phone to me. "You've come so far."

"It still hurts to remember sometimes." This was the door I didn't want to open.

"I know," Joanie said without hesitation, as if stating a fact. "But it's not you anymore."

AGE FIFTEEN

The counselors are diligent at Vanderheyden Hall, write down everything, document everything, and somehow after thirty days, they send me home to my parents, almost a year to the day since I went to foster care. It feels like returning to a country where I've forgotten the language.

The counselors also send Donny home to his mother. Hanging out with Donny becomes my weekend retreat, even as I fall back into my weeknight routines with Frankie, Eddie, and Tony. I come and go as I please, and at home my parents avoid me, not from a lack of love, but to save us both from my inevitable emotional and physical meltdowns.

Neil lives on his own in downtown Schenectady, a block away from the probation office. His apartment has anywhere from one to three pounds of pot at any given time. With my experience selling in the city, I become his dealer.

I can sell an ounce in less than an hour. I can talk to anybody, black and white, girls and guys, as a friend, making instant connections. I have a way of strutting up the street, my chest puffed out, and when people see me half a block away, they shout my name for all to hear.

I DON'T KNOW Butchie all that well. Not sure where I meet most of the people I know, mostly at random apartments, getting a nickel bag or some blow. Somehow, we all know each other, and somehow, I remember the faces if not the places or the names. But Butchie—Butchie's different.

He has this look, his hair tousled and down to his shoulders, and always wears a jean jacket, T-shirt, big silver belt buckle with a turquoise jaguar. A total street kid, never a penny to his name, but always has a little dope, or at least knows how to get some. He's a rock star; I think everybody wants to be like Butchie. Damn funny what looks like success when you're stoned all the time.

"Hey, Butchie!" I shout as I cross the street.

"Hey, man." We shake hands and stand side by side, bouncing on our toes and rolling back on our heels. "Got any dope?" he asks, smiling.

I shake my head. I have money but want to save it to buy some dope or coke later.

"No, man, not right now. I had some, got so high."

He nods and taps his fingers to his lips like he's smoking. "Got a cigarette?"

"Yeah, sure."

I pull out a pack and shuffle one out for him to take. We hang around smoking on the corner of Albany Street and Nott Terrace, the county jail in clear view.

"So, man, you want to get stoned?" He flicks away his cigarette.

"Yeah, man. Cool." The dope is wearing off, and I can use a lift.

"I know where we can get some weed."

Butchie walks down the street. I hang back a moment, hoping for something better than weed.

He stops and turns back. "Wanna go?"

I shrug. "Yeah, that's cool."

He steps back toward me. He's bigger than I am, broader shoulders, strong chest.

"Are you cool, man?"

"Yeah, I'm cool, Butchie." I laugh, playing it off like I'm just jonesing for a fix.

He smiles now, friendly and relaxed.

"'Cause I can't take you if you ain't cool."

"Yeah, whatever, I'm cool." I look him right in the eyes.

Butchie smiles big time.

We walk and hang a right, and all the way he's talking about how stoned we're gonna get, and now I'm getting psyched. He stops at a four-story red brick building with a glass door, like a convenience store, and the long, steep stairway inside leads up to a second floor without lights.

He rings the bell. After a few seconds, a black guy sticks his head out the window and yells down.

"Hey, Butchie. Who's that?"

"It's my friend." He turns to me, "What's your name, man?"

"Kevin." I just want to get off the street and get my fix.

Butchie yells back up, "Kevin. He's cool."

The guy comes down and leads us up to the second floor. Butchie never tells me his name. He rolls a joint, hands it to me, and holds out a lighter, a Bic in a shiny metal case. I lean in to take a long toke.

I hold in the hit as long as I can. "That's amazing dope," I say, exhaling little puffs of smoke with each word. "It's so damn good, it tastes so good." The smoke hits me fast, and I'm already feeling far away. "Is this laced?"

"It's Thai stick," he says as I pass it back to him. "No." He pushes my hand back. "All for you."

Butchie smiles at me, and he and the guy sit together by the window and roll another joint. I'm halfway done with mine, sitting in a big, soft armchair. I'm so high, floating, so happy.

"Hi." A voice drifts above me. "I'm Arnold."

"Hi." I look up.

"What's your name?"

"Kevin." I try to sit up, but the opium seeping into my muscles makes it hard to move.

"Can I have some?" He sits on the arm of the chair.

I look over at Butchie, smoking with the other guy. Everything is cool. I hand Arnold the joint and we pass it back and forth, and he's talking and I'm laughing, and I look across the room and the other guy is on his knees, taking off Butchie's pants, and Butchie is smoking the joint, smiling at me, in his jean jacket and T-shirt and shoulder-length hair, and his eyes are wild.

Arnold takes me by the arm and leads me to another room with a mattress on the floor. He sits me down and we talk, about how good the dope is, and how good it feels. He's nice to me. I kind of like him. I'm only fifteen, and he's probably in his thirties, but he treats me with respect. Kindness. He tries to kiss me, rubs me through my pants, and pulls up my shirt, and I'm so high and it all feels so wild and bad and I'm feeling sick but I'm hard as a rock and I feel so ashamed but now my clothes are off and he's all over my chest and sucking on my nipples and my legs are in the air and he's in me and it's ripping me apart. I vomit in my mouth and swallow it, yelling, moaning, sounding like a dog howling in pain. I'm pinned on my back with a man's penis all the way inside me and he's tearing my insides out.

Arnold gets dressed and tells me to stay there, he'll be right back. I curl up on my side on the mattress until the door opens and the other guy comes in.

"Arnold said you were great."

He's so big he can't fit in me. It's impossible, but he keeps trying, for a long time. By the time he finally gives up, my blood is soaking into the mattress. A tear squeezes out, and I try to hold them back.

"You want a blowjob?" he asks, rubbing my now-limp dick.

I shake my head in slow motion. He tries to jerk me off, but I can't keep it up, and he laughs. I can't stop the tears anymore, and then he stops laughing and gets up to leave.

"Get dressed." He turns, naked, and I watch him walk away.

I pull my clothes on and go back out. Butchie's gone, but Arnold's sitting on the arm of the chair again. The other guy has his pants on now. He looks at Arnold. "Too tight," he says, and disappears into the kitchen.

Arnold gives me a joint. "Do you want to smoke some more?"

"Yeah." I have to say yes. I can't let my mind know what my body feels.

"Come on then." He gets up and walks away without waiting for me, and I stumble after him, up the stairs to his apartment, where we smoke some more. After a while he takes me into his bedroom. I raise my legs up, and he takes me again. It still hurts, just as much.

I come back almost every day for the next two months.

NEIL LETS me crash during the day when I skip school. I sell dope for him on the Hill, so I can keep myself high until night comes and I can get with Arnold.

To start the night off we freebase, and my head explodes like a champagne party popper, then he takes me to his bed. He doesn't like that I keep getting sick from the Thai stick, but he lets me hit the pipe after he's done so I can sleep. That's my routine: Get high. Get fucked. Get unconscious. Repeat.

I hate getting fucked. His lumpy, hairy, black body smells at the end of the day, and his bald head drips sweat on my chest. He wants to kiss me, to pretend to be gentle, but in the end, he always just throws my legs up over my head and fucks me until he comes inside me. The cocaine helps, swirls around in my brain, and lets me forget the hardness pushing into me so I can stop caring about anything. When he gives me the pipe afterward, the opium takes me to a quiet, serene place. Sometimes he comes back from Billy's downstairs, drunk on wine, and tries to get me hard, wanting to be a lover. But in the end, he just fucks me.

I hate the fucking but love the freebase. Sometimes we line up straight coke on the mirror and snort instead, but that makes my nose bleed, and anyway snorting takes longer to ease into my brain, and I don't want to wait.

We've already freebased, and after he has me first in the bed and again on the couch, I want to be anywhere else but where I am.

"Can you get me a soda?" I ask, trying to sound nice, like I'm happy.

"Sure." He leans over and pulls me to him, hugging and kissing me, his tongue and mouth all over my lips and cheeks. It doesn't feel bad, just a bit off, like when a barber spends too much time tugging on your ear or holding your head at just the right angle, but you need a haircut so you just look down, you don't stare into the mirror. "Going to the bathroom first."

There's a little more than an eight-ball left on the table. I snort two lines, scoop what's left into the paper bindle. I can barely close the folds, but I manage and shove it down my shorts. I look behind the couch where he stashes the deseeded Thai stick, but all that's left is the dregs, nothing but seeds and stems.

I open the Marygin deseeder, grab a handful of dregs and shove it in my pocket. There's enough in the dregs to pick through later and get high, so I reach in again, and Arnold comes out of the bedroom. He stares at me, my hand stuck in the deseeder.

"What are you doing?" His eyes turn dark.

"Just wanted to get high," I mumble, trying to be casual, dropping the fistful back in the plastic box, stirring it with my finger. "This is all dregs."

"This was a good thing." His voice sounds like my mother when she's caught me pulling a twenty out of her purse. "We had a good thing here, and you rip me off? All you had to do was ask, and you rip me off?"

I just stare at him.

"Put it back."

He waits while I put the top on the deseeder and stash it back behind the couch.

"Get your clothes on."

Arnold's standing over me. I'm sweating, my heart is pounding now, just like when I'm twelve and in the back of the police car driving to the station. It's all over.

"Dump your pockets."

I pull the dregs out of my pocket.

"Keep it." He backs away from me. "And get the fuck out. Don't come back."

I stand there with the dregs in my fist, and the shaking starts.

"Please, I'm sorry, I won't do it again. I just wanted to get high."

I move close, try to hold his hands, put his arms around me, pleading.

"Fucking junkie. Fucking thief." He pushes me away, shoves me hard. "Get out."

He's animated now, in my face. I slump to the couch, and he grabs me by the collar, pulling me up and toward the door.

I stand in the hallway, lost.

"Get out!"

I walk down the two flights of stairs and feel the apartment door slam behind me. At the bottom, I drop the dregs back into my pocket and think about where to go, until I remember the bindle in my underwear. I pull it out and sit on the sidewalk, leaning against the brick, and snort it all.

12

LOSING

I woke up every morning knowing everyone wanted to help me, but no one wanted it more than I did. I focused on seeing my mother's face. I told myself, if a picture was all I ever found, I'd be happy for the rest of my life, but now, even after all this time, all my work, all my searching, even that picture seemed out of reach.

With Judy's advice and encouragement, I made the decision to pay a professional. Putting the search in the hands of someone for hire felt like handing over a newborn child to a stranger in a crowd. As soon as money came into the picture, it sucked the love right out of the room. I prepared myself for disappointments, and I was right. They came at a fast clip.

Then I called Pamela Slaton. We talked about her own search, how many people she had helped reunite, and she asked me questions. The right questions.

"Kevin, do you realize that this may not end how you would wish? You may be disappointed, or worse?"

"I know I can't hold on to my fantasies."

Pamela knew my words didn't match my heart.

"Kevin, I can promise you one thing, it's going to be okay no matter what we find."

"I cried last night." I fought the tears back again. "I know anything can happen."

"If you trust me . . ." Pamela began, then stopped and waited.

My heart ached, breath filled my lungs in deep, slow, quivering gulps, and the hope that had grown so deep over the past two years started to overflow.

"I have two daughters, and two sons."

"You must be very happy to have them in your life." She let the words linger. "It's okay, Kevin. It's really okay."

I summoned my will and found the air in my lungs to speak.

"Today is my oldest daughter's birthday."

"And you've been thinking about her all day." Pamela stated it as a fact.

I held myself upright in my chair as everything blurred and the sounds around me dulled, muted.

"Kevin. I believe your mother thinks about you every single day."

I took to Pamela right away. I had finally found someone with the strength and experience to bring my search through to the end. I hired Pamela, even though the cost was not easy to swallow. My mother and father had searched for a child, paid a fee, signed paperwork, and claimed me as their own. Now I did the same.

With the contract signed, I let the weight all fall off my shoulders. I did have a faith. Faith that I had done everything I possibly could and could now trust Pamela to do her best. Faith that God would guide and buoy me for whatever happened next, that I would be ready for the new chapter of my life. I embraced this faith like a son holding his father's hand, and for the first time in two years, I stopped and let the world flow around me.

The contract was clear. "Cases can be solved any time from the signing of the agreement (within a few days) through the four-month period." I had waited for forty-five years to meet my mother. I had searched for two years. Four more months was nothing.

SIX DAYS LATER, my phone rang. It was lunchtime, and I was about to leave to get some food, take a walk around the block, and enjoy the cool spring air. I turned back to the desk and grabbed the phone.

"Hello, this is Kevin."

"Kevin, this is Pamela Slaton."

Everything shifted. I lost my balance, the phone seemed to swell in my hand. The room felt stifling, even as the walls seemed to recede.

"Hi, Pamela."

"Kevin, is this a good time to talk?"

"Yes."

I couldn't comprehend the solidness of the phone in my hand, the clarity of the voice on the line.

"Kevin, I've completed your search."

I stopped breathing, then gasped for air like a fish plucked from a lake. I paced between the door and the desk. Words caught in my throat. I longed to listen, to hear what Pamela was about to say, but I couldn't. I wasn't ready, couldn't think, and to hear this I needed to be able to think and speak. Stars dazzled my vision, and I knew with certainty I was going to fall down.

"Kevin, are you okay?"

"I can't talk right now," I blurted. "I can't talk. I'll have to call you back. I'll call you back."

"Okay, Kevin. It's okay." Pamela sounded confused but responded with confidence. "I'll be right here. I'll be waiting for your call."

I balled my fists, desperate for something to hold on to as I hung up the phone. Stumbling down the hallway to the bathroom, I locked the door and sobbed. Awareness filled my senses—I was going to meet my mother. My knees gave out, and I leaned against the wall, then crumpled into the corner as all my strength and control gave out. Tears flooding, my mouth agape, my throat constricted, screaming without sound.

The tears dried, crusted, leaving a sticky, crinkly sensation on my face as I blinked. My breath steadied into its natural rhythm and my eyes began to focus. I wrapped my arms around myself, rocking gently on the bathroom floor.

I wanted to look fresh when I heard her name for the first time. I splashed cold water on my face, dusted off my pants, tucked in my shirt, straightened my belt.

Complete. The search was over. I was ready. I was going to meet my mother. The words echoed in my mind: *Kevin, I've completed your search.*

I closed the office door, sat down at my desk with deliberation, and dialed the phone.

"Hi, Pamela? This is Kevin. Sorry about that. I was surprised to get your call."

"I understand. Are you all right?"

"Yes. I'm more than all right."

Pamela took a long moment. I could feel my heart beating.

"Kevin, as I said, I've completed your search."

I smiled and breathed, ready.

"I'm sorry to tell you, your mother has died."

I sat perfectly still, not moving, not breathing, not thinking.

I felt my mother slip away from me before I even knew her name, the distance increasing as if I was being ripped in two from the top of my head, in slow motion, each second a millennium. Despair settled on me as thick as the gray ash and soot that blew over Brooklyn from Manhattan on that sky-blue day in September. I held the phone and cried, while Pamela waited without words.

"Thank you for calling." My voice was weak, not like my own.

"Kevin, I'm so sorry."

I couldn't make sense of it, so I cried. Time inched past as I sobbed, my breathing shallow, short puffs in my mouth.

"Kevin, are you okay now? Do you need me to call back later?"

"No."

"Are you sure?"

"I'm sorry. Yes, I'm sure."

"Kevin, I'm so sorry. This so rarely happens, and I didn't expect it this time. Your mother was so young, I was sure you would reunite. I know it's painful. I wish I could tell you something different. She died in a car accident on July 4, 1997."

Ten years ago.

"I found her obituary. She was married. I don't think he was your father."

I shifted again, without choice or option, like a boat with a rudder loosed in rough seas, jarring violently against the waves, lurching wildly side to side.

"I researched more and found another obituary from three years later, her husband's."

Though I couldn't compartmentalize, could barely comprehend, Pamela pressed on. Every bit of new information clamored for my attention, as if she were twisting the dial on a radio, and I strained to focus, tune in only to her voice.

"Her husband's obituary is very short. It doesn't say how he died, and I can't find any details anywhere. In my experience, a lack of details in the obituary often means the death wasn't of natural causes. I don't think he died well."

I had worked so hard to not let my dreams get away from me, to not chase my fantasies and allow myself to want more, and now I'd lost her. I had waited too long, and now I would never see her, hear her voice, hold her hand. All I wanted was a picture of my mother, an image of her when I was born, something I could see in my mind's eye when I talked to her at night. I had done everything right, listened and followed every suggestion, every bit of advice and guidance. I forced myself to remember that whatever happened, finding her, and knowing who she was, were all I ever dared conceive. That was what I wanted.

Pamela's voice again tugged me back. I forced myself to listen to her words.

"Kevin, you have two brothers and a sister."

AGE SIXTEEN

I con Tony Rotundo into driving me to New York City to pick up a quarter pound of dope from Great-Uncle Al's second wife's brother,

Tito. Uncle Al is my father's uncle; his wife Ada and Tito are all true, the pound of dope bullshit. I want to see Tito.

Ada is a beauty from Panama, Uncle Al's secretary, and forty years his junior. Tito is a few years older than me, just as gorgeous as Ada, and ever since we shared a joint in the parking lot at the wedding reception, I can't get him out of my mind. I don't care what story I tell Tony.

When we connect with Tito in the city, Tony's quick to pick up that Tito isn't the drug dealer I made him out to be. Tony bails, leaving me on a street in Spanish Harlem with Tito. And that suits me just fine. Even the one night we spend together is worth it, even worth pissing off Great-Uncle Al.

By the time I get back to Schenectady, Tony's told Neil about Tito, and Neil says to my face he doesn't want me hanging around anymore. I can buy dope from him, that's it. I'm not allowed in the building, much less Neil's apartment.

SCHOOL'S just another place to sell dope, so I don't put up a fight about waking up in the morning. My mother drives me to school before going to work, just to make sure I get out of the house. I spend the days hanging out in the hallways and bathroom, or behind the building.

Friday afternoon and I'm walking back and forth in the hallway, smoking cigarette after cigarette, waiting for the bell to ring. I still have a few bags of joints left to sell, and I don't like taking dope on the bus; I'd rather have my pockets full of money.

I see her, head down, looking at something. Never seen her before, so I turn my eyes away, and she walks past me to the end of the hallway and looks out the door.

"What time does the bus come?" she says, not looking my way. She's not someone I've grown up with, not from around here. She sounds like a white girl from the Hill.

I keep my voice low, put my finger up to my lips, knowing the acoustics will amplify the sound and get us caught. "Thirty minutes or so. Almost time." I light up another cigarette, and she doesn't flinch. That's a good sign.

"I'm Nessie," she says, her voice low, but clear, sharp, clipped, direct.

We look almost like brother and sister. Shoulder-length brown hair parted in the middle and feathered on the sides, her hair a few inches longer than mine in the back, brown eyes, strong eyebrows, tall nose, a long face. At five-foot-three, she's shorter than me—my chin meets up with her nose—but we probably weigh about the same. She asks for a cigarette, and we smoke together, me trying to get her to whisper, her teasing me for being so skinny.

"I bet I can pick you up."

She doesn't wait for a response, just bends her knees, wraps her arms around my waist, and lifts me off the ground. We both laugh, and as she puts me down, I lift her up, and she kisses me. I hold her off the floor, press her body against mine, deep kissing, her arms wrapped around my neck.

The bell rings, and as people start milling around in the halls we stand out of the way, holding hands. We aren't sure what's just happened. All I know is I want to see her again, so we trade phone numbers, and just as fast as she appeared, she walks out the door and onto her bus.

———

NESSIE LIVES at the opposite end of the school district. Her father is a drunk who beat her mother. Nessie and her three siblings were sent to live in four separate foster homes, and when she turned sixteen, Nessie decided to go back to her father's house. That's where our lives converge. The foster care system gives us a common language.

Nessie's father is a truck driver, always off on long-distance hauls, and even when he's in town he stays with his girlfriend, so his house becomes ours. Every weekend, I show up with a bag of weed laced with angel dust, and we fall into a slow trance of stoned passion.

One Friday, Nessie warns me that her father is coming home, so we have to wait to get high, and sex is out of the question. When her father comes through the door, he looks at me for a few long seconds. He's about my height, but big and broad and all muscle. I know he can break me in half if he wants to, but he shakes my hand, grunts hello, grabs a change of clothes, is gone almost as soon as he appears.

After he's gone, Nessie and I stand in the house kissing, shutting out every other thought and sound and sight, holding on to each other, almost tenderly. It feels like walking on the beach at sunrise. Nessie cooks some pasta and we eat, and suddenly I flash back to before my life got kicked in, when Dad is healthy and Mom cooks a meat, a starch, and a vegetable, and my parents and I have dinner together every night. My mom's cooking is good, plain but always hot and fresh, and then come the desserts, two or more flavors of ice cream, different cookies and cakes to choose from. Dessert is, after all, the point of the whole meal.

After dinner, Nessie clears the table, and I help her with the dishes. The wood stove is cranking out heat, but it doesn't reach her bedroom, so we stay on the couch and cover our nakedness with only the heat from the stove. We snuggle together after fucking, not talking, just being. Our breathing comes slow and easy. I never, ever want to leave.

When the school year ends, I know I won't be back in the fall. But without the daily routine of school, Nessie and I drift from each other, or more accurately fade away.

I get a job at Woolworth's in Schenectady, sweeping floors and cleaning pots and pans in the kitchen. The job is part time, but I'm dealing about a pound of marijuana a week now, fueling my own use with the profits.

I'm sixteen and making more profit than I can smoke, but that doesn't stop me from trying. Anything laced with angel dust, I keep for the nights when Eddie and Frankie bring over a bottle of whisky or gin or just a few six packs of cold beer.

Woolworth starts cutting back my hours, but the job is just a ruse so my parents leave me alone anyway. I show up stoned every day, but the manager doesn't seem to care as long as I stay in the back.

The day is warm for late September, and after a night of getting high together, Frankie gives me a ride downtown. I get out of the car at the corner and find Tony waiting for me.

"I should fucking kill you, you little shit!"

Tony grabs my shirt, throws me against the wall, and starts punching. As I crumple to the sidewalk, I see Frankie driving away.

"Give me your fucking money, you fuck!" Tony yanks me up, only to punch me in the gut and throw me against the wall again. I kick his left leg out from under him, and he goes down hard, but that only pisses him off more and he gets right back up, slams me into the wall, and throws me back down with a kick.

"Take it, take it, get the fuck off me." I throw all the money I have in my pocket at him.

He picks the money up but comes back swinging. I try to defend myself, kicking at his crotch, but he outweighs me by at least fifty pounds. He keeps pummeling me until I'm cowering on the ground, then the assistant manager from Woolworth comes running across the street, yelling for the police.

Tony won't quit. "You still owe me fucking money!"

The assistant manager pulls up short. "You know this guy, Kevin?"

He thinks he's coming to rescue me from a mugger. At first, he's confused, then angry, when he figures out I know this asshole. Tony curses me out some more, finally pocketing my cash before disappearing around the corner.

My shirt is shredded, blood soaking through from my shoulder, my face and nose scraped raw. I stumble across to the store, where the counter ladies are gawking and the manager and assistant manager whispering. I sit on the sidewalk and smoke a cigarette. Working all summer, and I've earned 746 dollars. I make more than that in two weeks of dealing. I finish my cigarette, walk away, and never look back.

THE PHONE RINGS, and usually I don't bother answering, but I feel lively, so I pick up the receiver.

"Is Kevin home?"

"Nessie?" I know the voice immediately.

"Yeah."

I see Donald and Bubby in the backyard, hear them through the open kitchen window. I have no idea what to say next.

"What are you doing?" she asks. Her familiar, matter-of-fact tongue makes my head spin, but I manage to respond.

"Getting stoned with a few friends."

"Figures." She laughs, kind of a cackle. Something inside me melts.

We warm up to each other for a few minutes, both remembering how to be together, how we talk, laugh, tease, coax. I feel my body respond, my mind taking a passenger seat to the conversation.

"Can I come see you?" The way I'm feeling, I'd steal a car to get to her. She doesn't answer right away, and I almost make the mistake of begging.

"You want to come see me?"

"Yeah. That'd be cool."

Another long wait, enough to make my knees tremble.

"I'm living in Albany now. I moved out of my father's house."

"Cool." I can get to Albany in a heartbeat.

"And I'm pregnant."

Now it's my turn to make her wait.

"Wow."

"Don't worry, it's not yours. I'm engaged." Her laugh pounds in my eardrum.

"Wow."

I let my breath out slowly, lightheaded, and have to force myself to breathe. "Congratulations." It's all I can think to say.

"Still want to come see me?" She stops laughing, but still I hear the smirk, teasing me, challenging.

This isn't what I thought it was. This is something different. Something I've never encountered before, never expected.

"Sure." I say it with conviction, and then with confidence. "When?"

NESSIE DROPPED OUT OF SCHOOL, too, and is back with her foster parents. Al and Abbey are odd, but we like each other right away. When I arrive, Al offers me a beer, which gets us off on the right foot. Abbey was the spitting image of Edith Bunker from the TV show *All in the Family*, right down to the whiny voice and giddy laugh. Al's last name is Bates, so both Nessie and Abbey call him Master Bates, and when the two of them get silly, I can't help but laugh along.

The afternoon goes by fast, and after dinner Al and Abbey say goodnight. Abbey tells me not to take the bus so late, to sleep on the couch, so Nessie gets me a blanket and pillow, and I stretch out and we talk. She's not due until April, but already she feels fat and bloated. I just tease her about how skinny she is.

"I want to lay with you." She doesn't ask, sitting next to me and waiting.

"Really?"

She smiles, and I see something new in her eyes, something older than a few months ago. Maybe it's the baby.

"Okay." I shift onto my side to make room.

"Just hold me." Again, not a request. She puts her head down next to mine, I put my arm around her back and hold her, nothing more.

We wake up to the sound of breakfast. I need to catch the bus, and I thank Abbey and Al for letting me stay the night. They ask when I'll be visiting again.

Nessie looks at me and smiles. "Tonight."

It isn't a request.

I HAVEN'T SEEN MUCH of Davey since going into foster care, but sometimes during the long summer evenings, if no one is around, he sneaks in, waking me up late in the mornings after my mother and father have left.

"I got messy on you today!" he laughs, wiping his cum off my stomach.

"I'm going back to Albany again tonight."

"To see her?"

"Uh huh."

Davey doesn't say anything, just throws the tissue away and bounces back on the bed next to me, rubbing my bare chest. I pull a Marlboro from the pack and reach for the lighter, but Davey grabs it and flicks the flame for me. Before it catches, he pulls the flame away, laughing, then holds it steady while I take a drag. The tip glows red hot, and Davey waves the lighter back and forth, sending hot sparks showering over my chest.

"What the fuck is the matter with you?" I scramble to brush the burning scraps of tobacco to the floor.

His face crumbles, and he tries without success to hold back his tears.

"I don't want you to go."

I don't respond, don't look up when he leaves.

Davey never stops by when I have friends in the yard, but one day he rides by on his bike while Donald and Bubby and I are sitting under the weeping willow tree drinking beer.

"Hey, Kevin," he says with a nod my way, but doesn't stop. Donald and Bubby stare at me without a word. I don't think, don't respond, only react.

I nod back to him. "Hey Davey."

He pedals on up the street, and I watch him ride away. I think he's gone, but instead he cruises up and down the street, making smaller and smaller loops until he's riding circles right in front of us.

"What's up?" he asks. His voice is still squeaky, his smile still goofy and sweet.

I feel the eyes on me. "Just hanging out."

I keep my tone casual so Donald and Bubby will know this is no big deal, just conversation, and hope Davey will ride away, and the moment will pass. Donald and Bubby are waiting, watching, cans held still in their hands.

"Just drinking beer, huh?" Davey stops his bike and puts both feet on the street, smiling.

"Yeah." I gulp a long swallow of beer.

"Hey, Donnie." It's the first words he's spoken to Donald since we met on the paper route, so long ago.

Donald stands up and turns toward the house, scowling. "I'm going back." He takes a few steps but doesn't leave yet, sipping at his beer. Bubby's waiting for my cue.

"See ya, Donnie."

Davey looks at me, but I turn away without a word, Bubby right with me. Davey waits as I walk away. Donald glares at Davey over my shoulder.

"What are you still doing here?" Donald spits out the words.

Davey's smile looks strange, crooked. The three of us watch as he puts his foot on the bike pedal, his hands back on the handlebars, looking down at the street.

Donald turns to me. "Why doesn't that faggot leave?" he says under his breath.

Davey starts riding again, big, slow circles. "Okay, Kev, see you later."

"I hate that faggot." Donald looks right at me. "Why do you let him call you Kev?"

Davey turns his bike away but stops again in the middle of the street, waving. Waving and smiling at me.

I try to think, try to breathe, my mind clouded with confusion. Tony's gone. Neil's gone. Eddie and Frankie still hang around with me just to get high.

I turn and march back toward him, raging.

"Get the fuck out of here, faggot! What the fuck are you standing there for? Get the fuck on your fucking little-girl bike and go home."

My words freeze Davey. I stand at the curb, staring at him, as he looks at me, over to Donald and Bubby, then back to me. I see his sweet smile dim, and he pedals away.

"You fucking faggot!" I yell after him. "Fucking faggot." The words come out of my mouth like an alien language, staining my tongue and lips with shame.

Donald and Bubby stop hanging around, and Davey never comes back.

13

FINDING

APRIL 2007

Gazette, The (Colorado Springs, CO) - July 9, 1997
   Deceased Name: ELIZABETH ANN "BETTY" BUCHANAN

ELIZABETH ANN "BETTY" BUCHANAN, 55, of Black Forest, died July 4, 1997, in Salida in an auto accident. She worked as a registered nurse for Pikes Peak Hospice.

   Rosary will be at 7 p.m. Thursday at Our Lady of the Pines, 11020 Teachout Road, in Black Forest. Mass will be at 7:30 p.m. Friday at the church. Mountain View Mortuary, 2350 Montebello Square Drive, is handling arrangements.

   Mrs. Buchanan was born March 1, 1942, in New Orleans to Francis X. and Betty Z. (Allen) Waguespack, who are deceased. She was married in 1962 in New Orleans to John K. Buchanan, who lives in Black Forest. She also is survived by two sons, James of Austin, Texas, and John A. of Colorado Springs; a daughter, Julie Elizabeth of Colorado Springs; three brothers, Robert M. Waguespack of Gulfport, Miss., Francis X. Waguespack Jr. of Bay St. Louis, Miss., and Steven James Waguespack of Calexico, Calif.; and two grandchildren.

Mrs. Buchanan was a member of Our Lady of the Pines Catholic Church. She enjoyed fishing, camping and gardening. She had lived in the area for 21 years, previously living in Tempe, Ariz.

Memorial contributions may be made to Pikes Peak Hospice, 3630 Sinton Road, Suite 302, Colorado Springs 80907.

*E*ri held me as I cried myself to sleep. I called in sick to work, couldn't face people, couldn't function yet. Conducting myself in a normal way, on a normal routine day, seemed impossible, an oddity. I felt like a freak attraction on a boardwalk sideshow.

Pamela sent more information about my family, and I soaked up the details that had become a mutable outline of my life. The days blurred as the new facts of my existence congealed, then became solid, though as-yet unfamiliar ground for me to stand on.

Adoptee, now natural born. Abandoned, now an orphan. Only child, now big brother.

John was the oldest of my three siblings, a year younger than me, and married to Kyung. They lived in Divide, Colorado, about twenty-five miles west of Colorado Springs, 9,500 feet above sea level.

My sister, Julie, lived in Colorado Springs, also married. She'd taken her husband's last name, McCutchen.

Pamela was unable to locate any information on my youngest brother, James. Other than seeing his name in both our mother's and his father's obituaries, he was completely unknown to me.

"The only phone number I found was for John's wife, Kyung." Even as she relayed facts and figures, Pamela's voice was kind, measured. "When you're ready, I think you should call the number and hope that it's your brother John's home phone. You don't have to rush, there's plenty of time. It's better that you be prepared emotionally. I can help you prepare, and to organize what you want to say."

"I understand the need to prepare, but I don't know if I'll ever again feel that there is plenty of time."

I wanted to listen to Pamela and call my brother's home. Judy counseled me to find the courage. Yet I read their names over and over, John, Julie, James. I had no pictures, no way of knowing who they were, or what they would be like, how they might feel when, and if, I could speak to them. I sensed that I was losing heart, unwilling to chance another failure, another dead end, or worse, another rejection.

John, Julie, James. John, Julie, James. I repeated their names to the point of obsession, my thoughts locked in a loop of compulsion, until suddenly something gripped my mind and held it still. I saw their names held in suspension, floating, and two names began to fade while one hung bold and unmistakable.

I called the number, taking a long, deep breath as the line rang. On the third ring, I heard a woman's voice.

"Hello?"

I picked up on Kyung's Korean accent. Summoning my best business voice, honed with two years of search experience and sprinkled with my devious past, I spoke as directly and forcefully as I ever have.

"My name is Jon Akins. I'm calling from Phoenix University." My words were quick but sharp, fully articulated. "We have the resume of Julie McCutchen. However, the phone number listed on the resume doesn't work."

"Jon Akins" is an amalgam of two people, an alias I used sparingly, easy to remember and assume on demand. I inserted a strategic, pregnant pause, barely a second, then asked for what I wanted.

"Do you have a number where she can be reached?"

My question was a directive, not an option. John's wife was caught off guard, as I expected. "Oh. Yes. Do you want her cell phone number?"

"That would be ideal."

I leaned back in my chair and let out a slow, silent sigh. Kyung paused, ever so briefly.

"Okay, just a minute." Less than thirty seconds later, I heard her voice again. "I've got her cell number."

"Great. If you could please give me the number, that would be very helpful."

"I have it here. Her number is ———."

Guilt nagged at the base of my skull, but shame had no place with my spirit. I can never speak to my mother. I wanted deeply to know both of my brothers, but not first. I wanted the first voice of my own flesh that I heard to be a woman. If it couldn't be my mother, I chose my sister.

I ASKED ERI TO TAKE the boys out of the house for the day. The cordless phone sat on the table, fully charged, a second phone in the charger. I spread out my three pages of handwritten script that Pamela and Judy helped me create, written in pencil, full of eraser smudges and crossed-out lines.

I had to accommodate the two-hour time difference between us. At 11:00 a.m. New York time, I dialed the phone.

"Yeah?"

"Hello. Is this Julie?"

"Who's this?"

"I was wondering if you have a few minutes to talk?"

"What's this about?"

"It's important to both of us, but if this is a bad time I can call back later."

"Yeah, later is better."

"Okay. When is a good time?"

"After 2:30. Look, I'm driving. I've got to go."

The line went dead, and I sat back in my chair, still holding the phone, utterly still. I locked in the sound of her voice, blocking out every other sound and thought.

At 4:30, I dialed her number a second time.

"Yeah."

"Hi, Julie? I called earlier today. Is this a better time to talk now?"

"Yeah, right." I could hear the sound of her driving. "What's this about?"

"Julie, I have to ask you, are you driving?"

"Yeah."

"You might want to pull over first."

"Oh my God!" Julie gasped. "Did somebody die?"

"No," I quickly assured her. "Nobody died, but this is a family matter."

"A family matter?"

"Yes. It's important to us both. Can you please pull over?"

"Yeah, okay." I heard the muted roar of traffic. "Okay. What's this about?"

"Did you pull the car over?"

"Yes."

"Can you turn off the engine?"

"Yeah. Okay."

"Can you take the keys out of the ignition?"

I knew I was increasing her anxiety, but I couldn't help but want her safe in the car.

"Yeah. Okay, I did."

I focused on the script in front of me, and read, word for word.

"Julie, before I tell you who I am, let me make sure you're who you are." I took a deep breath. "Your name is Julie McCutchen?"

"Yeah."

"And your maiden name is Buchanan?"

"Yeah."

"Your father's name was John Buchanan?"

"Yeah."

"And your mother's name was Elizabeth?"

"Yeah."

"Betty Ann?"

"Yeah."

"And her maiden name was Waguespack?"

"Yeah."

"Well, Julie, you are who I think you are. Let me tell you who I am. I've been waiting all my life to hear your voice."

In my script, I'd made a note to pause, to wait for an expected response, something like, "What do you mean?"

Instead, Julie screamed into the phone. "Are you my brother?!?"

My mind went blank. I could only look down at my script and read my planned response. "My name is Kevin Barhydt. I was born on June 27, 1962, in Schenectady, New York."

"Oh my God!" she screamed again. "Are you my brother?"

This wasn't what I had planned. I couldn't find my place in the script. Every nerve in my body jangled, every synapse in my mind fired. I willed myself to find my voice.

"Yes."

"Oh my God, I can't believe you found me." She sobbed, but with joy. "I'm so glad you found me! I've always wanted to meet you, always wished I could find you, but I didn't know how."

I couldn't—dared not—speak. I listened in tears, emotions driving me to my feet, unable to stay still. After the initial shock, Julie stopped short with a gasp. I knew what she had grasped—that I knew everything, that our mother was gone, and that I'd never meet her.

"Oh my God, our mother loved you."

My legs gave out, and I fell to the floor, unable to breath or see or speak, lying curled on my side but gripping the phone as though I'd never let go of it, of Julie's voice.

"She always wanted to see you. She missed you so much and loved you so much. She didn't feel it was right to intrude on your life if you didn't want her to. She said, 'If he wants to find me, he will.'"

"I was too late." I broke down in sobs again.

"I know." She wept with me. "But you found me. You found me. Oh my God, thank God you found me."

We talked for over an hour. I learned about Mom, clinging to every word so I could usurp Julie's memories for my own. I'd never imagined a thirst like this; it felt like it could never be quenched.

Julie's curiosity about me was just as relentless.

"I'm married. My wife is Eri, and we have two boys. I have two girls from my first marriage. They live in Ohio."

Julie wasn't shy, not at all reserved, and instantly offered her own details.

"I'm married too, well, divorced now, but I've got two kids, Jesse and Paige. Wait until I tell them they have an Uncle Kevin in New York."

My sister's voice was as gravelly as her laugh. I was instantly addicted to the sound of her. "What are my nieces' and nephews' names?"

"Kentaro is our oldest, and Tyler is his brother. My girls are Dawn and Sera."

"That's really cool." She paused. "You've got a really great life, brother."

"It's more amazing today." We both let that sink in.

"Well, I'm really glad you found us, but I don't want you to be shocked."

In her words I heard her arming herself for the assault, heard the swagger in her voice as she made herself vulnerable to a complete stranger.

"We're a pretty fucked-up family. You may not want us when you find out about us."

This wasn't in the script I'd written.

"So, I'm a fucking meth addict. I've been in prison. I'm on paper now," Julie says—out on parole, "but, hey, fuck it, I'm clean."

"Julie, I've seen my share of the back of cop cars, too." There was more to tell, but not today.

"Yeah? No shit."

"What were you in for?" This felt natural.

"Grand theft auto. Not the video game."

We both laughed. Our drug-addled, worn-out brains made these new connections effortlessly.

But I was standing at the end of a very long street, and knew I needed to turn the corner, and I didn't want to bring Julie with me. She'd already been there. She'd lived it. I didn't want to hurt my sister but knew I couldn't go there alone. The best I could hope for was to wait for her to take my hand and lead me there. I took a breath, and somehow summoned the courage I needed. "I found you through our mom's obituary."

"It was a car crash. My father was driving."

Julie felt the pain, but willingly continued. Her memories became our shared story.

"Yes, I read the obituary."

I was talking to my sister about our mother's death. The conversation felt right, as if we were remembering for each other, re-remembering together to make the memories more whole.

"She died instantly." She paused for a long time. "We had to have a closed coffin."

I didn't even try to hide my crying.

"Is this too much?"

"No."

"My father was in a coma. Our oldest brother—well, you're the oldest now—John was on his honeymoon."

"With Kyung?" I hoped I was pronouncing it right.

"Yeah. But we call her Linda. Well, John calls her Kyung, and sometimes I think James does too, but she tells everybody to call her Linda."

We both felt an emotional whiplash. I tried to be still and listen. Even though the room was warm, I couldn't stop shivering, like sitting on the porch as the sun goes down and a cold, unwelcome breeze cuts through.

"John and Linda were in Hawaii, and we wanted to let them have that happiness. James said we should wait to bury Mom until they got back, so he went to the airport and drove around all day until he found their car, and left a note to call him as soon as they got back.

"James did everything. He set up the funeral, dealt with our father in the hospital. We didn't want to bury Mom without our father there, but they didn't know if he would come out of the coma. When John got back, we all decided to have a memorial. The church Mom went to didn't believe in memorials, but they made an exception for her.

"You should have seen it, Kevin. They had to open up extra church seating like they do for Christmas and Easter, there were so many people. Mom was a hospice nurse, and she helped so many people. These were the families of the people. The people she helped were dead, but the families remembered her. They all loved her so much. People I didn't even know were coming up to me in tears."

"I'm sorry I wasn't there for you, Julie." Saying it felt like a prayer.

"It was so awful."

She moved the phone away, and I heard her trying to catch her breath. I waited until I heard her breathing steady.

"I wish I was there for you then."

"You're here now, Kevin."

"Yes. I am."

Our stories kept tumbling out, the fucked-up and the funny. As I became a big brother to Julie, my little sister began her own journey, back to something she'd lost far too much of already.

"Mom told me about you."

I held my breath.

"When I was sixteen. I remember it. I was going through a lot of shit then, and she sat me down, we sat at the kitchen table and she said, 'Julie, people make mistakes.' And she told me about you."

"Did she tell James and John?"

"No. She told our father, I know, but nobody else." I heard in her voice, she was right there with me and someplace else far away at the same time. "Even when I got all fucked up, and Mom and I fought, that still made me feel close to her. She trusted me."

"So you're the only one alive who knows I exist."

"I never told anybody." She let out a long, slow sigh. "Kevin, to be honest, I was really fucked up. John takes my calls, but James will hardly talk to me. I don't blame them."

"And I called you first. Somehow I knew to call you first."

"Yeah, you called me first."

"Yeah. I did."

———

JULIE PROMISED to call our uncle and give him my number but thought it best if she talked to James and John separately the next day. I didn't want to push, had to trust that this was exactly what was supposed to happen. I told myself the same thing I tell parents with a newborn child: Don't blink. I don't want to miss one single second.

Eri came home and sent the boys upstairs to play so I could relay every moment to her. I was almost gasping for breath but couldn't stop talking. I wanted to replay every moment, to etch the details into permanent memory.

Thirty minutes later the phone rang.

"Hello, hello. Is Kevin there?"

I'd never heard a Cajun accent before. My mother's brother.

"Yes, this is Kevin."

"Kevin, this's your Uncle Bob."

"Yes, sir, I thought it was you. How are you?"

Uncle Bob chuckled, his voice low and cigarette-scratchy.

"Isn't this just fucked up? Betty Ann never told me shit!"

I'd found my family, and they were just like me.

Uncle Bob was a hoot, straight out of Louisiana, a down-home, down-to-earth kind of guy. He referred to my mother—always—as Betty Ann, never just Betty and never, ever Elizabeth. We shared the same middle name, Michael. My other uncle is Stephen, the name my mother gave me. She said in her letter that she named me after St. Stephen and St. Michael. Nice to know it went deeper than that.

He was my historical memory, and I didn't want to rush anything. Uncle Bob was fifty-three and in good health. Time seemed to be warming up to me again.

Uncle Bob loves to talk, and it was impossible to keep all the details in my head. I scrambled between laughing and asking questions and scribbling notes as fast as I could. He never knew about me, but he remembered when I was born.

"Yeah, I remember that. We called it Betty Ann's summer in New York."

"Uncle Bob, do you know who she lived with?"

"Yeah, yeah, sure, an old gambling friend of your grandparents. Her name was Ruth, a Polish Jew, emigrated with her parents. His name was Pete. Pete was Sicilian." He pondered out loud. "Yeah, he was a professional gambler. He and his wife'd come down to New Orleans and get together. They was kinda like family to us. They musta taken your momma in. Huh. No shit."

I imagined him scratching his head.

"Yeah, Ruth was a waitress, and Pete a gambler. Was good at it, too, ya know? They had two daughters, Roberta and Deloris. Moved down to Cocoa Beach in Florida. Your mom and Roberta were friends when they were kids."

"I found my mom's address when she lived here. It was 300 Main Street, about twenty minutes from where I grew up in Rotterdam."

"Yeah, yeah, right, they lived in some place called Rotterdam Junction, or something like that. They called it Rotterdam Junk Yard."

He laughed loud and hard, and I with him.

JULIE CALLED me back later in that evening. Our brother John agreed to take my call tomorrow at 6:00 p.m. Mountain Time. She said he took the news okay but asked for a night to sleep on it and process the revelation. Both Julie and Uncle Bob said John was the mellow one, easy to get along with.

In the morning, Julie texted me a picture, and I sent one back to her. We talked several times during the day, her assuring me I'd get used to her rambling. She referred to herself as a real "flibbertigibbet," something our mom always called her. I wonder silently what word Mom would have used to describe me.

Our brother James said he'd take my call at 4:00 p.m. Mountain Time. He took the news better than she thought he would. Everything was moving quickly now. The pace kept my mind focused, and I was too occupied to let my feelings get the better of me. Julie had already mailed me pictures of our mom and brothers, and of herself. They should arrive by Wednesday; she'd sent them priority.

"You didn't have to do that," I said.

"Yes, I did," she replied. "You've waited long enough."

Julie and I were already ending our calls with "I love you." I've always gone with my heart.

AGE SIXTEEN

"You can stay with me," Nessie says, putting sheets on the twin bed we share.

"What about money?"

"Al likes you. Abbey likes you, too. That's all that matters. You can live here if you want. It's up to you." Her belly now shows a nice, round six-month bulge tugging against her blouse. "Are you going to be the father?"

"Do you want me to? What about Michael? What about that?" I point at the diamond ring on her finger.

"It's a ring. It's just a fucking ring. When are you going to get me a ring? When you get me a ring, I'll wear that ring. I don't want nobody to think I'm some knocked-up mother without a man."

I let that sink in. "So . . . do you want me to be the father?"

"Yes."

"You're sure?"

"Yes."

Over the past months, I've brought back some clothes from my parents, but now I pack up an old suitcase with the rest of my clothes and put it by the door. My mother asks me to stay for lunch, and I open a beer and sit at the table.

"Where are you staying?" she asks me. My father is eating, silent.

"At Nessie's."

I eat chicken soup as quickly as I can, but it's hot, and it burns my tongue. With my head down, blowing gently on the steaming spoonful of soup, I feel them looking at each other, contemplating.

"Nessie's pregnant."

"She's what?" My mother spits out a mouthful of soup. "Oh my God, Kevin. How are you going to be a father? You don't even have a job!"

"Neither does he," I quip, turning to look at my father, daring him.

"I worked for twenty years!" my father bellows. I've woken the sleeping bear.

"That's not the point, Kevin." My mother tries to regain her footing. "When is she due?"

"April."

My mother sits back, and I can almost hear the calculation in her head. "I thought you broke up with her after school ended?"

"We did break up. It's not mine."

I push the empty bowl away and pick up the grilled cheese sandwich on rye that my mother had neatly cut in half.

"What do you mean, it's not yours? It's not your baby?" My mother asks, her voice rising, not in anger but confusion. And a bit of hope.

"We broke up after school, and she got with this guy Michael. He's the father. But he left her, and now we're back together." I sit back in my chair and stare past them out the window.

"But if he's the father, he has to take care of her and the baby." My mother looks back and forth from me to my father. "You can't take care of a family."

"Right." My father crosses his arms, nods his head.

My mother, confident that she's right, sits straight up in her chair and looks directly at me.

"Nessie is trying to get you to take care of her. You shouldn't do that. She should get back together with the father, and he should—"

"She's not getting back together with him. She's never getting with him."

I raise my voice as loud as I can and still stay in control.

"He's not a good father. He doesn't care about them. When he found out she was pregnant, he never showed his face again. He gave her a ring and left. I can be a better father than that. I show up. I come every single day. I'm a better fucking father than he is. I'm a better father than a lot of fathers!"

I push the plate away and sit back, my hands clenched on the arms of the chair, and glare at both of them as my mother struggles for words.

"You can't just say you're a father. You have to be one. You have to have a job. It costs money to take care of a family. She wants you to pay for everything? Does she know you don't have a job?"

"She doesn't care!" I stand up and stalk toward the door, turn around and jab my finger at them across the kitchen. "She loves me."

"Mom's not saying she doesn't," my father says.

"No, I'm not saying that. I didn't mean that."

"She's never asked me for a dime!" I come back to the table and my fingernails dig into the chair. "She doesn't care about money. She doesn't care about all the shit you care about, she cares about me. She cares about us being happy. She cares about this baby. So do I."

"Just come sit down, Kevin," my mother pleads.

"No!" I jab my finger at her again. "She's not like that, she's not using me. You don't fucking care about the baby. You don't fucking care about her. You don't fucking care about me."

I grab my suitcase and fling the door open, banging it against the wall as I stomp down the steps.

"You don't fucking care. Fuck you."

NESSIE'S WATER breaks on April 2 in the early minutes after midnight. I lie next to her and rub her huge belly, but the contractions are slow to come and far apart. It feels as though there isn't an inch left inside for the baby to move. Nessie rolls from side to side, finally propping herself up on our pillows.

"The pain isn't bad. Kinda hardly there, like small muscle cramps. Like after you swim."

"They're only lasting a few seconds." I keep rubbing her belly, feeling for I didn't really know what, but the baby still isn't moving around.

"I don't want to go to the hospital."

We turn out the lights and lie in the darkness, waiting.

Nessie pokes me awake just before six.

"I want to go to the hospital." She keeps poking until I get off the bed, already dressed from the night before.

"How is it?" I ask.

"It hurts worse. It's going slow, but it hurts worse."

Abbey and Al drive us to St. Peter's Hospital in Albany. Nessie holds my arm while we walk circles in the room, until the pain comes again, and she grabs my arm hard and lies back down. The contractions are lasting longer now, but still not coming faster, so by lunchtime the nurse tells me to go home and eat, and they'll call me when she's further along.

It's just a short walk to the house, so I eat and update Abbey and Al and head right back to the hospital. Nessie tries to smile, but then the pain comes again. After it passes, she laughs.

"I'm going to crush your hand."

"Do it. Squeeze as hard as you want."

The contractions last nearly a minute each now. After an hour, my knuckles feel like a ball of wet sand at the beach, waiting to disintegrate.

I sit next to her all through the afternoon and hold her hand during the contractions, eating some dinner while she sucks on ice chips.

By midnight, she can't get up except to go to the bathroom. Despite the contractions, her body isn't ready yet, she's not dilated enough. When the pain comes, I hear her teeth grind, her eyes shut tight as she moans, the tears running down her face. At seven o'clock the next morning, after nineteen hours of labor, they tell us it's time for a cesarean. Neither of us has slept for twenty-eight hours. Nessie sobs, exhausted, begging, whimpering, "No. Please, no."

St. Peter's doesn't allow fathers in the operating room. When they bring Nessie out, still medicated from the surgery, the nurse takes me down the hall. I sit in an armchair, and she brings Dawn to me. I hold this tiny human with my two hands under her arms, resting her on my lap, and her head droops into her chest. The nurse smiles at the blank look on my face and shows me how to hold her, cradling her head in my left arm.

Abbey is as happy as a foster grandmother can be. Al and I drink beers to celebrate, but I want to get up early so I can be at the hospital by the time Nessie finishes breakfast.

Everyone laughs when I try to change Dawn's diaper, but my lack of skill is more unwillingness than inability. I'm good at holding Dawn tight when she cries, and I love to make her burp, walking up and down the hallway until she sleeps, her head heavy on my shoulder.

On our last day in the hospital, the nurse brings in some paperwork to fill out. Nessie's nursing, so I hold up the newborn ID form for her to see. Some parts are already filled in.

Infant's Birth Date: 3/4/79
Time: 1:00 PM
Sex: Girl
Color or Race: WHITE
Weight: 6.9 lbs.
Length: 15 in.

I read aloud the blank sections, and Nessie dictates what I should write.

MOTHER'S NAME: Bisset
INFANT NAME: Dawn Amy

Because Nessie and I aren't married, she doesn't think she can give the baby my name, but she doesn't want to give the baby her last name either. We've already argued about it, because Michael wasn't around for the entire pregnancy, but in the end, I agree that for now the child will take his name.

The form has imprints of Dawn's left and right foot, and one final line to fill in.

I CERTIFY that during the discharge procedure I received my baby, examined it and determined that it was mine. I checked the Ident-A-Band® parts sealed on the baby and on me and found that they were identically numbered and contained correct identifying information.

I hand Nessie the pen, but she shakes her head and hands it back to me. "You do it."

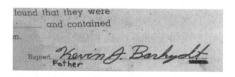

"YOU'RE NOT THE FATHER. You helped her until she had the baby. That's enough, Kevin. You shouldn't have to support her. It's not your responsibility."

My mother looks across the dining room table for reinforcement, but the most my father can manage is an occasional nod.

"I'm going to get work. I just need some money until I find a job."

"What? I can't hear you," my mother snaps.

"He says he needs some money."

"You don't have a job. You don't have any money," Mom prods.

"I know."

"You did enough. You can't take care of a baby. You're not even married."

"I'm not leaving them." I stare at the table, not moving.

"She's the mother. She should get the father to help." My mother leans toward me, her elbows on the table, almost pleading now.

"He's gone." I lift my head up and look straight out the window at the backyard.

"Where is he?"

"He's gone."

"Where?"

"He's gone. He left them. He didn't even come to the hospital. I was there. He didn't walk her and feed her. I did. He wasn't there. I was. I'm there. I'm here." I cross my arms and lean back hard in the chair, letting it hold me upright. "I'm the one who's here."

"But you're not the father."

"So? So what?" I point across the table at my dad, my words defiant. "He's not my real father."

Her head droops down, eyes not focusing on anything.

"And you're not my mother. You're not my parents, but you are my parents. It's the same. It's just the same."

The table goes silent. All of us stare at nothing, unwilling to look at each other, and my eyes drop to the floor.

"Why don't you come home? You can find a job here."

She sounds like my mother again, not judging, giving me an out. I lift my head, still not looking at them.

"I just need a hundred dollars for now."

"Just give him the money," my father bellows, throwing his arms in the air and leaning back in his chair, shaking his head in frustration.

My mother walks to the bedroom, comes back clutching her purse, and hands me the cash, her face unreadable.

"Thanks."

I put the money in my pocket, and we sit in silence a few moments longer. Then I stand up and push my chair under the table.

"I'm not leaving them."

APRIL 2007

"Hi, James?"

"This is James."

James lived with his wife and two children on a mountainside with no cell service, totally off the grid. He stopped to take my call at The Ever Open Cafe on his way home from work, on the very northern edge of Fort Collins, Colorado.

"Hey, how are you? This is Kevin."

"I'm good, thanks."

"Julie gave me your number."

"Yeah. She told me that you were out there."

"I guess this is a surprise."

"Yeah, a bit."

His voice felt familiar, comfortable. I could feel myself smiling.

"A good surprise?"

"To be honest, no," James said without missing a beat. "I mean, nothing personal, I just don't know you."

"I know."

"My first thought, actually, was bullshit, not my Catholic mother, there's no way she had a child out of wedlock." James's gravelly baritone rose and fell, and even behind the sometimes sharp tone there was always kindness. His words flowed, pulling from a keen intellect and deep emotional wellspring, every vibration of his vocal cords sounding like an old, favorite song.

"What made it okay for you to take my call?"

"Like I said, at first I didn't believe her, I said no way." He paused long enough to sigh, then continued. "But then Julie told me a story about when she was sixteen and wanted to have an abortion, how Mom confided that she had a child, pretty much the whole story about you."

James was skeptical, but his honesty gave me a sense of calm.

"I didn't know that."

"Yeah, well, man, this is the family you found." James' sarcasm was charming, but he caught himself and continued without the edge. "I was at work when Julie called. I told her I was headed into a meeting, and she said 'James, we have a brother.' My first reaction was, 'Are you high again?' Part of me was taking it all with a grain of sand . . ." His voice softened. "Julie's a liar. She has that disease from being an addict."

"Yeah, she told me about that."

"I don't really have a lot of faith in her, to be honest."

James listened as I relayed the tale of my birth, my adoptive parents, and my life-long wish for a picture of my mother. I had already decided to approach all three of them with absolute honesty, and now instinct told me to hold nothing back.

"How many brothers or sisters do you have?" he asked. I heard only curiosity.

"None."

James was silent. I tried not to read his mind, simply had to trust that the next moment would make clear what to say.

"So you didn't have any idea about us? Your parents didn't tell you anything?"

"They didn't know anything."

We talked about the car accident, and he shared the details, the church memorial, the funeral.

"I wish I could have been there for you."

"I wish you could have known her, man, but I'm glad you didn't have to be there when she died. It wasn't good. It was brutal."

"And then your dad died."

"When he came out of the coma, he was blind, never regained his sight. John and Linda stayed and took care of him for almost a year. He hated being blind, but he learned to deal with it, kind of. Had a girl-friend and seemed pretty happy sometimes, but he blamed himself for Mom.

"Three years after Mom died, he walked out in the front yard at three in the morning, called the local sheriff and said, 'I'm really sorry to do this to you, but I want you to get over here and clean up the mess before my kids get here.'"

It wasn't my pain, but I couldn't help but cry.

"It was winter, so there was all this blood and pieces of bone on the white snow."

He didn't hear my tears. I held my hand over the phone as I listened.

"The body was gone by the time I got there, but I didn't want Julie and John to see the blood and bone. So I shoveled snow on top and covered it up."

"James, I'm so sorry."

We were both tired after almost two hours together. I wanted to never hang up the phone but trusted that we would have more talks like this. James hesitated for the first time, and when he spoke again, I heard a new tenor in his voice.

"You sound like Mom."

I couldn't speak for a moment. Again. I'd already learned to listen, in a way I never had before.

"The inflection of your voice, like . . . it's just Mom. I can just hear her in you. It's really beautiful, man."

"James, this is a lot for me."

"Me too!" James laughed loudly, but with kindness. His laugh was infectious, and together we recognized and embraced the tremendous strangeness of the moment. "I saw a picture of you, Julie texted me one, and you look so much like Grandma and Ma. Just like, crazy resemblance."

"Did you see the copy of the letter your mom wrote?" We'd broken past nervousness now, both of us excited, bouncing off each other.

"Yeah. That was Mom's handwriting, it never changed."

"Julie said the same thing."

"Look, Kevin, you keep saying 'your mom,' and I get why you'd do that, I appreciate your respect, but you can say it, man. You can say 'our mom.'"

I could not find words to say what I felt, and if I had, I don't know if I could have uttered a sound. I tipped my head back, letting the torrent of emotions and thoughts flood through my body and wash over me like a warm summer thunderstorm.

"I don't want to rush any of this, James."

He was quiet, just long enough for both of us to take a breath. "Our family has only been shrinking, my mom and dad passed, Julie is all fucked up, and now you show up and our family just got bigger. Like, something I thought was completely impossible." James' voice dropped as if I were sitting next to him in the quiet of his car. "I can't even describe how quickly you've gained my trust. How quickly you've become my brother. You just are my brother, it's like blood, blood is thicker than water, you know? I just feel it balls-to-bones, man. You are my brother."

"Hi, is this John?"

"Yes."

"John, this is Kevin."

John talked fast, jumped right in, dared me to keep up. He's been a big brother a lot longer than I have.

"Yeah, Julie called me. She started off with the classic 'Are you sitting down?' and I said, 'No, I generally answer my cell phone standing up.'" He laughed, and it's a hearty laugh, not gentle like James, almost abrupt, but jovial. "She had to be melodramatic about it, you know Julie. Well, I guess you don't know Julie, but she can be pretty melodramatic."

"It's a lot to take in."

"Right. So, she told me about you, that you called her. To be honest I was like, 'What? Our mom had a kid? Our mom?'"

We both laughed. I'd had time to prepare, but he'd gotten the shock treatment.

"Right, I know, she told me she was sixteen when your mom told her." I want so badly to be careful with my words.

"Well, yeah, that was also around the time that Julie had gotten pregnant."

"When she was sixteen?" I asked, trying to reconcile the facts in my head.

"Right. I can't believe Mom never told us anything about it. I mean, what was she going to do if you found her?"

"I wish I had. I waited too long."

"Yeah." John sounded caring and kind, but I got the sense that emotional upheaval was not comfortable for him, and that was fine with me. I'd cried enough already. "After I talked to Julie, I talked to James. I think she called him first. I said 'Wow, do you believe this?'"

"It's pretty unbelievable, I know."

"Yeah. And James said, 'Why would anyone *lie* to be a part of *our* family?'" He chuckled, and the chuckle exploded into a deep belly laugh, unexpected, as if he'd let go of a fully blown balloon, enjoying watching it spin and whiz in chaotic circles and scrambling to catch it in midair. "There was kinda this realization, we've lost so many people, it was like, wow, did we just gain another family member?"

He laughed that big laugh again. I was already getting used to the sounds of my family.

"I'm hoping so."

We told stories for two hours, feeling like bobbleheads, our minds bouncing from one memory to another. John wanted to know about my mother and father, about Eri and my children, and I wanted to know about him, what he had done as a child, his best and worst memories growing up.

They grew up on a horse ranch that Mom loved. Their dad was a strapping cowboy from Wyoming, but James looked more like him than anyone else. John loved books, loved to read, loved role-playing games.

John knew I had a lot of questions about our mom, and he promised to talk again, whenever I wanted.

"I can get you some pictures." John was innately a big brother, even to his new, bigger brother. "I have lots of them here at the house, I'll just have to dig through them."

"John, how do you feel about all this? I know it's a lot."

"Just kind of accepting."

He was not resistant at all, and I was so grateful.

"I think it's a little different for us. We've already had brothers and sisters, are finding another brother in a family we already have. You're finding a whole new family for the first time. It's just kind of, 'Wow, this is a weird turn the universe took.'"

"John, thank you."

"Hey, man, you're family now."

"Those words mean the world to me, John."

"I'm glad you found us. I'm glad you called Julie first. I don't know what I would have said if you had called me."

"If it's okay with you, I'll try to call you sometime soon, maybe next week. I'm open to whatever you are comfortable with."

"Listen, as far as I'm concerned, you're Mom's son, so you're my brother. I know Julie and James will feel the same, just give us time. Like I said, that you called Julie and she called us? Bro, that's a miracle. You have to understand, Kevin, we not only got a brother, but we got our sister back, too."

AGE SIXTEEN

The next time I visit to ask for money, my father says he's found me a job in Albany, a six-week bricklaying training program, only a short walk from Abbey and Al's house. I say thanks, ask for twenty dollars to hold me over, buy some dope, and get high in the back of the bus on the ride back to Albany.

News of the job tilts things in my favor with Abbey. We celebrate with beer and a nice dinner, and on April 23, I wake up and go to work. When I walk home for lunch, I feel different—I have stories to tell about the men who train me, about the other apprentices who, like me, are there to make a new start.

My first $122.00 paycheck comes on a Friday, and Abbey wants me to sign it over to her. I want to show my parents the check first. Nessie and Abbey both scream at me as I walk out the door.

Even with the check I have no money for a bus, so I stick my thumb out. Not a lot of traffic, but before long, a guy pulls over and I jump in the car.

"How far you going?" He's in his thirties, black, casually dressed.

"Downtown Schenectady."

"No problem." He smiles. "Is that where you live?"

"No, I live in Albany."

"What's in Schenectady?"

"My parents."

I smoke a cigarette while he asks questions. He's nice, polite. Like Arnold.

"Is that a style?"

"What?"

"Those holes in your jeans?"

He reaches over, poking his finger into a rip in my jeans on my left thigh.

"No, these are my work clothes."

His finger stays in the rip, his hand resting on my leg as we drive in silence, then he pulls his hand away slowly and leans back in the seat. We're almost downtown by Woolworth's now.

"You can let me out anywhere." I point at the corner just ahead. "There's fine."

"Is this where your parents live?"

"No."

"Let me take you home."

"They live in Rotterdam."

"I'll drive you."

His voice falters now, the firm, confident tone gone. Begging almost.

"Okay, take a left on Broadway."

I sit back, my legs splayed on the seat, and feel the heat in the car, hear his quickened breath. I look out the window as we pass Jay Street, half expecting to see Butchie smiling at me, standing on the corner in his ripped jean jacket and silver-and-turquoise belt buckle.

"Is this okay?"

He reaches over and puts his hand on my thigh again, higher up my leg. I lift his hand and move it lower, nearer my knee.

"Only on the hole."

He puts two fingers in the hole this time, stroking my leg hairs. I smoke, letting my arm hang out the window, feeling in the breeze as he drives, my left arm across my lap. We drive past the WAITT House, turn left past the Little Super, on streets I've known all my life. The car slows.

"You can let me out here."

I flick my cigarette out the window. He pulls over, a few houses down from my parents' house.

"Can I suck your dick?" he asks.

"No. I've got to go."

"I'll pay you."

"No."

"Ten dollars."

"No." I close my legs, but his two fingers stay in the hole, pulling at the frayed material.

"Can I just rub your leg then?"

I reach for the door handle. He pulls his hand away, takes out his wallet, and hands me a twenty without a word. I pocket the cash but don't look at him.

"Just my leg."

I light another cigarette, blow the smoke out the window, and let my legs hang open. As he fondles my leg he rubs himself through his pants and keeps trying to move his hand up my leg, but I keep stopping him, and he whimpers but keeps rubbing, rubbing, working himself up, and I move his hand down and he moans and gropes my leg harder. Finally, he finishes and pulls his hand away with a huff, yanking on the fabric so it rips the hole more.

"Get out." He spits the words out, staring straight ahead.

"Okay."

"I gave you a ride."

"I was hitching."

I look back at him, one foot out the door.

"I gave you a ride all the way to your house. To your parents' house!"

"I didn't ask you to." I slam the door and stand on the curb.

"Fuck you." He's trying hard to look angry.

"No." I laugh as he drives away, tears in his eyes. "Fuck you."

———

BRICKLAYING IS HARD WORK but learning how to lay brick is even harder. I try to not get high in the morning before the training, but by noon I have to take the edge off, so I smoke a joint on the walk home for lunch.

Abbey is home from work because on Fridays she cashes her paycheck. Dawn is giggly as I raise her up in the air, each time a little higher, set her diapered butt on my head, and lower her back down to wiggle our noses together. The mood is so light, from outside the kitchen window anyone would think there was a birthday party going on inside.

My buzz is settling in, and I wish I didn't have to go back to training, wish I could just spend the afternoon getting high. Abbey is at the sink, Nessie feeding Dawn, as I sit down to eat a bowl of chicken soup and a sandwich Abbey has set out.

I sit in Abbey's usual seat, where her coat and purse are hanging on the back of the chair. I'm happy, floating on air, everyone else preoccupied, and my instincts take over.

I lean forward to slurp a spoonful of soup and see Abbey's purse hanging open, the bank envelope with her paycheck tucked inside, and almost on its own my left hand reaches for it, even as I keep eating soup with my right, blowing and sipping and blowing and sipping and swallowing. Without missing a sip, I open the envelope and finger through the bills, my eyes still on the soup and Abbey and Nessie.

I pocket over three hundred dollars and shove the envelope back down inside the purse, making sure to leave half of the bills, lean back and take a long, slow breath, smile, and finish my soup.

Abbey sits across from me eating her lunch while I work on my sandwich and Nessie bounces Dawn on her lap. After we're all done, we sit and drink and talk, watching Dawn's smile, her eyes, her tiny hands fluttering and pawing at the air. I get up and take my empty bowl and spoon to the sink.

"I'll be back tomorrow or Sunday."

"You're not coming back for dinner?" Nessie asks, smiling, not challenging.

"No, easier to just go back tonight and stay over."

I kiss Nessie goodbye, pick Dawn up and swing her up high so she giggles and squeals before I hand her to Abbey. The two stare into each other's eyes as I grab my jacket from the living room and make my exit.

I skip the afternoon training, making a beeline for Schenectady. With cash on hand, I'm laser focused. I spend the next thirty-six hours freebasing on the Hill until I've burned through the three hundred dollars, and finally get to my parents' house late Saturday night.

Nessie's been calling all weekend. My mother stands in the kitchen and tells me I should call her back right away, and just then the phone rings.

"Abbey is throwing us out." Nessie's voice is loud and hard.

"What? Why?"

I hold the phone away from my ear, but even so I can hear Abbey shouting in the background.

"She fucking accused you of stealing from her purse. Taking fucking money from her purse. There's no way! You couldn't have done it! We were all sitting right here in the kitchen. I would have seen you. She would have seen you! She just lost the money, and she's trying to blame you. She doesn't even care about the money, she just wants us out."

I take in a breath, slowly, willing my body to be still. "What about the baby?"

"She doesn't fucking care about the baby." Nessie is screaming now. "She doesn't care about anybody."

I hold the phone and wait until she runs out of steam, her anger and fear spent, quietly sniffling, lost. We both hang on the phone, listening to each other breathe. I can feel her willing me to speak, waiting, catching her breath between tears.

"I'll come tomorrow." I hear her breathing slow. I say the words again. "I'll come tomorrow."

My father agrees to drive me to Albany after church. My mother smiles up at me from the passenger side. "I'm going along for the ride."

I lock up the house, slide into the back seat.

When we get there, I lean over from the back of the seat and point out the house, so Dad pulls to the curb.

"I'll be right back."

I walk into the living room where Abbey has planted her feet, her arms crossed like a prison guard, and glares without speaking as I head upstairs. Nessie sits on the bed holding Dawn, her face tear-streaked and drained of color, her hair tangled, uncombed. An empty bag of chips and a scattering of crumbs on the floor. Everything she owns is packed in one large suitcase and two paper shopping bags.

I carry the suitcase down to the front door, climb back upstairs and grab the shopping bags. Nessie follows me down, Dawn clutched to her chest.

I put the bags on the floor and take Dawn from Nessie, then turn to face Abbey still standing in the middle of the living room floor. "Sorry," is all I say, and I see tears roll down her face before I walk out to the car.

My mother looks up into my face as I open the car door and hand Dawn over into her arms. Dawn bounces a little on her lap, looking at my mother, up at me, and back again. My mother stares at me for a long time. I've never seen her face look the way it does when she looks at the baby in her arms. Dawn wiggles and coos, and as she adjusts the baby on her lap, a smile spreads over my face.

"Watch your leg." I get up and carefully close the car door. "Watch the baby."

I turn back to the house and Abbey, who watches from the doorway as we load the suitcase and bags in the trunk. Nessie and I get in the back seat, and my father drives away.

MAY 2007

A few days after my talks with John and James, I sat at the dining room table with my parents after dinner on a warm Saturday evening. My mother had the windows open to let the breeze in.

"Can you wait for dessert?" It wasn't really a question, and they both grew quiet as I put the ice cream back in the freezer.

"You guys know that I've been curious about my birth family, that I've been looking for information over the past two years."

I paused as they both nodded, looking at each other, then back to me.

"I completed my search."

Their eyes lit up.

"Sadly, my birth mother passed away ten years ago."

My mother's eyes welled up with tears. I let the news settle in for a few seconds.

"She died in a car accident in 1997." I waited again. "Her name was Betty. Elizabeth, but everyone called her Betty."

I took out the pictures and handed the picture of my mom to my mother.

"Oh, Kevin, she's beautiful." Her eyes brimmed over. "She looks like you. She's so young."

"The pictures are from her thirtieth wedding anniversary, and from her son James' wedding."

"She had a son?"

"She had two sons and a daughter."

"The man is her husband?"

"That's her husband, John Buchanan. He's not my dad. She married him right after I was born."

We passed around more pictures as I introduced my parents to my two brothers, my sister, my nieces and nephews. My father couldn't keep the names or faces straight, but my mother got it down pretty well.

We shuffled through the pictures, my mother commenting on each picture, how pretty my mom was, how much I look like her. She said the names over and over, and my father stayed confused, so she kept correcting him, each time making it more real for herself.

"You need a photo album for those." My mother looked at the stack of pictures. "Do you have one?"

I shook my head.

"I think I've got one."

Five minutes later I went looking for her. She found a brand-new album, still shrink-wrapped, and with it she carried another album, older, with photos of Kentaro and Tyler, Eri, my father, and her.

We brought both downstairs and flipped slowly, page by page, easing through the memories. How cute Kentaro was when he was born. How we don't have enough pictures of Tyler, how the second kid always gets cheated. We found our favorite pictures, and they grounded us, brought us back for the moment to a familiar comfort.

Then the room quieted, pictures of my new family scattered in the center of the dining table where we ate together for almost forty-five years.

"This is a nice album." My mother handed me the new album.

I pulled off the shrink-wrap and handed it back to her.

"You're better at it, Mom."

"You want me to do it?"

"Yes, you're better at it."

Don't blink. I didn't want to miss one second.

My mother carefully, easily, arranged the pictures in the album—on the first page the pictures of my mom, then ones of my sister and brothers. She looked over every picture, so focused on getting them just right that some went in upside down, and we laughed at her absentmindedness, distracting us for the moment.

When all the pictures were in, she handed me the album, and I held it in my hands.

AGE SEVENTEEN

When Dawn is three months old, we all pile into the car for a week-long Cape Cod vacation. Babcia comes with us, riding in the back with my mother, Dawn lying on their laps as we head for a house north of Chatham, a mile-long drive from the beach.

Dawn never leaves the house without her little bonnet so she won't burn, and all three women hide from the sun under an umbrella. Nessie sometimes comes into the water with me, but only up to her ankles, and any time a wave rolls in she locks up, bracing for the swell, screaming and laughing, high-stepping back onto the hot sand.

The sun shines the entire week without one cloud or drop of rain, and the beach is our afternoon ritual after mornings spent relaxing at the house. A few evenings, we put on some nice clothes and go out to dinner. The nights are as warm as the days, and we eat outside enjoying the breeze, laughing and handing Dawn around the table.

After we get back to Schenectady, Nessie misses her period. I want to keep it between us, but she blabs it at the dinner table, and the conversation quickly turns to my job. Nessie knows I have extra money, that I'm dealing dope more and more, and now with another baby on the way our dinners end with fights more than desserts.

Sundays, my parents take Dawn to church. She never makes a fuss during the service. Nessie and I have been arguing since the night before, and we wake up screaming at each other. I lock myself in the bathroom to get away from her, still drunk from last night, and sit on the toilet snorting blow as she screams through the door. The cocaine shoots through me like a dozen sparklers sizzling through the top of my skull, and I flush the toilet and put my head back and smile at the sound of the water swirling below.

Nessie slams her fist on the door, harder and harder until the hollow core creaks and splinters under the assault. I know she knows where the key is.

The pounding stops, and I hear her drag one of the wooden dining room chairs up the hall and climb up. I yank the door open just as she leans down to jiggle the key in the lock.

"You fucking bastard! You fucking bastard!" She screams, eyes bulging out of her head as she falls backward and crashes into the louvered closet doors behind, the slats cracking where her shoulder hits.

"What the fuck are you doing on the chair, huh?"

I kick the chair over and throw it against the table, grim satisfaction at the sound of wood crashing against wood. I turn to pick up the chair, sure it's cracked.

"Fuck the chair!" Her tears come hard now, still crumpled against the broken door.

Dropping to one knee next to her, I reach for her arm. She lunges, claws my face, knocks me back and I twist on all fours out of reach. Apart but at the same time we stumble to our feet and she stabs with her nails again, backing me into the kitchen and her fists pummeling my head, my face, my arms as I block her blows.

"Fucking stop! Stop!"

I corral her wrists together and clamp them against her chest, slamming her against the refrigerator, a sickening thud when her head pops off the metal. I push away and see her eyes cloud, her jaw go slack. She's crying still, but now the volume is turned down low, and everything's in slow motion—pulling open a kitchen drawer, fingers fumbling, grabbing a long knife with both hands.

She circles around me and backs away, past the bathroom and my parents' bedroom, into the spare room, my childhood bedroom.

"I'm leaving." She glares. "Leaving and taking Dawn, taking our baby, and I'm done. I'm done. Fucking done."

I pace up and down the short hallway, in and out of the spare room, before kicking at the broken closet door.

"You're not fucking leaving." I block the doorway, stabbing my finger in her face. "Where you going to go? Huh?"

Nessie backs away, me standing in the middle of the hallway and screaming at the empty doorway, then suddenly she's there with a knife above her head, a manic, screeching scream, her mouth gaping like a jagged knothole in a shattered tree, zigzagging toward me in just a few steps. I grab hold of the door frame for leverage and kick her square in the chest. The force lifts her clear off the floor, and she lands on her backside in the middle of the room, hurls the knife at me. It bounces off my right arm, cutting through my shirt into my bicep.

A WEEK BEFORE THE BABY arrives, we sit around the living room discussing names. My father had been kind enough not to name me Herbert John Barhydt III, but if I have a son his name will be Kevin John Barhydt Jr. There are no other options I'm willing to discuss.

"What if it's a girl?"

My father sits in his recliner, tossing out ideas. "Do you want to have a name with a 'K'? Like K for Kevin, but for a girl?"

"Katherine?" my mother suggests. "That was my mother's name." She dismisses the thought immediately. "No. That's too old a name for a girl."

"I like Victoria." Nessie's thinking aloud.

"Too much like Virginia." My mother smiles. "We already have two too many 'Vs' in the house."

"But then we can use each other's luggage forever!" Nessie quips.

My mother's maiden name is Sendzicki, Virginia Sendzicki Barhydt. Nessie's is Storm. If we marry, Nessie's name will be Vanessa Storm Barhydt.

"No," I say. "No more VSB's."

"How about Sarah?" My mother throws the name out of nowhere.

"Or Seraphina," I muse.

"Seraphina?" My mother's eyes look up to the heavens. "Maybe."

"No." Nessie shakes her head.

"Seraphina." I say the name out loud, slowly. "Seraphina."

"Sarah?" My mother looks at Nessie, and Nessie nods. "I like Sarah."

"No. It's Seraphina." I sit up on the couch, staring straight out the bow window. "Seraphina."

After a quick round of no's from my mother and Nessie, they're ready to move on.

"Seraphina?" my father asks me.

"Yeah. Seraphina." I say the name with finality. The room goes quiet.

Slowly, each one in turn says the name aloud. My father looks at me again, and we nod confirmation.

"What's your middle name, Mom?"

"Josephine?" She speaks the name as a word that feels odd on her lips. "No, not Josephine. That's as bad as Katherine. Worse! I thought you liked Seraphina?"

"I do."

MY FATHER DRIVES us to the hospital three months before my eighteenth birthday, and three days before Dawn's first. My mother stays home with Dawn.

I walk back and forth between the waiting room and the nurse's station, and finally they let me sit in the hallway outside the OR. Every time the door opens, my father and I catch our breath, but the minutes drag by without word. Finally, a young woman comes out, smiling at us sitting on the benches.

"Excuse me." I stop her from walking past. "Is the baby born yet?"

"Are you the father?" She smiles again.

"Yes. It's been a long time. Are they all right?"

She wrings her hands, uncertain.

"Did something happen?" I ask, suddenly panicked. "Is something wrong?"

"No, no, no. I just don't know if I should say anything."

"Please." I look up at her, my nerves on edge. "The baby's born?"

"Yes."

"It's okay? They're both okay?"

"Yes."

I let out a breath, and my father rubs my shoulder. "Thank you." I smile at her, then drop my head into my hands, elbows resting on my thighs.

"Is it a boy or girl?" my father asks, and I look up at her face.

"I'm not sure if I should say." She looks at the closed OR door and back to us. "I think it's a boy."

She walks down the hallway in the wake of our stunned silence. As the news sets in, both our faces broaden first into smiles, then grins larger than life, then laughter as my father slaps my back. I wipe away the sudden tears running down my cheeks, and as one we drop back on the hard seats, his arm across my shoulder.

"You did it," my father says into the space between us. "You did it, Kev."

The tension in our bodies unwinds and time slows down, the seconds loitering and deliberate, my lips mumbling barely coherent words. I'm no longer shaking, ready now to sleep for a hundred years, when the OR door opens again. A nurse comes out to ask if we're the family of Vanessa Storm.

"Yes. I'm the father."

"Mr. Storm?"

"No, my name is Barhydt."

"Bar . . . ?"

"Bar-height. Like a high bar."

"Mr. Barhydt. Your baby's mother is fine. She's going to be in post-op for about an hour."

"The surgery was okay? They didn't have any problems? Because it took a lot longer than our first daughter."

"No, sir, Mr. Barhydt, everything went fine."

"Good. Thank you."

"Do you want to know what your baby is?"

"Oh." My father and I smile at each other, his hand patting my back. "We already know."

She pauses, surprised. "How do you know?"

"The girl told us!"

"Mr. Barhydt." She took a slow, deep breath. "I'm very sorry. She shouldn't have said anything to you."

"No, don't worry. That's okay. We're just glad everyone is all right." I grin at my father again and lean back in my chair. "And it's a boy!"

"No, sir. Mr. Barhydt, you have a daughter."

The hallway goes still, my ears blocking out all external sound—the buzzing of the dull fluorescent lights, footsteps, voices in the distance no longer exist.

"What?"

"The baby is a girl."

The volume starts to rise again, but time stutters and jumps, seconds crowding in after each other, then dragging, crawling. I can't move even hearing her apologize, that the young girl had misspoke.

"I have a daughter," I say aloud.

"Yes, sir."

Something shifts, both inside and out. Time finds a new path to follow, undetermined by the rising and setting of the sun, indifferent to my inability to adjust to the newness of everything around me.

"Thank you, nurse." I look up and smile. "I have a daughter."

She nods, smiles a huge smile, and lets out a relieved breath.

"I have a daughter. Her name is Seraphina Josephine Barhydt."

14

SINKING

SEPTEMBER 2007

I stared through the windshield, transfixed by the view. To keep from driving off the highway, I took the next exit and pulled off to let the sheer scope and splendor of the Rocky Mountains overtake me. I stood in the middle of nowhere, on my way to somewhere, my tears mirroring the impossibility of the journey and of my destination.

I felt so high. Oh dear God, I felt high and beautiful and light, and there was no place else in the world I would rather be. For the past two years, I'd been chasing a dream that had now, after so long, become a miracle, and though my heart was pounding, running wild, I felt no fear.

I called Julie as I drove into Colorado Springs. "Hi, Sis, I'm almost there."

"Hey, Brother! Did you see John already?"

"I want to see you first."

Two blocks more and there she was, standing in the parking lot, just the way she said she would be. I dropped the transmission into park, ripped open the door, jumped out with the engine still running, and wrapped my arms around my sister. I held her close, tight, head to toe, and cried into her hair.

She whispered and laughed. "I'm real. I'm really real."

"Me too."

We took each other in, giggling and laughing and crying, and now the magnificent Rockies seemed like nothing in the middle of nowhere compared to the woman who stood in front of me, my flesh and blood. *She is my family, and I am hers.*

Julie couldn't hold still, wiggling in my arms, clasping my hands in hers.

"Oh my God, it's like looking into James's eyes! You have the same eyes."

We took a half step back, still holding each other, but seeing each other for the first time, and her eyes rounded as her jaw dropped, then snapped shut.

Julie turned her face away. "I can't look at you. Oh my God, I can't look."

Overwhelmed and confused, but not hurt. I just didn't understand. She wouldn't look at me, sobbing, tears streaming down.

"You have her eyes. You have Mom's eyes."

All these years I'd been looking for my mother, our mother, wanting to see her face, for her to see me, yet I'd always felt she was with me throughout my life, somehow by my side. Until now, I'd never known how close she was. She was right there, a part of me. She was with me always.

Julie wrapped herself around me again, her face pressed against my shoulder, both of us shaking with tears and laughter and complete joy. We wanted to never let go.

As we drove to visit John and Kyung, I soaked up every second. Every moment was a miracle—not a dream, really, truly happening. Like a kid taking a first plane ride, staring out the window as the jet leaves the ground, watching and listening, forgetting to breathe. Don't blink.

We rode and talked, building on the easy rapport we'd developed over the phone for the past four months. We climbed into the mountains above Colorado Springs and turned down a long dusty road with open fields of tall grass waving on either side. As I pulled up to the house, John and Kyung came out to greet us.

Julie reached to open the door but hesitated when she saw me sitting frozen with my hands in my lap. My sister sat next to me, happy to have me in her life, and my brother was waiting twenty feet away, smiling, with my new sister-in-law smiling by his side, her eyes huge with wonder, and I could hardly breathe with the knowledge that I didn't deserve this happiness. Even though they were right there with me, welcoming me into their family, everything that I was and still am screamed with absolute surety that they would leave me, and that their rejection would be final, absolute.

Julie grabbed my hand, whispered *It's okay, it will be all right.* I breathed deep, focusing on every day that I'd spent looking for our mother. I willed myself to trust that Mom was with me now, and it was her hand that held so tightly to mine.

Every memory of my past fought, battered me down, told me that I'd gone too far, that I wasn't worthy of this moment. Still, somehow, I sensed that this well of joy and welcome was only the beginning of what would be beyond my wildest dreams, if I could only stay strong.

I walked into my brother's arms, full-body embrace, and he did not let go. John is not like our mother, not prone to emotional affection, but he let me hold on as he held on to me, his hand cradling the back of my neck. I brushed away a few tears as we stepped back and smiled, and he chuckled in a way I imagined he has since he was a child.

Kyung waited until John and I had our fill of each other for the moment, and when I eventually turned to her, she opened her arms.

"Welcome, Brother."

I was overwhelmed with their generosity, and the clarity of who they believed me to be. I was family.

We headed out together for dinner, John insisting on treating. I might be the oldest brother, but he was still the elder of the pack. I struggled to eat the spicy Mexican food, but that made little difference, because we talked so much, none of us finished eating before the food got cold.

After we dropped Julie off at her apartment and drove back to John's house, Kyung excused herself, and John and I settled down in the comfortable living room. I had already learned to love my brother's voice, his laugh, and his quirky way of seeing the world. He's smart, and he knew it, and loved to share his philosophy of everything. Tonight, though, he tried to catch himself whenever he started on an intellectual tangent, dialing it back to focus on us.

We both had more questions than answers, and even less of that than rambling ponderings. What would it have been like growing up together? How different would our lives have been? What if Mom had kept me and never married their dad?

As the night accumulated both time and meaning, John and I eased through the pauses in our conversation, and the silences became comfortable as we settled into each other. We knew we couldn't make up for all the years apart, and intuitively grasped that we shouldn't rush our time together, not one single second. Instead, we began to sense that our history was being built through these seconds, one at a time, with great strength and care. We wanted it, believed this foundation was good and necessary. Mostly, we knew that our mother would have wanted this.

KYUNG INSISTED on taking me up Pikes Peak. John insisted on driving.

At over 14,100 feet at the summit, the air was so thin that moving quickly was not an option. I slowed down, measuring the importance of each breath with John by my side, feeling as though together we could float off the top of the mountain, with not one cloud to block my view.

The effect on me of the mountain's sweep and grandeur was an inescapable consequence of having made the trip at all. The gravity of being with my brother encapsulated any and all small moments of worth, as new and permanent memories blossomed, unencumbered by anything from my past, present, or future.

Driving up the mountain had strained the car's transmission, and as John navigated back downhill, the van refused to shift into lower gear. With the vehicle stuck in drive, John had no option but to ride the brakes as we swung around the hairpin turns, Kyung turning white in the back seat, silent, holding her breath. John and I put on brave faces, talking about the rest of our plans for the day, but none of us bought the ruse.

At mile marker thirteen, we saw the sign for the mandatory brake check. The ranger didn't even need to test the temperature; smoke and the stink of burning pads was enough for him to require a ninety-minute timeout. After an hour, we got antsy about being late to pick up Julie, and John and I had the same idea at the same time. We purchased extra-large drinks, loaded the cups up halfway with ice, filled them to the brim with water, and headed to the van.

As casually as possible, John poured his water over the brakes. Even after an hour's rest, steam rose off the still-hot pads. My cup went on next, then we let the dry air and heat of the day evaporate the evidence of our conniving.

The rangers retested the brakes and gave us the go-ahead. When we finally made it off the mountain, more than grateful for our lives, we had descended 6,715 feet of elevation, navigated 156 curves with not a single guardrail—John driving, Kyung frozen in fear, and me wondering what our mother would think if she could see us now.

AGE SEVENTEEN

On May 27, exactly one month before my eighteenth birthday, I wake up in the U.S. Naval Recruit Training Command, Great Lakes, Illinois. Our RPOC is screaming at us fucking pathetic scumbags to get the fuck out of our bunks, and his second in charge marches up and down the barracks, banging the shit out of an empty garbage can.

I pull assignment to a 900 division, training separately from the rest of the new recruits. Our division will carry the state flags, marching in parades with the drum corps and drill team.

In addition to new recruits' regular duties, the "sticks," as our state flag's division is called, are required to drill on Saturday afternoons and to perform at all graduations. We drill every day, with the exception of Sundays, and after a month, we march in a local parade. We're shuttled back to the base and sent straight to the drill hall to put away our equipment.

"Recruits! Line up! Nut-to-butt!" RPOC screams. "Left face! Attention on deck!"

Our Master Chief and Lieutenant JG come into the hall.

"You all did exceptionally well today." JG faces us, his polished, mellow officer tone welcome after the RPOC. "And it was noticed." He paces up and down the line. "If you hadn't shined today, I wouldn't be here right now. If you hadn't shined today, you'd be outside drilling.

"But you did shine. So next week, you'll fly out to St. Louis. This is not another parade. This is something that only the best get invited to. This is an honor. Do you understand?"

"Yes, sir!"

"RPOC, you will conduct one extra drill each day, starting right now."

"Yes, sir!"

"Recruits, you were exceptional today. Next week I expect you to exceed exceptional."

"Yes, sir!"

We board a transport early Thursday morning, July 3. The plane, a hollowed-out shell where we sit on the floor and strap ourselves against the wall, is barely pressurized, but none of us care because we were off base, in the air, and away from the dull monotony of bootcamp.

After landing, we're loaded onto a military bus, each of us responsible for holding our equipment on our laps for the ride to Busch Memorial Stadium.

The St. Louis Cardinals are playing the Philadelphia Phillies, with game one of a double-header already underway. We have to hurry, because the Cardinals are losing and losing faster than anyone expected.

Wearing our dress whites, gold braided aiguillettes on our left shoulders, we wait in the cool air of the cement hallway until RPOC orders us into formation, and we march onto the field.

Even with the crowd on its feet, the stadium is hushed as we march in perfect lockstep, our flags stiff and upright, right hand over left, elbows at a ninety-degree angle.

"Company halt! Left face! Present flags!"

All eyes are on us as "The Star-Spangled Banner" plays. All of the minutes, hours, and days spent drilling pay off when we lower the POW and MIA banners, the U.S. Navy flag, and the flags for every state in the nation in absolute unison. For twenty seconds the crowd holds its breath until fifty-seven thousand fans all start screaming at once, their cheers crescendo-ing in an instant, seeming to last forever.

For the second game, we have seats in the upper deck. Because we're not allowed to bring cash, each of us receives chits for two hot dogs and three drinks. By the third inning, I've eaten one hot dog and guzzled three beers, my first drinks in over a month. I trade my other hot dog for more beer chits and grab as many as I can from anyone who doesn't want theirs. By the bottom of the sixth, I'm on my ninth beer.

I black out before we get to the plane and pass out cold on the flight back to base. I come to when we land, soaked in my own sweat and piss. Because the sweat's pooled in my ears, they didn't pop on the way down, so I don't hear a thing for hours.

AFTER GRADUATION FROM BOOT CAMP, those of us whose families couldn't make the trip for the ceremony take a train to Wisconsin and hire a limo for the night to celebrate. Our driver drops us off in front of a nondescript building with a red door on the bank of the Milwaukee River. Fairly sure he's just trying to get rid of us, we pile out of the car, hooting and hollering and already drunk.

A man dressed all in black answers the door and asks us for the secret password, the start to the goofy, elaborate indoctrination to Milwaukee's famous SafeHouse Bar. As soon as we get inside, I order and guzzle the Spy's Demise, a sweet concoction consisting of a shot of gin, a shot of sloe gin, some 7UP, and another shot of some secret ingredient. The last thing I remember is hammering down a second Spy's

Demise as if it's a fruit smoothie. I wake up the next morning lying in my own puke in the bushes outside a hotel back in Illinois.

AFTER TWO WEEKS AT HOME, I ship off for two months of training in Jacksonville, Florida, where I'm assigned to VP-44, an anti-submarine squadron based out of Brunswick, Maine, and from there fly straight to Okinawa, Japan.

It's been two months since I finished boot camp. Kadena Air Base is a new beginning of a new end for me, one that takes my excesses to a new level with some of the hardest partiers in the squadron.

Papa Gino is our red-headed, round-faced, self-appointed leader. Papa's my height, but outweighs me by seventy pounds, wears a bushy Navy beard, and walks with a swagger like John Wayne's. From the south side of Boston, he throws his accent around as if he's channeling Whitey Bulger.

Kaiser Bill is Papa's gentle, soft-spoken sidekick. Papa plans our bar hopping, leaving Kaiser Bill in charge of getting us through the night. He has a girlfriend in Brunswick, but he's the man to talk to if you want to get a whore back to the barracks.

I'm assigned to work the midnight shift at the geedunk, a snack bar in the hanger. My buddy Mark, "The Kielbasa Kid," works the line shack, in charge of launching and landing planes throughout the night.

After our shift, we stay up until the liquor store opens at 11:00 a.m., buy a bottle of Seagram's Seven Crown, and pass the bottle back and forth on our walk back to the barracks. The bottle's empty by the time we get to our rooms.

We spend nights out pounding watery drinks and listening to our favorite band, Condition Green. The lead singer gives us the microphone to scream out "Stairway to Heaven" or "Highway to Hell." We're too toasted to get the lyrics right, but nobody cares.

Some nights, I break off from our group and walk up and down BC Street, like when I walked the streets in Schenectady, but here no one speaks my language. That doesn't seem to matter, though; the old woman standing in the doorway calls me inside. I hand her twenty dollars, walk up the stairs and down the hallway to a dingy room, and the door closes behind me.

A young woman, awkward and shy, with gentle eyes, sits naked on an old mattress on the floor in the corner. She speaks no English, and her round face is hesitant, but her body is plump and soft, her skin smooth. I take off the St. Anne's medal my mother gave me "to keep you safe," and lay it on the stand next to the window.

The heat of the day lingers in the room, and the air feels empty. My body responds as I touch hers, but I feel weak, broken inside, as I look down into her face. Her eyes betray the slow destruction of her inexperience. I move gently, letting my chest rise and fall against her, trying to melt the cold, hard knot I feel in my belly, but as sweat drips from my forehead her eyes sink deeper into darkness, away from me.

Afterward, she waits, standing by the window in the corner, while I sit on the mattress and cry. I leave the room but not the building, finding another room, and another, trying to fuck away the look in her eyes.

I wake up in my barracks the next day and realize I left the St. Anne medal behind.

It's Friday night in Okinawa, and TJ, one of the guys that works with me in the geedunk, wants to go drinking, and I have no one to hang out with, so what the fuck, why not? We hit the usual spots on BC Street, laughing at the whores, taking our drinks from bar to bar. Nobody cares what we do. We're Navy.

I'm wearing a button-down, short-sleeve shirt over my new black T-shirt with "Fuck Off and Die (BITCH)" embroidered in large, gold block letters, and at first it's like any other night of blackout drinking. The night is warm, and my head gets fuzzy. My insides align with the outside world for once, and the world feels right, and I settle into a genuine happiness.

TJ's just as drunk but seems to be making the decisions. He picks the bars we stumble into, and when he gets sick of the bar girls, he pulls us back out onto the street, laughing and falling into the walls, smacking each other in mock fights, until the locals yell at us to shut up and we laugh in their faces.

Sweat pours from our bodies as we run down the street, down an alley, him in the lead and me trying to catch his ass. He darts into a stairway, and we end up on the roof, where I corner him, and both of us laugh as I pretend to shove him over the edge.

He grabs onto my shirt, feigning fright when I grab him by the shoulders, and he drops his hands to my hips and holds my wrists and smiles, his eyes going deep, and pulls me close. We're still. Still smiling and sweaty and out of breath, he slides his hands down, me so fucking drunk I feel the sensation down to my toes, how perfect life is for a change, for this one moment. No wife or kids or work, and everything else fades when he puts his hands on my face and pulls me to him and we kiss.

I open my mouth, and our tongues go deep. We're nowhere and anywhere, maybe not even on this planet, and no one knows us, and no one cares what we do, and the kiss goes on and on for what seems like hours. His hands caress my chest inside my shirt, and I snatch his body everywhere, and he rubs himself against my pants, and it's so peaceful up on the roof.

We hold each other, kiss and giggle and bump and grind. Somehow, we're off the roof, and one of us hails a cab, and then we're in his room, his roommate gone on flight duty.

When I come to, we're both naked, and the sheets are stained and tangled up in our legs. Still blitzed, I get dressed, but can't lock the door because it only locks from inside or with a key, so I shut it behind me, stagger to my room, and crash the rest of the morning.

The sun is hanging high that afternoon as I suck on a beer and eat barbecue outside the barracks, and I see TJ walking toward me flanked by two big, lanky, ugly thugs, one of them his roommate. He pulls me away from the grill, the two guys glaring.

"Last night we came back with those two girls from town, right? Man, I was so fucking drunk!"

I give them a blank smile.

"Where did they go? Did yours run out on you?" The pleading look in his eyes cuts through my hangover haze.

"Yeah, man." I answer with a swagger, and his relief is palpable.

"Mine too! Man, she went nuts on me! Must've left when I passed out." He looks at the two guys, trying to imitate my nonchalant stance. "Those girls were crazy!"

The thugs look me up and down.

"You both had these girls last night?"

"Yeah." TJ is wild eyed, and I give my best poker face. "Yeah, man, we found them at some bar. They came back with us, and I don't know about your room, but it was a real wild time in mine."

That seems to satisfy, but as they turn and walk away, TJ gets in my face, his smile turning to fury.

"Man, you left me! You left the fucking door open. You left the motherfucking door open! Why did you leave the door open? They walked in and there I was naked with dried fucking cum all over me!"

TJ never speaks to me again.

SEPTEMBER 2007

We picked up Julie, her son Jesse, and daughter Paige, and on the drive our voices faded, leaving only the sound of the breeze through the open windows. My thoughts narrowed to Eastonville Cemetery.

The graveyard was smaller than I had imagined but, bordered by beautiful blue spruce, it seemed like the right place for Mom to be. It was ringed with a wooden fence, an iron gate guarding the entrance, and an American flag flying high overhead. You had to have lived in Black Forest for at least twenty years to be buried there.

John parked the car on the short gravel pathway and took the lead, telling Julie's kids about the cemetery and the caretakers, husband and wife, who lived across the street.

Not long after I'd found Julie, I had called to speak with the caretakers and sent flowers on Mother's Day, and they so kindly sent me a picture of the arrangement by the gravestone, along with a loving note. I knew the flowers would be gone, but some part of me still expected to see them, fresh and beautiful even now.

As I walked, my eyes found the gravestone I had only seen before in that picture. Julie, Kyung, and the kids were still talking and standing around me, until John saw my face, hushed everyone, and led them back to the car.

I wailed inside. My heart disintegrated at meeting her this way, even though I was so grateful to have finally found my way to her. I willed my feet to move forward and lost sight of the headstone as my eyes flooded with tears, and nothing I could summon in myself stopped them from flowing.

I wiped the tears away, took the last few steps forward, and fell to my knees at the grave. "I want you back. I want you with me." I mumbled through sobs. "Why did you have to go?" Childish, choking, I gasped for air. "Oh, God, I miss you so much."

I wanted her with me more than I wanted to breathe. I fell with my face to the ground, crying in the grass and rough dirt that covered her grave. Incoherent sounds poured from my throat—a soft, wailing cry like a child lost in the woods, tired and without hope.

Eventually I pushed myself up to my knees and sat back on my heels on the soft earth, looking at the trees that peppered the grounds. In the quiet and beauty of the place, I talked to my mom—not to the stone, or to the earth, but to the trees and the clear air, the blue sky and the soft clouds.

Finally, I knew it was time to leave. I'd said what I needed to say for now, and we would have more time together, I knew that. In my pocket I found the coin I had brought, the coin that had been passed on to me, and turned it over in my fingers, feeling its emotional heft and the power of its blessings rather than the physical weight of it. I read the inscription one last time: "To thine own self be true. Unity / Service / Recovery."

I scratched at the earth a few inches away from the stone, dug as deep as I could with my fingers, pushed the coin down until it was as close to her as I dared, filled in the hole, and patted the tough, weed-like grass back into place. A piece of me was here now, where the sun could warm this place, and in this small, simple way, we'd always be together. No one would know but us.

Close to her this way, I felt at peace. I sat and looked around at this small and consequential place, breathing in the pine scent, and pictured the years to come, the rain as autumn settled in, the snow that covered the ground until spring came again.

My family all felt a sense of sadness at visiting the grave, but I had only just found her. I wanted to stay by her side, never wanted to leave her, and my grief overwhelmed me. When she abandoned me, she left me, and I lost her. When I finally found her and learned she had died, I lost her all over again, this time forever. I wanted to feel for my family, to feel *with* them, but my own loss was compounded beyond what I could tolerate. They had known her, and I never would. No one spoke as I sobbed in the front seat while we drove away.

JOHN PULLED the van onto the shoulder across from the small, neat house in Black Forest. I looked at what might have been my home, the house where my brothers and sister had played. Where our mother had lived. Where their father had died.

The house had been sold after their father's death, and the new family had made it their own. The barn still stood, but the horses were gone now, and both John and Julie seemed to feel the remoteness of the land they once thought of as their sanctuary, and their legacy. Now, even after so many years, the ground still held their father's blood, and the pain and loss of everything they ever knew, and loved, and depended on.

We stood quietly, taking in the tranquility. The warmth of the sun, the thin, fresh air filling my lungs, clearing my mind, finding a way to move forward from the grave with an almost spiritual sleight of hand, toward something new, something better.

The owner spotted the six of us lingering and walked up the dirt driveway. John crossed the road, Julie and I trailing behind him.

John waved a greeting. "Hi, we used to live here."

"This used to be our home," Julie added, sounding a little bossy but full of strength, and maybe pride, too.

The woman remembered. Julie had come back several times after the sale, many times high and incoherent, but the owners had always been gentle and gracious.

"Sure, come on over."

As I walked onto the property, Mom was with me. Every place my feet touched, I felt her steps under mine. I saw her strolling in the yard, standing in the pasture, taking a walk under the trees near the stable.

"Would you like to come inside?"

I stepped through the front doorway and stopped just inside, then Julie led me through the house.

"The table was right here."

She moved through the empty space left behind, near the sink with the windows looking out over the yard.

"The table was square, and we all used to have breakfast here. I sat here, and Mom sat there, the day she told me about you."

I stood as still and as tall as I could, quieting my mind, basking in my sister's words, claiming the essence of her memory for my own.

John and Kyung walked through the family room, a few wooden steps up from the kitchen. I wanted to see it all, but knew that time was limited, that we were only guests here. I didn't need much, just something to call my own. My heart told me I'd never be here again.

"John." I called him over to me, pointing to the worn pine boards. "Are these steps the same? Have they changed?"

"No, these are exactly the way they were. Mom loved the pine in the house."

I put my hand out to touch the door frame that my mother had passed through thousands upon thousands of times, and a peace ran through my body. I smiled, sinking down to sit on the steps, and closed my eyes and thought of all the times John had chased Julie and James back and forth from room to room, felt myself running with them, whispering something childishly serious. Imagined how we might have played together, what it would have meant to me to be the oldest, how everything could have been so different.

I saw in my mind the fullness of the moment, and my heart broke at being so alone and abandoned, so frail in my limitations, and the truth that I could never shoulder the full weight of all that I had longed for, all that I had missed, all that I had lost—the past I had never had.

The pictures of Mom that my siblings gave me are only images of memories for me, memories that will never be mine. Experiencing Mom would come, as it always had, in my imagination and through her absence. And in time, through John and Julie and James, that absence would mingle joy and sorrow. Even our time together at her grave had been more of a goodbye, a leaving behind. Now I needed to have her with me, to accept her into my being, and this place was where my soul told me that acceptance would come to pass.

She had abandoned me. Nothing could ever change that fact. I would always be a living reminder of what was left behind. That emptiness was my past, had become my whole life, but now, here where she had lived, I chose to not let the emptiness define my future. I chose to take only what I could contain within myself, something simple, significant. I laid the palm of my right hand on the step and closed my eyes, committing to memory the texture and grain of the wood, and completely and deeply opened myself, letting her come to me.

I see Mom as she laughs and cries here. Mom loving her children. Mom fully passionate and alive. Mom missing me, longing for me, wishing for me to knock on this door.

Now she is with me, and we sit together on the steps. She listens to me as I tell her about Roz and Beth and David Luck, about Sister Charla and Mary. She tears up with joy when I tell her about her grandchildren Dawn, Sera, Kentaro, and Tyler. She holds me tight when I speak the name Eri, and she tickles my nose and teases me, how lucky I am to marry a woman whose name means Blessed with Wisdom.

Mom holds me now, and I pour out the story of all my days, some days better, many worse, and as I weep, she weeps with me. Sitting on the steps she listens, letting me take my time. We both fall quiet. I lean against her body. She is soft and not too strong, and I'm careful not to put my full weight against her. She runs her fingers through my hair. I tell her how good that feels, that it's just what my mother did to comfort me when I felt so lost and broken and alone. We sit together, and I feel her breathe in and out, her chest rising and falling, her fingers stroking through my hair, my hand resting on the step.

I opened my eyes and looked down at my hand pressed against the wood, burning the image of these two steps into my mind's eye. It's all I'll ever have, and it will never be enough, but it will be mine. It will be ours.

AGE EIGHTEEN

As soon as I get back from Okinawa, Nessie and I get married in a ceremony on the second floor of my father's favorite Chinese restaurant. Papa Gino, Kaiser Bill, and the Kielbasa Kid come to Schenectady to be my wedding party, and we arrive early and go straight to the bar for a drink. The bartender reminds me that the bar opens after the ceremony, until I not-so-gently remind him I'm the fucking groom and start with two shots of Jack Daniels followed by a rum and Coke. The next day we fill up a U-Haul and head north.

On the base in Brunswick, I work the day shift in the kitchen. I'm stoned and hungover every day, and the chief knows it and works me to the bone. At the end of each day, I can hardly hold my head up by the time I park my car outside our apartment.

Dawn and Sera are so full of life and joy, bouncing at the chance to romp with me. When I walk in the door they sing *daddy, daddy, daddy,* and even Nessie smiles. In those moments, everything feels strange, like something is right and the day just might turn out okay, just might not end in a fight or a blackout or with cops at the door. And if one day ends well, maybe I can hope that the next might be the same.

As we settle into domestic Navy life, that small hope begins to grow. Getting drunk and high still is the center of my existence, but somehow other parts of the day become more than just random scenes in our drama. The girls are calm and draw or play quietly on the floor while Nessie makes dinner, happily pouring pasta sauce on our plates with

Dawn cheering, "Yeah, *pisgetty* and meatballs!" and we all roar with laughter.

But the partying takes its toll, and over days and weeks, the fights start again. Without rhyme, reason, or intention, we yell and push and hit and scratch and smash breakables. Sometimes the fights end in laughter, drunk and stoned out of our minds, and fucking each other before we pass out. Sometimes they end in tears, mostly Nessie's, me smoking out of the bong or pipe or joint to keep the sound of her crying from ripping my heart out.

MY LAST NIGHT STATESIDE, we have a party. No crystal meth, just beer and wine and lots of pot. At the end of it, Nessie's toasty, really hot for me. My mind is so numb my body won't respond right away, but we know how to solve that. She gets rough with me, and I grab her tits, my mouth biting at her nipples, and she screams and hits me, not to let go, just to hit.

I bite all over—her neck, down her sides, her hips, the hair between her legs, tearing at her hair and skin. She hits me, grabs my body and pulls me to her mouth, in her mouth again and again, finally hard. We suck each other raw, I grab her ass and lick between her cheeks, and she sucks on my balls until the pain is too intense, and I yell and throw her on her stomach, spread her legs, bite her back. Wet between my legs, both of us moaning, lust and pain, passion and pleasure indistinguishable.

Entering her from behind, my history, the memory of TJ, of Arnold and Billy, of Davey, blocks out every thought. I forget who she is, forget my marriage, thrusting and driving as hard as possible, again and again, one hand on her back, the other wrapped in her hair to force her head down into the mattress, and she just holds on, endures the pain, endures my self-loathing.

Finally, done and spent, I let go, and she turns and screams at me, the kids crying, *mommy, mommy what's wrong,* and me still naked, throw up on the floor next to the bed and pass out. Black out the shame, black out the hurt and humiliation she feels, black out the screams and the tears.

Nessie hates me. Dawn and Sera fear me. Blackness envelopes me, takes away my sight, then my hearing, until I feel nothing but my heart beating and my lungs drawing in, pumping out air. The rest of my body hoping to not wake in the morning. When my eyes do open, Nessie drives me to the base to catch my flight to Rota, Spain, and kisses me goodbye.

ONE MONTH later Nessie leaves me.

I have four months left before going stateside, and I beg my Master Chief to let me go home, but he won't budge except for a death in the family. The first week after she breaks the news, I call her every day begging her to take me back. After that, she won't take my calls.

Papa and Kaiser Bill come to my room, which is littered with half-eaten baloney-and-cheese sandwiches and empty Seagram bottles. I'm slumped in an overstuffed chair, a lump of Moroccan hash shaped like a chicken egg on the wooden bench in front of me. I've bought the eggs, between fifty and seventy grams each, so I could start dealing, but all my profits have already gone up in smoke.

Papa picks me up out of the chair and carries me to the couch, sits down next to me, and holds my face up to his.

"Kevin! Hey!" His voice is sharp, loud, in my face. "Snap the fuck out of it!"

"What?!" I blink, trying to focus, and try to turn my head to look for the pipe on the table.

"Don't fucking look away." Papa slaps my face. "Look at me!"

"Okay." I slump back on the couch.

"You need to listen to Kaiser Bill. I want you to listen to him. It's important. Do you hear me?"

I nod. Kaiser Bill sits down and leans forward, his hands in his lap.

"Shelly called me. She told me that you and Nessie had some big fight the night before we left."

I start to reply, but he holds his hand up and keeps talking.

"She said that Nessie didn't blame you for it. She knows it was both of you, not just your fault."

Adrenaline pumps through me, and I fight to claw through the fog in my brain.

"Then why won't she pick up the phone?" I start to cry.

"Listen!" Papa shakes my shoulders, and I pull him back into focus.

"Nessie took the kids." Kaiser's voice is a mix of pain and anger. "She moved out of your apartment, that's why she's not answering the phone."

I stare at them both. I can't cry, frozen on the couch. I've lost my will to think.

"Kevin, I'm sorry. I don't think Shelly is helping. I think she's the one who talked Nessie into leaving. I know she's my girlfriend, but she's really not a good influence. I'm sorry, man."

I shake my head but still can't understand.

Papa grabs my shoulders again to prop me up, holding my face toward his.

"Nessie took the girls and is shacking up with some guy, living in a house outside of Brunswick across the Androscoggin River. Do you understand?"

I let out a wail and sink to the floor. Papa rages and stomps around the room yelling, but not at me, cursing out Nessie and Shelly and the Navy and the world. Kaiser Bill tries to calm him down, but Papa storms out, and I hear him yelling all the way down the hall.

"Who is she with?" I try and fail to muster Papa's anger.

Kaiser Bill is always calm, the flip side to Papa's bluster, but now his face turns red, his lips curl, he looks like he could kill someone.

"Some guy from the base."

"One of us?"

"He's a Navy guy." Kaiser Bill nods and hangs his head. "I don't know what squadron he's in. I don't know what the fuck is wrong with him."

"What the fuck am I supposed to do?"

"I don't know, man. Do you even want her back now?"

"I don't know what I want."

Kaiser Bill stands silent as the fog slowly lifts, and then tears explode out of me.

"My family!" I don't recognize my own voice. "Oh my God, the girls. Little Dawn. Little Sera. My baby girls. I lost my family."

Over the next days I vacillate between anger and longing until I'm lost in the wanting. Wanting to be forgiven and to forgive. Nessie finally agrees to talk, and I call her after I get off my midnight shift at the line shack.

"Hey. It's me. Are you there?"

"Yeah, I'm here." I hear no bitterness. She just sounds tired.

I beg, plead and scream, yell and cry, but Nessie refuses to leave him, refuses to wait until my deployment is over, refuses even to try to work things out.

"But we're married. What about the girls? Don't you want to try?"

"You should have thought about that before," she snaps at me. I know that tone.

"I don't want you to leave. How can you just give up? How can you leave me?"

I have no more words.

"I don't love you." She cries softly.

"Why?"

"I just don't."

We both cry together, like old friends who know they won't see each other again for a long time.

"Can you at least not live with him?"

"He's a good man. He doesn't hit me. We don't fight. He's not a drug addict."

"What the fuck!" Something in my brain clicks, and everything looks black inside and out. "Those are my kids, not his!"

"One is."

I slide off the chair, sob into the phone, alone and lonely, abandoned again. Blackness covers me like a heavy wool blanket, scratches at my skin, and I sink lower onto the floor, deeper into despair.

"I was with her before she was born. I'm her father."

"No, you're not. You're not even a good father." Her words tear at me, and I lift my chin even as she takes aim again.

"Please don't leave me."

"Get your life together, Kevin."

"Please don't take my children away." I choke out each word as if it will be the last I ever utter, snot running from my nose, drool spilling out of my mouth, folding myself into nothing.

"They're not your fucking kids. They're mine."

Neither of us speaks and the quiet becomes the distance between us. My tears stop, and I lower my head, my voice hardly a whisper.

"What did I do? Don't do this."

"I don't love you."

MY GROSS PAY is 585 dollars every month. The Navy lets me send up to eighty percent of my paycheck home, so when I first started my deployment, I sent 468 dollars home to Nessie and lived off the rest. As soon as I get off the phone with Nessie, I go to personnel and switch the percentages.

In Spain, a forty-gram egg of hashish only costs seventy dollars, and I cut it up and sell it for triple that on the base. That works for about a month. I buy a new egg every week, but smoke most of it and spend the rest of my money on sex in Seville, on Jack Daniels, Seagram's Seven, Bacardi 151, and cases of beer. My room is one-stop shopping for hashish, and every buyer leaves with a drink in their hand.

The image of Nessie living with some other Navy guy runs on a permanent loop in my imagination. Papa Gino and Kaiser Bill won't leave me alone unless I'm at work or passed out. They listen as I scream about Nessie and let me lean on them when I cry over my daughters.

After a drinking binge from Friday morning straight through to Sunday morning, I come back to base before dawn with no memory of where I've been. A few hours after I pass out, the night watch shakes me awake, telling me I have to relieve him. When I don't show, I get written up and reported, busted down from an E3 to E2 paygrade.

The next time I show up for watch, I realize that I have the keys to every room in the barracks. If they were going to bust me down, I'd sure as hell make up for it the best way I know how. Once I'm sure the hallway is clear, I let myself into Willy's room. I'd been partying there earlier, sold Willy and his buddies some hash, and know he left some cash behind when they went out on the town.

I wake up to somebody banging on my door. Papa Gino and Kaiser Bill and two guys I don't recognize say they want some hash, but their eyes watch my every move, scanning the room, without a sound.

The 350 dollars from Willy's room is shoved down my underwear. They say they just want a few grams, but one of the strangers pulls out a hundred-dollar bill. I fish in my wallet and pull out a couple of twenties, then dig through my drawers looking for ones, fives, and tens.

I ask Papa Gino or Kaiser Bill if they have some cash I can borrow to make change, but they hesitate, so then I ask if they'll vouch for the strangers. The room goes real quiet, and they exchange a look and a nod. If Papa and Kaiser trust them, I say, then so do I, so they can take the hash and come back when they have the right change.

I know I have to take my deceit to the next level, so I go down to Willy's room. The door's open, and I wander into the crowd there and start chatting, casual as can be. Willy's face turns beet red as I keep talking about nothing, relaxed, not reacting to his anger.

No one confronts me, but they talk about the theft, all eyes on me. First shock and dismay, then anger, then resignation and condolences. The red slowly drains from Willy's face as his anger begins to ebb, until I pat him on the shoulder, take a twenty out of my pocket, and with a smile suggest we all pool our resources to help Willy out. Several guys have to hold him back as a couple others usher me out of the room.

Back in my own room, Papa Gino and Kaiser Bill start to rake me over the coals. I've dug myself into the lie so deep I believe it myself, and I'm so convincing they buy my story. We break out the hash and smoke what I know is the beginning of my next binge.

AGE NINETEEN

I signed up for a three-year tour and make it less than two. With only a few days left in the deployment, Navy brass refuses to let me fly back with the rest of the men, for my own protection. I beg the CO to let me finish my deployment in Rota and travel home with the squadron, but he rages at me from behind his desk and throws me out of his office. The legal officer brings the paperwork to the barracks and tells me I don't have to sign the papers, and I perk up for a moment, remembering how Father Ralph asked me if I wanted to stay at the Bridge Center. I was ready to say yes, but this time the choice was different. I could sign the papers and leave with a discharge, or refuse to sign, face a court martial, and spend the rest of my time in the brig.

Name (last, first, middle): *BARHYDT, KEVIN JOHN*
Department, Component, Branch: *NAVY - USNR*
Last Duty Assignment: *PATROL SQUADRON FORTY-FOUR*
Decorations: *EXPEDITIONARY MEDAL; SEA DEPLOYMENT RIBBON*
Date Entered Active Duty: *Year: 80; Month: May; Day: 27*
Separation Date: *Year: 82: Month: Mar; Day: 29*
Type of Separation: *DISCHARGE*
Narrative Reason For Separation: *BURDEN TO COMMAND DUE TO SUBSTANDARD PERFORMANCE OR INABILITY TO ADAPT TO MILITARY SERVICE*

BACK IN BRUNSWICK, it takes less than an hour to transition from military employee to civilian.

ONE OF MY Navy drinking buddies, Bob, drives me the thirty minutes across the river to where Nessie and the girls live, and we find my blue AMC Hornet parked in the weeds, still half-covered with snow. The battery's dead, but the car starts with a jump from Bob. The brakes are gone, and the tank is on empty. Wisely, Bob has brought a five-gallon can of gas. Just in case.

The next morning the squadron flies back from Rota, and I'm on base waiting. I don't know the guy well, but he's smuggling in some hash for me. I'll sell it, and we'll split the profits.

I stop at Bob's, smoke a gram with his wife, Kathy, shoot some crystal in the bathroom, and head for Schenectady with enough hash to sell and keep some money coming in. I know what I want my future to be. I'm heading home with a plan to return to the things I know best and do well. Dealing drugs is only one of them.

Three days later, on April 1, 1982, I'm caught breaking into a house and end up back in Schenectady County Jail.

ON APRIL 2, my parents put up their house as collateral for the ten-thousand-dollar bail. At the bail hearing, my lawyer asks Rotterdam Court Judge Longo for permission for me to leave the state to pick up my belongings in Maine. I leave straight from court, stop off for a quart bottle of Jack Daniels and a six-pack of Coors, grab the leftover hash hidden in my parents' attic.

A little after five in the morning on April 3, I wake up with my body in freefall, the car in mid-air, flying upside down off of I-95 in York County, Maine.

When the car lands on its roof in a ditch ten yards off the highway, my lip is split open, my teeth are bleeding, and I have a gash on my forehead. With my door in the dirt, I hand-crank the passenger-side window down to crawl out.

I sit on the car's underside, squinting in the morning sunlight, and wave at the driver of an eighteen-wheeler to let him know I'm okay. Not one bone is broken. While the driver calls for help, I light up a cigarette, take a deep drag, and blow smoke into the fresh, crisp, Maine air.

MY PARENTS PAY to tow the car back to New York. Because I'm out of the Navy and broke, my father convinces my mother, and himself, that I need transportation to find a job, and he pays for the repairs.

As fast as he had appeared, the new boyfriend disappears, leaving Nessie and the girls homeless. I bring them back to Schenectady to stay with my parents, hoping for reconciliation, but she already has plans to follow another Navy man to Norfolk, Virginia. I stand in the hallway, leaning on the doorframe, and watch her pack.

"You love him?"

It's almost better now that it's over. It feels almost like when we first met, like we were just friends, except for two children and four years of getting high together, and now we've crashed to our lowest low.

"I don't know."

"You don't have to go, you know."

She glares at me, smashing the yellow-and-white skirts, the green blouse and white undershirts, into the suitcase.

"Well, I can't stay here." She rubs her eyes, physically willing her tear ducts to hold tight.

"I'll leave you alone. I won't try anything; I won't touch you. You can sleep down here with the girls, and I'll sleep upstairs."

"No."

"Or you can have the upstairs room. I don't care. I'll use the couch."

A few tears have dried on her face. She empties another drawer, folding and packing my daughters' clothes, taking them away from here. Away from me.

"I want you to stay. I want the girls to stay."

"Your parents hate me."

"They don't." She stops packing and looks full at me, daring me to deny it again. I drop my gaze. "They love the girls."

She turns back to packing, her hand gathers Dawn and Sera's socks.

"You're not losing the girls. They're your daughters."

I sit in the doorway, my head against the jamb, tears streaming with no sound. Nessie folds and packs and lets me be until I'm cried out.

"You would like him." She smiles, and I can't help but breathe a bit easier.

"Yeah?"

"Yeah. He's a skinny drug addict. Just like you."

I FIND A JOB at the local Price Chopper. The manager's thrilled to have an ex-Navy man, but I only last a month. Next is a gas station, pumping gas and delivering used tires to the dump. Most of my old friends are gone, or want nothing to do with me, so I call Donny and we drink all night, driving around the back roads with his girlfriend, Ruth.

The next day Ruth calls me and invites me over to her pool. Without Donny there, we spend the afternoon swimming, the night drinking, and end up fucking in the back seat of my car in the woods. Donny's pissed when he finds out, but more sensible than I'd have given him credit for. I think he should probably beat the shit out of me, but I know he won't. We sit outside her house talking until he runs out of words, then we just smoke cigarettes for a while. Finally, he stands up and says, "She's a slut. You can have her." He walks away, and I watch him until I see him hitch a ride. I go into the house, and Ruth gives me a beer.

Ruth doesn't get high, but we both love to drink. I sleep over that first week and move in the next. Her father, Marvin, hates me at first, but his wife loves me. Marvin warms up, and as long as I stock the fridge with his favorite beer on payday, we get along just fine.

Most Fridays and Saturdays, Ruth and I drive from bar to bar along with Donny and his new girlfriend. The girls don't mind when we leave them on the dance floor while Donny and I go out to the parking lot to snort coke. We burn through an eight-ball in a night.

I KNOW I'LL BE IN JAIL SOON, the only question is for how long, and all I want to do is forget. Five days after my plea bargain on attempted burglary, Donny and I splurge on tickets to see Elton John at the Saratoga Performing Arts Center. We down a case of Miller High Life Ponies in the parking lot, find a spot on the lawn with the girls, and pass joints back and forth.

When the band starts up "Saturday Night's Alright for Fighting," the place comes to life. Donny and I put the girls on our shoulders, and the whole crowd dances and screams the lyrics at the top of our lungs.

We mellow out to "Daniel" and pick up again for the encores, "Crocodile Rock" and a medley of "Whole Lotta Shakin' Going On" and "Twist and Shout." Donny and I wrap our arms around the girls and tuck their heads under our chins to watch the band take their bows.

On the way out to the car, the girls are still buzzing about the show, and Donny and I are ready for another case of Ponies. But when we get there, I can't find the keys. We run back to the lawn but can't find them anywhere in the grass. Security gives me a number to call in the morning, but that doesn't help us now.

I work in a gas station, but Donny knows cars. With some wire found on the side of the road, he gets the door unlocked and cracks the cover of the steering column when he kicks to release the steering wheel. He tries to hotwire the car, but can't get it going, and by now all the other concertgoers have left. Though traffic is sparse, a local guy pulls over and offers to push us with his car.

Donny gets behind the wheel, and we navigate the road at about thirty-five miles per hour. It works better than we could have dreamed. Pretty soon we're laughing, sure this plan is genius, at least until we see lights flashing behind us.

The cop takes maybe sixty seconds to come to terms with our genius plan before bursting into a guffaw at the ridiculousness of the circumstance. We all laugh along while he goes to his patrol car to call a tow.

He calls in my license and registration and comes back to ask if he can search the car. I say sure, wanting to stay on his good side and confident the car is clean. What I don't know is that the last time Ruth's brother Roger was in the car, he stashed his nunchucks under the passenger seat, and the cop spots them and now has probable cause. I have a bag of joints stuffed in my socks, but Donny's carrying his in his pocket. The cop searches us, and we're busted for possession. Donny had been driving, but it's my car, and both of us fail the breathalyzer. We're handcuffed in the back of separate cars, and the girls are taken to the station to wait for a ride.

The next day SPAC security calls and leaves me a message. They found my keys fifteen minutes after we left.

On Monday, I call into work and tell them I have car trouble. The owner is nice about it, offers to have the car towed to the station, fixes the steering, and only charges me cost for the parts.

On Tuesday, the owner sits in his office with the door closed while his wife calls me into her office. She hands me some cash and says, "We'll pay you for today." On her desk is a newspaper, with the headline "Man Guilty" circled in red.

The Daily Gazette

Man Guilty On Burglary Attempt Count

A 20-year-old Schenectady man, originally charged with theft and the possession of marijuana, pleaded guilty in Schenectady County Court yesterday to a single charge of attempted second-degree burglary.

County Judge George W. Stroebel ordered a pre-sentence probation report and deferred sentencing of Kevin Barhydt of Brentwood Lane until Aug. 30.

Barhydt was permitted to plead guilty to the attempted burglary charge in satisfaction of an indictment containing counts of second-degree burglary, third-degree grand larceny, fourth-degree criminal mischief, fourth-degree possession of marijuana and possession of a hypodermic needle.

The indictment accused Barhydt of the April 1 theft of property from the 41 Bayberry Road home of Mary Daigle and the possession of a syringe and more than 25 grams of marijuana.

From the Daily Gazette, *Schenectady, NY, April 1982. Used with permission.*

*At a term of the County Court held at the Courthouse in the City of
Schenectady, in and for the County of Schenectady, and State of New
York on September 1, 1982*
PRESENT: Honorable GEORGE W. STROEBEL JR.
THE PEOPLE OF THE STATE OF NEW YORK Indictment 382-8
Against
Kevin Barhydt
*THE DEFENDANT HAVING BEEN FOUND GUILTY BY PLEA
ON July 20, 1982 withdraws the not guilty plea and enters a plea of
guilty to attempted burglary in the second degree in full satisfaction.
SENTENCE: Schenectady County Jail for forty-five (45) days with
credit for time served and Probation for five (5) years.
A TRUE EXTRACT FROM THE MINUTES:*
Edna McKay - CLERK

I'M PUT ON A TIER with guys my age, punks one and all. Each tier has ten
cells, and we spend our time playing spades and hearts, betting for cigarettes, telling stories about our crimes.

David Gelato takes to me right away. He's an inch shorter than me,
but with a barrel chest and biceps three times the size of mine. He's only
eighteen, but cool and handsome as hell, and knows it.

He'll be out in two weeks, but within a day, we're already making
plans to meet up on the outside. First, I'll get a tattoo. David has a giant
eagle on his right upper arm and a lizard on his left calf, both from
Tommy Spaulding in Albany. We'll get drunk, get high, and I'll get the
best fucking tattoo ever. David is the best friend I've made since I met
Donny at Vanderheyden Hall. We click right away, and the two of us run
the tier.

The guards never bother us after dinner except to lock us in our cells
and at lights out, but they keep an eye on us, watching us through the
grates on the air vents at the top of our cells. They leave us alone when

they see us jerking off, so we do it all the more just to piss them off. Or turn them on. We don't care much either way.

MY PARENTS VISIT ME, sitting across the metal table, my father trying to keep a smile on his face.

"I brought you a carton of Camels." He jerks his thumb behind. "They said you can pick them up after we leave."

"Thanks."

I smile, light up a cigarette, and sit back in my chair.

"You need anything? Can you get matches? I brought you a lighter, but they said you can't have lighters."

"They give us matches."

The noise level in the visiting room rises—everyone talking with their visitors, laughing, arguing, crying. I finish my cigarette and light another.

"It isn't this bad on my tier." I laugh. "It's quieter than here, that's for sure."

My father laughs, strained and hoarse, but he's trying. My mother stares around the room, then looks at my father.

"Aren't you going to talk to him?" my father asks her. "Tell him about the car." He looks back at me.

"She got in your car to move it in the driveway, and thought she was in her old blue Mustang. Remember that old car? It was a stick shift, and she kept looking for the clutch. It took her a few minutes to realize she wasn't driving her old blue car."

My father laughs, teasing her, then stops cold when he sees the tears running down her face.

"I can't take this."

She walks quickly to the door, not looking back, leaving me and my father alone at the table. We watch as the guard closes the door behind her and sit awkwardly for a minute without speaking. I light another cigarette. My father says he'll come back soon, and leaves.

THERE ARE seven of us on the tier when I arrive, then a few days later another guy comes in near midnight, after we're locked in our cells. In the morning, we ask his name, but he sits on his bunk without speaking, even when we taunt him. At breakfast, the guards make him fall in line and walk down to chow with the rest of us.

He's skinny, more of a kid than any of us. I weigh 135, and he's maybe 110. When he finally decides to come out and mingle, it's too late.

"Hey, man, can I have a cigarette?"

"You *want* a cigarette?" I give him a withering stare.

"Yeah."

"Yeah?" I say, a smirk on my face. "How's it feel to *want*?"

The tier breaks up laughing, and the kid retreats to his cell.

He comes out for lunch, but by now the word's out, and no one will give him a break.

"Gonna get fucked tonight, sweetie?"

"Damn, you're skinny."

"Your ass is gonna crack up the middle!"

"When they done with you, come to my tier."

"We'll be sweet."

"You gonna love us."

The guards watch, but don't interfere. They know all too well, better to let him fend for himself than look like they favored him.

The kid skips dinner, and we come back to find him sitting in his room, facing away from the door. David and I move our table right outside his cell, ignoring him while the guards make their rounds. Once they're gone, we keep our card game going, taking turns walking into his cell to abuse him—punching him, knocking him down, harassing him.

Guys who don't want to, David threatens they'll be next.

After a few rounds, the kid's face is swollen, his left eye closed, but on David's orders he isn't bleeding. He sits on his bunk crying but never makes a sound.

We move the table back in front of David's cell, playing cards and smoking, talking about fucking girls and stealing and getting high and all the partying we'll do when we get out.

A few minutes before lights out, David and I walk back to the kid's cell and stand outside looking in. He's no longer crying, just slumped against the concrete wall, slack, listless.

"Don't go to sleep, kid," David says, and walks away, whistling. I watch, waiting, but still the kid doesn't move a muscle, his eyes never wavering from me, and he doesn't seem to blink.

In the stillness that settles in after lights out, we can hear the kid in his cell moan and cry, quietly at first, then louder, and we hear the familiar irregular thudding sound as he bangs his forehead against the concrete wall.

A few hours later, the guards respond to the kid's howling, unintelligible screams.

They take him out before sunrise, half-carrying, half-dragging him with a blanket over his head and body.

After our cells open, David and I check out the kid's cell. The guards have taken the kid's sheets, pillow, and belongings, but we can still see the burnt edges of white cloth in the metal grate overhead where the guards used a lighter to burn down the sheet the kid tied up to hang himself.

Word naturally gets out to the rest of the tiers, and David and I sense a new respect in the yard at rec time and sit by ourselves at meals. The rest of the guys on our tier leave us alone, partly out of fear, but mostly because every one of them now hates us.

After David gets out, the monotony of the days is interrupted only by visits from my father. I'm glad for the cigarettes, and the money in my commissary, but we mostly sit in silence.

ON SEPTEMBER 29, at 12:01 a.m., I walk out of jail and my parents are outside waiting. The look on their faces when they see me makes me want to hug them, to run away with them to some island and celebrate our lives and being a family.

Instead I wave behind them, and my parents turn to see David, his girlfriend, and Ruth across the street. My mother starts to cry as my father hands me the keys to my car, looking helpless. I mumble a thanks and ask for some money. "No," he says, with Mom repeating "No," over and over. "No, come home, please." I shake my head and cross the street to where David is waiting for me.

Two months later, I meet my father in a parking lot. He and my mother keep up my car insurance and fill my tank if I drive to the gas station with them, but until now they've been unwilling to give me cash. I've already told him why I need the money.

"I bought some Camel filters." He pulls out two cartons. "That still your brand?"

"Yeah. Thanks a lot. I need 'em."

"So, what happens next?"

"I don't know."

"Will you come back to stay at the house?"

"I'll think about it, but probably not."

He nods and digs his wallet out of his pocket.

"How much?"

"A hundred seventy-five."

He counts out two hundred. "Get some gas with the rest."

"Thanks. That really helps."

I pocket the money, and we stand for a long moment, the sun warming us both. We could be a father and son together in any other place and time. We could be on vacation, or shopping, or just hanging out.

He looks away, then back at me. "You know this is against my religion."

"I know. I'm sorry."

"You do what you think is right."

"I am."

"Okay. Come back to the house and see your mother."

"I'll come this weekend."

"When?"

"Maybe Sunday. If I can."

"Okay. Try, will ya?"

"If I can, I will."

"I love you, you know." He chokes on these words, his chest heaving. He grabs his chest as I step back toward my car, away from him. "Call me if you need anything."

"I will. Thanks, Dad."

I turn and walk back to my car, wave goodbye. Even from here I can see the effort it takes him to move his feet, as if he's a tree ripping himself up by the roots. I drive away and don't look back.

When Marvin finds out about the abortion, he throws me out of the house. Ruth cries, even though I assure her it was the right thing to do. I find a job at Ponderosa Steakhouse, and when the assistant manager tells me he's moving, I take over his apartment in Schenectady.

For a few months, I drive back to pick up Ruth on weekends, hanging out with David and his girlfriend, drinking in the car and bar hopping. I tell her I have to work on Sunday, but that's a lie. I don't tell her about the apartment, or about Michelle.

***

IT'S A PERFECT DAY. I'm on my way to my apartment after early Sunday dinner with my parents, and the sky is so blue and clear, everything seems possible. For this one moment, the day seems to belong only to me, driving my car, smoking my joint, a bunch of firecrackers and bottle rockets on the passenger seat. I feel so free, happy, the breeze blowing, and the music cranked with the windows down.

I take a deep drag on a cigarette, and for some reason it seems like a fun idea to drop a lit firecracker out the window. I light it off my cigarette and casually drop it out, watching in the rearview mirror the reaction of the cars behind me. The quick lift from the shower of sparks and crackling and swerving is fun, but after a few, I want more of a rush.

So I light a bottle rocket and hang it out the window, holding the rocket just until it starts to whistle, watching with a grin as it flies down the street behind me.

I laugh out loud at the perfection of my life. Then I catch a red light, and a man pulls up next to me, waving and shouting. He shows me his state trooper hat and gestures for me to pull over.

I nod, smile, and wave back at him, my mind racing, or at least I think it does. Through my stoned haze, it seems completely plausible that my four-speed Chevy Chevette can outrun this trooper car. My drug-addled mind puts me in a movie where the car chase ends well for me.

I drop the clutch and jam the gas pedal to the floor. The engine wails through the gears—first, second, third, back to first—as I swing the steering wheel right, then left, then right again, blowing through every stop sign.

I imagine other cars jumping into the path of the trooper as he tries in vain to follow me, but when I check the mirror after four or five turns, there he is just half a block behind me.

I yank left and slam the gears again until I suddenly find myself facing a cul-de-sac, and I'm hanging on to the steering wheel for dear life; my car bounces up over the curb, the sidewalk, a lawn, tearing up the grass, and the trooper waits and watches me from behind.

By now I realize the fool's errand this chase has become, know the bag of weed in my pocket will royally screw me. The best idea I can come up with is to drive on the left side of the road across a bridge and throw the bag over the side.

I know these roads well, recognizing the neighborhood that was my playground at WAITT House. Still, something has to give and finally, as I round one last corner, either my car or my own free will surrenders, and I slam into a telephone pole.

I get out of the mangled Chevette, looking as confused as possible, feigning ignorance.

"Why are you chasing me, man?"

He pulls a .357 Magnum and aims it at me, but now the inane question takes over my mouth, repeating over and over, as innocent as a kid who skips math class and gets caught in the bathroom.

He grabs my T-shirt and throws me to the ground, yanks my head up by the hair, presses the barrel against my temple, digs his knee into my back. The gun goes back in the holster so he can punch me in the back and kidneys, grabs my hair again to push my face into the road.

He leans down close, so only I can hear.

"You know you could have killed somebody? You fucking little asshole, you could have killed some kid, you stupid fuck."

He picks me up like a ragdoll and slams me into the trunk of his car, pulls me out, slams me in again. Repeat. Repeat. In broad daylight, on the Hill, a residential neighborhood, a state trooper. Kids and adults gather around to gape.

He shoves me into the back seat of the car and calls his dispatcher, and more cops show up, and the crowd cranes to get a glimpse. One girl catches my eye, and we smile at each other, but somebody pulls at her arm.

"Don't smile at him. He might be a killer!"

Somehow that makes me feel better. I prefer that story to what really happened.

The State Trooper drives me to his barracks. My joy ride has fucked up his undercover job, and he's pissed. Someone could have been killed.

THE BARRACKS ARE CROWDED FULL, the shifts changing, so he handcuffs me to a metal table that's bolted to the wall. Finally, only a sergeant and the Trooper are left.

The sergeant pulls up a chair next to me and talks calmly, like an older uncle.

"You really should sign the confession he's typing up."

My buzz has long since worn off, my only response a request for my lawyer.

"You don't want to do that, son."

I won't say a word. He stands and looks down at me, and I see no pity in his eyes before he turns away and leaves me alone in the room with the man who brought me there.

The Trooper finishes typing his report and hands it to me. "Sign this statement."

"No."

"Good."

He picks up a telephone book, rolls it into a bat, and beats me off the chair, hanging from one arm, still handcuffed to the table. I curl into a ball, my face against the wall, so he beats my back and sides until my free hand moves to protect my sides instead of my head, and then he beats my head back and forth, back and forth, and my eyes close and my hands go limp. Not because of how much it hurts, but because I know this isn't going to stop, so it must be what I deserve.

I wake up in the back of the car, on the way to County Jail.

"You got smashed up in the crash," the Trooper says, his face serious.

"No. You did this."

"That right? No one will believe that."

"My lawyer will."

"Tell your lawyer, sure, that's good. He'll tell you the same thing. You're a fucking liar."

Finally, I say what he wants to hear.

"No one will believe me."

"That's right. Good."

They find the bag of dope I threw out the window, but by the time they get to it, it's empty. Still he smiles at me in the mirror, because of the roaches in the ashtray, and the firecrackers and bottle rockets, too. My silence speaks to my inability to understand.

Sitting in the back of his car, my only thought is how cool it is that my Rush T-shirt is ripped. My blood stains the Permanent Waves graphic like a suit of armor.

AGE TWENTY

Michelle's family despises me.

She's a hostess at Ponderosa Steakhouse; I wash dishes. The first time I come to her house, every female member of the family is there to meet me, along with little brother Tim and older brother Michael.

When they finish inspecting me, Michelle takes me in to meet her father.

Her father sits me down in the parlor, a dark room with plastic covers on all the furniture, and after eyeballing me, finally speaks in what I guess is an accent he learned from watching *The Godfather Part Two*.

"One thing I wanna to know, what are-uh your intentions a with-uh my daughter?"

I stare at him for a moment. Sure, I'm stoned, but I try to guess the right answer.

"Well, we're probably going to, uh, go see a movie."

He keeps eyeballing me.

"Then, we'll maybe go out to get some ice cream."

Still no response.

"And, after that, we'll be back here by eleven?"

I wait. He leans forward, holding his thumb and middle finger together and pointing at me with the other three fingers, like he's flicking snot at me, waving his hand back and forth toward me. Finally, he speaks.

"No."

"No?"

"No." He points a stubby, boney finger right at my face. "I wanna to know, what are-uh your intentions a with-uh my daughter?"

This is a fucking Twilight Zone episode.

"Are you asking me if I'm going to marry your daughter?"

He gets more animated and raises his voice.

"I wanna to know, what are-uh your intentions a with-uh my daughter?"

I've been drinking since noon, wear two earrings in my left ear, flaunt tattoos, and smoked a joint on the drive over. No amount of booze and dope could have prepared me for this shit.

I sit back in the chair, throw my head back, and laugh out loud.

"Sir, I don't know. We're going to go out on a date tonight. If we have fun, maybe we'll do this again, get to know each other, and after a while . . ."

For once, I run out of words. I close my lips tight and hold my breath as he leans forward in his chair, eyeball to eyeball with me.

"I wanna you to know one-uh thing."

He points at the closed door that opens into the long hallway to the kitchen where Michelle, her two sisters, her two brothers, her sister-in-law Joanie, her mother, and her grandmother are waiting.

"You hurt-uh my daughter," he points at his chest, "you hurt-uh me. You hurt-uh me," he jabs the bony stub at me again, "I hurt-uh you."

"Yes, sir, I understand." The words come out, but I'm still holding my breath.

"I'm-uh gonna tell-uh you one-uh more time!"

His voice notches up a level. I bite my tongue and see spots from lack of oxygen.

"You hurt-uh my daughter, you hurt-uh me. You hurt-uh me, I hurt-uh you."

Michelle and I back her little Chevy hatchback down the driveway with the whole family watching and speed off down the road. We bag the movie and ice cream, buy a quart of Jack Daniels instead, park in the woods out by the power lines where my parents live, and I fuck her in the ass.

I NEED A WAY to get to work. With ten moving violations, no driver's license, and several thousand dollars in fines and landscaping costs, the bus is my only option for getting to work. That doesn't work for me.

Michelle takes to staying at my apartment more and more, driving me to work at Ponderosa. I make enough money to buy dope, but not enough to also pay my rent, so Michelle pitches in and eventually takes over all my bills.

We pool our money, and I start dealing coke, an ounce a week at first, then two. I stash the dope in Michelle's car and never deal out of my apartment, only out in the open on the street, walking up and down through all my old neighborhoods.

One night I go into an apartment around the corner from my place, sell a few grams, and step into the kitchen to teach some high school kids how to freebase. I'm not gone more than thirty seconds, but when I get back to the living room, the front door is open and an eight-ball I left on the living room coffee table is gone.

I know who took it, a sleaze who hangs around the stoop and his runt-of-the-litter brother. I grab Michelle's car keys, my father's old Robeson U.S. Navy knife, and my .303 British rifle and, along with two other guys, spend the next few hours driving up and down the streets and banging on doors.

A gang of teenage whores say they saw the Runt in the Brandywine Diner, but not his brother. We stake it out, and when the Runt comes out of the diner, we jump him.

Not too much shoving and screaming and squirming and smashing later, we throw him up against a chain-link fence at the back of the lot.

The other guys hold him there as he screams bloody murder.

"Shut the fuck up, asshole." I hold the knife blade to his throat, but he still won't stop screaming, so I get the rifle out of the car and crack him in the head with the butt. That shuts him up, eyes rolled back in his head.

A group of four guys comes out of the diner, heading toward us. I ditch the gun in some leaves behind the fence but hold on to the knife behind my back. Then I see the leader of the pack.

"Hey, Louie."

I haven't seen Louie DiBraccio since I ran away from his aunt Thelma's foster home, but he recognizes me right away.

"What's the story?"

The Runt moans and sits up, groggy but coherent.

"I didn't do nothin', Louie. I was just in the diner, and when I came out, they jumped me. He's got a knife."

I let the knife show from behind my back, slack in my hand.

"That true?"

"This fuck and his brother ripped me off."

"No, we didn't."

The Runt screams as I smack him above the nose with the knife hilt. Blood runs into his left eye.

"I was stupid. I left some dope for a few seconds in the other room. His brother ran off, but we caught up to this one."

Louie steps up to look the Runt in the eye. "Did your brother rip him off?"

"I don't know."

"Did you rip him off?"

The Runt is squirming now, won't look at Louie. "No." He looks at me and spits out the words. "I didn't rip you off, man."

The Runt watches, his head drooping, as Louie confers with his gang, then comes back to me.

"You got a gun?"

I nod over toward the fence, and one of my guys pulls it out from the leaves.

Louie watches as my guy puts the rifle back in the car, looks at the Runt one last time, turns and walks away.

The eight-ball is gone, but at least we have the satisfaction of taking it out on the Runt. We beat him unconscious and throw him over the fence. He doesn't know where his brother is, or he isn't telling. Either way, we don't care.

I know the word's out, and if the cops find a gun on me, that violates my probation and I'll end up in prison. So I sell it, cash on hand, to one of the guys and tell him to get it out of my sight.

Back at the apartment, I grab another eight-ball from Michelle's car and go right back out on the street to deal, keeping an eye out for the sleaze, though I don't expect to find him. By two in the morning, I'm sold out and I have a pocket full of cash and a rock for myself.

Michelle's passed out, so I lock the doors and crawl onto the porch to poke my head over the edge, looking for cops. I crawl back inside, lock the porch door, and sit on the kitchen floor with a mirror and a rolled-up hundred-dollar bill.

I want to make every line last, take it slow, but if the cops come, I'm busted. I decide to stop freebasing because that's what made me sloppy, the only reason those fucks got my eight-ball. Snorting blow isn't the same high, and my nose is all blood, all the time, but at least I can keep my head straight.

I blow through the rock and yell Michelle awake. Nothing seems enough tonight. Michelle puts a beer in one hand, a glass of Jack and Coke in the other, packs me a bowl of pot, and even holds it to my mouth and lights it for me. I drink and smoke until everything finally goes quiet inside, then fuck Michelle into the floor, as hard as possible, trying to hurt my dick, hurt myself, but I can't feel anything anymore, just keep trying to break her open, trying to make my outside feel as numb as my inside.

When Michelle finally leaves, and there's nothing left to pound on, I go back out toward downtown, listening for cars, slowing down and looking over my shoulder to let the drivers see my ass and my face at the same time.

It doesn't take more than five minutes before a car takes a right on a side street and waits for me to come around the corner. He rolls down his window and looks at me, leaning on the car door, and says with a lisp, "Want to suck some cum?"

His dick is the size of a small cigar, about five inches long. Pencil dick, we would have called him in middle school. It's all over in just a few minutes. I sit in the passenger seat, waiting and wondering if he'll let me do it again, or maybe fuck me. Instead he looks into my eyes and his mouth opens, his lips move, and his lisp is tinged with shame. "Get the fuck out."

I walk some more, looking for more cars, wanting more, but instead go up to my apartment and sit in the old ratty armchair, smoking pot with the same mouth that swallowed him, rubbing myself through my pants, hitting myself again and again in the crotch, trying to feel anything, just anything.

He was from Texas, he said. I wonder if he's still out there, driving around, wonder if he'd let me do it again, or even come upstairs and let me do it all night, until, still tasting his salty cum, my eyes close without any dreams.

15

SURRENDERING

SEPTEMBER 2007

I spent the next day with Julie's kids, my niece Paige and her older brother, Jesse, and in a heartbeat became Uncle Kevin.

Julie had a sour stomach, so the day was just me and two teenagers at a giant indoor arcade. Jesse and Paige had a good laugh when we played laser tag and their uncoordinated Uncle Kevin walked straight into a wall in the dark. The kids were both very sweet, helping me find a bag of ice while I went to the restroom to wash off the blood oozing from the cut on my nose.

I drove to Julie's holding the ice on my nose to keep the swelling down, and the kids had a good time teasing me in the car. Julie had slept the day away, and after a quick shower, she was up for going to dinner according to our plan.

My brother James walked in, straight up to me, and wrapped me in a nose-to-toes hug. The room disappeared as we held on to the moment and each other as long as possible.

His wife, Tracey, hugged me, too, and handed me a gift, a beaded necklace she made. She explained the significance of each bead, then reached from behind to fasten it around my neck. James has one just like it.

Their two children, Breandan and Peggy, each a year younger than Kentaro and Tyler respectively, captured my attention, and my whole heart. Breandan, handsome and awkward at the same time, wore a glowing smile and tried to stand as tall as his six-foot father. His little sister, Peggy, climbed into my lap, and I wanted nothing more than to tuck her into my jacket pocket and keep her with me forever.

This was my family, kind and loud, sweet and funny, cute and cuddly, bouncing around Julie's apartment snapping pictures. I felt instantly at home, simultaneously completely content and lost, overwhelmed in the emotional commotion.

John met us at the restaurant and, as if by agreement, everyone left the seat at the head of the table for me. Wordless, I let my family teach me what it means to be with them. I heard their voices more than the words they said and had to fight off the desire to simply close my eyes and soak in the music of my siblings and their families. But I knew the time for listening was past. I struggled to shed the cocoon I'd built, comfortable in the knowledge that for them the assimilation had already transpired. The long wait to belong was over. Now it was time to insert myself into the space they'd already made for me. I was their family now.

"You really look like Mom." John sat a few seats away, between Kyung and Peggy, his hands still for once, resting on the arms of his chair. "It's really spooky. You look more like her than we do."

"He has her eyes," Julie offered. "He has James's eyes."

Instinctively I stood, feeling something new inside, something natural and right, and slowly found my footing and the words.

"I'm so glad I found you. I'm here now. I'm here, and I'll never, ever leave you." I raised my glass. "To Mom."

"To Mom!"

As I sat back down, Kyung turned to John. "Do you think it might be easier now that Kevin's here?"

"Easier?"

"That you won't have all the responsibility now. Being the oldest."

The table went quiet and I felt sad, yet grateful.

"No." John was thoughtful, deliberate. "I don't think so. I don't feel different." He looked at me and gave that big, goofy laugh of his. "Maybe less alone. Just happy you're here."

For the first time I felt the weight of all their eyes on me. "John will always be the big brother to you guys. That won't ever change."

Everyone breathed, taking their cue from John's nod. A sly smile crept up from deep within me. "But we're both older brothers." My smile spread wider. "I'm just *really* old."

AGE TWENTY-ONE

Most male prostitutes work downtown by the town hall. The men who spend money there are usually regulars, mostly husbands with a day job and kids in school. I'm older than most of the other whores, but they all know me, and I'm welcome there. I know if I want, I can make enough around town hall in a few hours, head back to the Hill, and use the cash to buy more blow.

Instead, I opt to walk on, a little farther, where I can jump in a car, give a blowjob and get a half gram, or maybe even a gram of blow, and be right back out there in less than fifteen minutes. Three or four blowjobs in an hour or two is easy to make happen.

Blowjobs are quick and safe in a car, but anything more than that, and they have to take me to a room. If they have a room for the night, I'll get at least a few lines before we even get started and be back on the street in less than an hour with a gram or two in my pocket.

Local guys usually take me back to their apartment. Once, I end up at a nice house, on a rural road out past where my parents live, but all I see is the basement couch.

I've already sucked enough dick to get high for the rest of the night but decide just one more and let a car follow me down a side street. I slow down and speed up, playing coy, feeling almost giddy except that word is better suited for people who don't give blowjobs for cocaine. Michelle would call me perverted and laugh. My mother would just say, "You make me sick," and slam the door.

He wants the whole ride, blowjob and a fuck, lives just a few minutes away, and promises an eight-ball all for myself. I've hit the jackpot. It'll be a long night.

He's shy, so I strut around his apartment with my dick hard and hanging out. He feeds me two lines at a time, and I suck him for a while. After my third or fourth round of snorting and sucking, my nose gushes, and I get blood all over the chair, the floor, his dick, as he curses and pushes me away to the bathroom sink.

At six the next morning, he's fucking me for the third time, and I can tell he's crashing. When he finishes, he gives me the eight-ball, which I shove in the pocket of my cutoff jeans, and kneel on the floor next to his bed. I cover him with a stained sheet and a sweet smile, just to keep him warm, and keep rubbing him through the sheet, slumping to the floor and resting my head on the edge of the bed, and he phases in and out.

His pants are under the bed right by me, and as I stroke him through the sheet, my other hand feels around and pulls his wallet out, fingers the thick fold of bills, slides them into the pocket of my shorts along with the eight-ball. I crawl up on the bed, sucking him gently, cooing how sweet it will be for him to fall asleep in my mouth.

I FIND A NEW two-bedroom apartment with a roommate named Skip, who drools when he's drunk or high, pockets of white spittle collecting in the corners of his mouth. When he's really excited, the foam splatters so he looks like a St. Bernard, his eyes bugging out, wiping his chin on his sleeve, coughing out a laugh with a huge, stained-tooth smile, like someone has trained him, slapping him in the snout and rewarding him with a treat.

A job on the night shift at a factory lets me give blowjobs in cars until sunrise, and Michelle gives me cash from her paycheck so I can deal at least an eight-ball every weekend. I still need to rob at least a few hundred each week to keep the blow, pot, Jack Daniels, and beer flowing at my required level. Michelle's afraid I'll get arrested, or robbed, and asks me to stop dealing. We strike a bargain—I stop dealing, and she'll give me enough money for two eight-balls all for myself, and she always chips in more when I run out.

Both Michelle and Skip know where I go at night, but neither says a word. As long as Michelle's with me I stay home, but after she leaves or passes out, I hit the streets. I'm afraid to open the curtains while I do blow in the apartment, but whenever I run low, a greater fear consumes me, and I have to go back out on the street to find a cock to suck or someone to take me home to fuck.

I don't even care anymore how much blow they give me, as long as they get me high and let me bend over and take them in my ass. The more it hurts, the more I want. No matter how much I drink I can't black out; the cocaine keeps oblivion at bay, but if I can get them to hurt my body hard enough and long enough, my mind shuts down, like giving them a knife and asking them to stab me again and again, knowing they're killing my body, only allowing my mind to casually notice the pain.

I snort blow until my nose won't stop bleeding, shove toilet paper up each nostril, guzzle a bottle of Jack Daniels, drive blind drunk to the all-night corner store on Albany Street, and send Michelle in to buy two more cases of beer.

I'm browning out—the alcohol blocking out all but random glimpses of sight and sound, while the cocaine keeps my eyes pinned wide open, my mind missing big-picture things but following whatever triviality pops into my head.

While Michelle's in the store, I stumble out of the car and crouch in the middle of the road, leaping up and throwing my hands in the air to stop a car that swerves around me. The driver rolls down his window, laughs and bellows, "Happy New Year, asshole!"

"Fuck my asshole!" I scream at him. "Come back and fuck my asshole, asshole!"

I run full speed and straight as an arrow down the middle of the road, except that it isn't, and I trip over the curb and smash my face into the sidewalk.

My eyes open. Michelle is behind the wheel, driving, crying. I'm in the passenger seat, blood streaming from my face, and I scream, raging at I don't know what, kicking the dash, smashing my head against the window. I grab the wheel, swerve the car right as she screams in terror and slams on the brakes just before we hit a line of parked cars, and I fly headfirst into the windshield.

My eyes open. I'm slumped against the wall in the apartment, my head in Michelle's lap. I vomit on her lap and against the wall and on the floor and down my shirt and pants.

My eyes open. Michelle's covered with caked vomit but wiping off the wall and floor around me. I'm soaked with sweat and puke. Tears pour down my face. I'm ashamed and scared she'll leave me, beg her not to go, vomit again, roll up on my hands and knees and dry heave, as her hand rubs my back, softly, the way my mother did when I was little and sick.

My eyes open, caked with dried tears. I hear a cackle, a hyena laugh, and look around and see Skip in the other room.

"You motherfucker, I'll fucking kill you!"

I lurch across the room, my shoulder slams into the doorframe, my face hits the wall and knocks me on my back.

The hyena laugh roars in my ears as I push off the wall and stagger forward again, waving my fists in his face. Skip wraps his left arm around me in a headlock, shoving my blood- and vomit-covered face against his belt, and punches the top of my head until I fall to my knees, arms limp at my side, my neck compressing, squeezing, squeezing. His laugh fades as blood and oxygen stop flowing to my brain, his fist like a jackhammer against my skull, cheek, ear, nose, mouth.

SEPTEMBER 2007

Julie wouldn't let me go. We stood in the parking lot, just as when we first met, her arms around my neck, and her face buried in my shirt. Then Kyung held Julie while John and I embraced, and as I wiped the tears from my cheeks, he gripped my shoulders and smiled that big smile, and I laughed out loud. He pulled me to him again, that big, booming laugh splitting right through my head, and told me everything would be okay. It was all okay now.

Tracey led Breandan and Peggy to their car as James jumped in the rental van with me for the drive to their home outside Fort Collins, Colorado. By this late in the day, the traffic on I-25 had thinned out, the sky overcast and dark without a moon. I was with my brother and was never so grateful for a long drive.

With Julie I felt the same loving apprehension I had with Kentaro and Tyler; I instinctively wanted to reach out and hold her hand to cross the street. John's natural aloofness gave me all the room I needed for the dust of the day to settle, to just sit back and observe and let my emotions and mind be still.

With James, my spirit felt naturally at rest, without any fear or apprehension. It seemed too soon to know this, too fast to have this sense of belonging, this oneness, and I took long, deep breaths and embraced this new, intuitive connection.

I let him do the talking as I drove, stealing sideways glances at him in the glow of the dashboard. His bushy, shoulder-length hair was dwarfed by his full and untamed beard. He had his father's rugged frame, while I reflected our mom's softness, but the spirit of who we are was all Mom.

He grew up with our brother and sister for his entire life yet held a distance between them. I grew up always alone, with only imaginary family, feeling the gaps in my own existence. We both found more than comfort together. We were each other's missing link.

"Thanks for making the trip down, and for bringing everybody with you. I know it's not the best time. You doing okay with me here?" I know I'm being more cautious than necessary, but I'm new at this, have no roadmap for being a brother.

"Hey man, I'm really glad you're here."

"Just checking. Hope you don't mind me asking."

"I never mind."

Our smiles eased the moment, and we drove for a while lost in our thoughts. I didn't mind the silence. When he spoke again, I felt as though I'd been hearing his voice all my life.

"I had a bad morning, just felt very dissonant. Tracey and I aren't doing great. So hard to know what the right thing to do is. Can I be happy again with Tracey? I don't know."

I didn't try to parse my thoughts, wanting to be as genuine with him as he is with me. "My least favorite word is happiness. It's totally subjective. Happiness is never something that comes from outside. I know you know this. I know it in my head, but I've still spent most of my life looking outside." I couldn't tell if I sounded like a big brother, or patronizing, or just rambling, but I could tell he was listening, so I continued, embracing the blessing of this time together.

"A lot of my stuff revolves around abandonment. Being adopted is only one small piece. I've been betrayed, abandoned many times, and I still struggle. Sometimes that struggle is how I know I'm really alive."

I heard him cry now, softly but without suppression, his face turned toward the dark window.

"James, it was so powerful to hear Julie tell me that Mom loved me, that she always wanted to see me."

"I can imagine, man."

"I waited all my life to hear those words, and now I have you, and John and Jules. This is way beyond my wildest dreams."

His tears filled the space between and around us, and I brushed away my own. I was grateful for them—tears of belonging. He grabbed my hand in his, and we squeezed and held our grip longer than men do.

My brother was wonderful, so open and expressive. We drove through the darkness and let our struggles, hopes, fears, and dreams flow from our hearts, naturally and easily, beyond either of our expectations.

As we neared the last leg of our drive, I was on fire with how much history we'd already created, and for what lay ahead.

James turned his head and I felt him watching me, felt him choose his next words with care. "You know, Kevin, we can talk about anything, man. You are family. I don't distinguish between you and John and Julie. You're my brother, man, which means I will be both a pain in your ass and a great support, hopefully at the right times."

"Perfect."

"I don't want you worrying about managing what you say with me, okay? Just say it, whatever it is. Share what you want to share."

"That's exactly how I would want it. I'll never worry again."

AGE TWENTY-TWO

I move into an apartment in Albany with Timmy, a guy from work. I promise Michelle that I'll stop prostituting, and she promises to keep me supplied.

My routine becomes complete oblivion. I show up thirty minutes early at work to drink and do blow in the parking lot, get high and drink at every break, and somehow drive home at one in the morning.

Michelle's there, without words, filling my glass with Jack Daniels and lighting my Camel filters until I fade into blackout. She always keeps the bottle of Jack filled, and when I wake up, I start over again. Open my eyes, light a Camel, cough and hack up bloody mucus, light another cigarette, and take swigs of Jack until I stop shaking enough to walk to the bathroom. My piss is brown, sometimes with clots of blood. My shit is always full of blood. I flush without looking.

Winter passes, and spring, and summer. Michelle cries more, mostly because I'm not eating. I can't keep food down, what most people eat without thinking about it. Michelle keeps donuts in the bedroom, and when I'm quiet enough at the end of the night to not fight her she feeds me small pieces, like a sick bird. I promise I'll eat at work, and I try, but mostly I just manage coffee with milk and three or four sugars.

She cries every time she gives me money. We both cry, a lot.

"We never go anywhere."

"I don't want to go out."

"We could go out for dinner."

"I can't eat."

"What about a movie?"

"It costs too much."

"I've got money."

"I don't care about any movies."

"I know."

"I need something."

"I know. I'm sorry."

I can't have sex anymore without Michelle slapping and hitting me. The pain breaks through the numbness that has invaded my senses, and even then, I can only manage once every month or so. I never even get morning piss hard-ons anymore. My body is shutting down, and nothing seems to work.

At night, Michelle watches me cry, yell at my body, curse my cock, trying anything we can to break through the despair. If she hits me enough, between my legs or on my chest, slaps my face, punches me, degrades me and speaks the words of hate I've taught her, only then can I stop feeling the sickness in me, and only then I might be able to get it up. By the end of the summer, we're both almost ready to give up.

It takes an hour to get me hard enough even to start, but that doesn't last more than a few minutes before falling into numb, flaccid uselessness. My mind and body no longer connect anymore, just misfire chemicals that simulate manic emotions and utter confusion. I curl up and cry while Michelle retreats to her usual spot in the corner by the closet, wrapping her arms around her shins and pulling her knees up to her chest, her head drooping, her forehead on her thighs, waiting.

"I don't want to see you cry. I want you to be okay." She sounds tired, her voice muffled, not raising her head.

"I need an eight-ball."

She picks her head up, watching. I feel shame, sunk deep into myself, lost, gone, distant from anything and everything I ever was before and hopeless for what could have been.

"Okay." She pulls out her purse and hands me cash.

When I return, she meets me at the door, nervous eyes compromising her hopeful smile.

"Did you get it?"

I pull it out of my pocket, holding it up for her to see.

"Good." She stands in the doorway, blocking my way, and hugs me, then takes a step back, looking up into my face. "Will it help?"

She wants to have sex, to feel hopeful, if only briefly. All I want is to get high, but I want to believe, as she does, that we can have something more.

"Yeah. It'll help."

"How?"

"It makes me feel like Superman." My face feels strange, contorted, but I recognize the sound of my own laugh. I haven't smiled in a long time.

Her eyes light up the room, and her goofy grin infects me. We've found a cause we can rally around, a place we can put our hope and our effort. We believe in Superman.

Michelle and I take over the living room, spreading pillows stolen from my roommate's bed around everywhere. She brings out a bottle of Jack Daniels and a shot glass, lights some candles, and turns out the lights while I sit cross-legged on the floor at the coffee table, manicuring the blow—fifteen little test bumps on one side with thirty full-size lines for the big hits.

When half the lines are gone, I substitute bowls of pot for the Jack. My eyes blur, but my mouth keeps kissing, trying to be sensual, romantic, loving. I'm off balance, missing her lips, slurring my words, but she keeps holding me steady, propping me up at the table for the next line.

"Do you want to try now?" She feels between my legs, but my cock is shrunk, my balls contracted into my body, shriveled, like I'm in an ice bath.

"In a minute." I kneel up and do another bump, then two more big hits, and sit back on my heels.

My heart pounds, but it feels as though it's pushing only empty, cold air through my veins. My lips are cracked, and I can't feel my tongue; everything from my chin to my eyebrows is numb. Michelle scoots over and straddles my thigh.

"Do you feel like Superman?"

Her words cut me, almost a physical slice, filling me with shame and failure. I feel a shock in my heart as a hot, dark rage replaces the cold void, my skin burning as adrenaline shoots through me like a bullet. As quickly as the rage fades, her childish, expectant eyes transform my shame to bottomless self-loathing.

We lie naked together, trying again to make love, kissing and cuddling after each round of a bump, a shot of Jack, two big hits, sit back and light a cigarette, and in the ritual our hope grows. She follows me blindly, her wish for nothing more than one single happy night evaporating as the drugs wind me up and tense my whole body, twist me like an old, bent metal Slinky, until I'm shaking all over, sputtering words with no vowels, sentences without nouns.

"You don't feel cold." Michelle puts a blanket around me, drapes her naked body next to my shriveled self.

"Mm. Hmph." I look up at her eyes, try to speak, my lips quivering. I try to smile. "Brrr."

"Do you want to get dressed?"

"Shh . . . shh . . . mm . . . mm-mm."

I shake the blanket off, push Michelle off me, sending her sprawling feet away, and crouch back over the table for the last two lines. I suck them both up my one unclogged nostril, take money from Michelle, and leave to get more.

SEPTEMBER 2007

I woke up the next morning to a cacophony of sounds. Peggy was sitting on the floor surrounded by what seemed to be every toy in the house. I was in her bed, and she had been told not to wake me, but as soon as I opened my eyes, she started talking in what seemed to be a complete stream of consciousness. Just like her father.

Their home, the "Earth Ship," as they all called it, was completely off the grid, built with James' own hands, mostly out of recycled cans and tires, with geothermal heat and solar power. They had run out of money and much of the interior was unfinished. He didn't want me to think badly of him for living the way they did, which didn't make sense until he told me that he'd used the inheritance after his father's suicide to pay for everything.

The thirty acres of mountainside in Livermore, Colorado, that was their property had been pitch black when we arrived. The house was literally built into the landscape, the back up against the hillside, but the front side was a wall of eight-foot-tall floor-to-ceiling glass panes. The sun, along with the whole family, was already up as I walked into the main living area, and the view stopped me in my tracks.

The Continental Divide. My breathing slowed as I took in the panorama of harsh, jutting cliffs, rugged peaks, and green slopes miles in every direction, the brilliant sun shimmering across sprawling meadows and bouncing off tens of thousands of evergreen treetops. The front door was wide open, letting me fill my senses with the cool morning air, even as the geothermal heating kept the interior a perfect seventy-two degrees. I felt as though walking out the front door across the open grass toward the dense, majestic forest would lead me straight into Eden.

"Morning, bro," James called with a smile.

He was cooking in the kitchen, the house already bustling, Breandan flopped on a couch reading, Peggy still talking, a little bouncing cherub right by my side. Tracey swept into the room and gave me a morning hug, and I forgot all about the view.

"Uncle Kevin, will you read to me?"

Peggy snuggled into the overstuffed chair with me and wrapped my arm tight around her. She's delayed and couldn't yet read on her own, but her love for words drove her to consume language in every way possible. As I read each page, she mouthed the words with me. She could memorize and recite entire dialogues, expressing pure joy for the spoken word.

I mentally recorded every sight and sound, fully immersing myself in the moment. Tracey's footsteps as she scurried back and forth to check on me, then the kids, then James, then back to me. The subtle whisper when Breandan turned another page, completely engrossed in his reading. The sound of eggs frying in the kitchen, James pausing to silently observe his daughter and his new brother making memories. Making our history.

After breakfast, James helped pry me loose from Peggy, and we walked the lower fence line of the property, just the two of us, to a small clearing with a well-worn fire pit surrounded by free-standing logs cut to serve as benches and stools. We didn't have much time before my flight, when I would leave him to focus on his marriage and face some hard choices, but for right now both of us had each other.

"Right down there is Sand Creek." He pointed past some small pine trees and mountain shrubs. "It runs down Devil's Canyon."

"Why Devil's Canyon?"

"The creek's about a quarter mile long. It overflows along the road and freezes up every winter. It's a car-eating canyon, so we call it Devil's Canyon. Cars go sliding off every year."

"You ever slide off?"

"Nah, man. It's not really that hard, but I'm not gonna go down there, especially with the kids in the car. You gotta know what you're doing. Nobody dies, but about ten or twenty people get hurt every season. After Mom, I don't fuck around in a car."

"Was the drive last night hard?"

"Driving's always hard. Not really when I'm alone, but if anybody's with me, and I'm behind the wheel, my anxiety spikes. I didn't really sleep last night. My body won't come down from the fight or flight."

"You're afraid when you're driving, or a passenger?"

"Both. When I'm a passenger, I just try to zone out. It was hard last night because I didn't want to be in a trance when I was with you."

"I'm glad we're not in a car now."

My cockeyed, wry smile told James all he needed to know about his new brother, and he laughed a rocking-back-on-his-heels laugh, stretched his lanky frame, threw his arms overhead. I watched the tension ooze out of his body like sweat, evaporating into the breeze.

"I'm always waiting to lose somebody. That's what driving is to me, and if it's me behind the wheel . . ." I wait for him to finish, but he trails off.

I saw his father better now. The gentle features of our mother creased, those beautiful, soft eyes framed by deep, tiny lines that didn't belong to a face so young, his inner joys scarred and frozen behind a tense, unnatural hardness.

I felt the arc of the sun shifting, the heat and intensity peaking before the day slipped away.

"Is this the family fire pit?"

"Not really. Sometimes, but usually it's just me. We do a drum circle, but Tracey doesn't come." He looked away again over the treetops. "She used to. Not anymore."

"Maybe tomorrow will be different."

I expected an objection, or at least a polite brush off.

Instead he went in an unexpected direction. "Why would you want to be a part of such a broken family? I mean, I'm stuck with it, I've already paid admission, but you're choosing us." He shook his head, with deep compassion. "Was it that bad for you?"

"I'll tell you someday. I don't want to bring all that stuff here."

"I understand."

"It's just that I don't want to . . ."

"You can talk about Mom. It's okay. It's been a long time, I've already grieved. It's harder for you, I understand, but don't worry about me."

He waited a long time for my reply.

"When I was struggling, especially when I was a kid, and things went pretty far off the rails, the first thing anyone ever asked was if it was because I was adopted. Was there something about me that was rebelling. Just the angry-young-man shit."

"People can't see past their own assumptions."

"But I don't feel sad about that now. I care about today. I care about you guys."

James didn't try to comfort me or tell me it was going to be okay. He just sat with me.

"I don't want you or Julie or John to ever feel sad, that Mom letting me go caused all this shit that happened after she left. I'm not afraid that you'll see all my broken pieces. I just don't want you to ever think I'm sad because she left me. It's not like that."

"I don't think anyone would blame you if you were sad."

"I am sad. It hurts every single day. And this trip? Seeing where she lived, where you all lived, without me? Thinking what could have been for me? That kills me, you know it does.

"But I'm sad the way she was sad. It had nothing to do with her doing something wrong, because she did exactly what she had to do, and here I am, with parents, and Eri, and my kids, and now you guys, and my life is just one giant amazing wave of crazy energy. And it's my life. And even when I hate it sometimes, I still love it.

"Every part of her life, with you, and John, and Julie, and your dad, and all your horses and cowboy yahoo Black Forest Colorado yuk-yuk life, all of it, was exactly what I think it was supposed to be. I'm not sad that we had these different lives." He looked away again at the treetops, knowing I'm speaking from my soul. "You miss her."

The morning air braced me, the sun protected me, and the words tumbled out.

"I'm sad that we never got to hold hands. I never, not once, heard her voice. Never looked into her eyes when she laughed or shot daggers when she was pissed. I miss her, and I know she missed me, still misses me. I understand how much you miss her. Nothing else matters. You know that."

"I know."

"Because if I could have her here just for one day, just for one hour—"

"I know."

The breeze reminded us how little time we had left.

"You know." I heard a smile in his voice. "She never got pissed. Mom never, ever, had daggers in her eyes."

"Even though you gave her good reason to."

"Hell yeah!" James let loose a big, warm laugh.

"You know, man, I know you're broken. We're all pretty broken, so you fit right in. I see all the pieces, man, and you know what? I like the pieces."

"There are a lot of pieces, that's for sure."

"You want to see broken? Man, our sister is broken. Even her broken pieces are broken."

"I know."

"You put the pieces back together. I'm putting the pieces back together." He laughed and threw his arms up in the air again. "Shit, I don't know if I'm putting them together or smashing them apart right now, but you know what I mean."

"I hear you."

"You show me all your pieces, man. I know they were all broken, but I can't see them anymore. I know they're still there, still broken, but you've healed, man. All I see is you, and man, you're a beautiful man. I know all the pieces are there, but I can't see the cracks anymore."

"Trust me, they're there."

"Trust me, I know. But I can tell, you're not anything like what you seem to think you were. Whatever you were, I don't know how you did it, but you ain't that person anymore."

AGE TWENTY-THREE

I quit smoking cigarettes for Thanksgiving.

I'm always broke, and Michelle's tapped out days before her paycheck comes. My two-packs-of-Camels-a-day habit seems like a good way to save cash. I'm neither able nor willing to pay a buck twenty-five a pack.

To get through the nicotine withdrawals, I double down on the blow and pot and Jack. I tell Michelle it's only until I get past the urge to smoke a cigarette. Two weeks later, my system is saturated.

At the warehouse, I'm responsible for packaging the pool liners for shipment, running the box through the banding machine, transposing the dimensions from a spec-sheet, and printing my name on the box.

I can't remember how to spell my last name. I can say the sounds aloud—bar-height—but when I try to sound out the letters, I get lost. It's a Dutch-German spelling, and it shouldn't be all that difficult, but I come up with a quick-fix solution. Every night at the start of my shift I take my driver's license out of my wallet and tape it to the banding machine.

Work is a relief, a way to keep moving, to stay on my feet. Friday is our short night, when I get home by 8:00 p.m., Michelle is waiting for me.

She's already eaten dinner, made sure the room is cleaned up, and filled the beautiful Jack Daniel's Old No. 7 decanter that sits on my nightstand. I have enough blow and pot for the weekend. Somehow, I've left my driver's license taped to the banding machine at work, but I don't have to drive again until Monday. Michelle will make trips to the store for beer.

All she does is watch me get high and keep the drinks flowing, and she's bored. We spend hours side by side, both of us completely alone.

She wants to have sex, and I want to try, but not because either of us has any strong physical urge.

I try, but as always fail to stay hard. It only gets worse every time we try. She's patient at first, then cries when I collapse in a ball on the bed, hitting myself between my legs, beating my dick and balls, screaming in pain and self-hate, and she holds me, rocking me through my desperation.

"We could try something," I say, wiping my nose on the sheets, rubbing my wet eyes.

"What?"

"Get on."

"But you're not hard."

"Just sit there."

"You won't cry?"

"I don't know. I want to try."

She straddles me, pushing her dry pussy on my limp, useless dick.

"Tell me a story." I spread my arms out to the side, limp on the mattress.

"What story?"

"Just tell me what I tell you to say."

I close my eyes and let myself remember aloud. The details are fuzzy at first, cars with no color or smell or size, apartments with all the lights on, but no furniture except for a chair, a bed, maybe a mattress on the floor. She listens, then her voice embodies the parts that matter the most.

"I'm bending you over the chair . . . my hard, black cock is slamming you in your ass . . . you suck off the guy with the small dick."

"His friend waits his turn . . . when I'm done, he fucks you while you suck your own shit off my cock."

"Swallow my cum in my car . . . I shove your face down into my wet balls."

I TEACH her all the stories, and she practices because they help. With my eyes closed, she puts me inside her and I stay hard, lying back, listening to her words, remembering.

Every day is exactly the same. I forget my name, she fills my decanter, I snort my blow, she tells me stories, I close my eyes, I forget my name. I forget my name.

Quitting cigarettes only increases my intake of everything else, and my inability to pay my bills. Michelle borrows money to pay my rent while I sit in my room and cry.

"I don't have any money, and I can't go home for Christmas without presents."

"We can spend Christmas here."

"What about your family?"

"I won't leave you."

Michelle decorates the apartment with a three-foot plastic tree, and she buys presents so we have something to give to each other—a blue Care Bear for her, a purple one for me. We name them Micha Bear and KB Bear, and spend the night talking to each other through the bears and fall asleep on the couch together.

We're almost completely broke, so I promise to take it easy on the blow for the rest of the week. I figure I have some pot to smoke, so if I can make that stretch, and Michelle keeps the Jack and beer stocked enough to get through the nights, maybe we'll be okay.

Christmas is on a Wednesday. I know I'll never get ahead until I get back to dealing again, so I make a New Year's resolution. I will stop using drugs and alcohol for one year, so I can save enough money, so I can buy enough drugs, so I can deal drugs and never have to buy them again. This is my grand entrepreneurial idea.

I'm a high school dropout. I can't spell my last name, much less the word *entrepreneurial*, but nevertheless this is my plan. Super Genius.

WE MAKE IT THROUGH Christmas and the rest of the week, go wild over the weekend, then on Monday I ease up on my drinking. I keep smoking pot to compensate and track exactly how much I use so I can be sure to have just enough to finish everything by January 1. Michelle and I maintain our storytelling routine, but we spend time playing with KB Bear and Micha Bear.

All day Tuesday I'm not feeling well, and we wonder if I have a cold, maybe a fever. I'm down to the last of everything, with the plan to finish it off and quit at midnight, but the day has gone by without much chemical use. At midnight, there's no big moment of throwing out the pipes and bags, flushing everything down the toilet, dumping the booze down the drain, swearing off the stuff for good. It's a typical New Year hoot-n-holler jump up and down with the TV blasting out the scene from Times Square, and then it's over.

"Happy New Year!"

My New Year's resolution is simple. It's not about the drugs or drinking or any sense of turning a corner, it's simply about the money.

"I'm done!"

I say it to Michelle, but really to myself, or even more likely to the spirit of Christmas future.

"I'm done. No more for a year."

We stand in the first moment of the new year, kissing and smiling, then Michelle puts her hand over her mouth with a gasp, looking shocked.

"Wait! I forgot! What about the gift I got for you?"

"What gift?"

"From my trip to Italy." She smiles, runs to the bedroom, and returns with a box she had hidden in my closet. I hold it as she opens the lid and pulls out a beautiful leather-clad two-liter flask, metal hooks built into the sides of the leather, and four shot glasses hanging off the hooks. I grab two shot glasses, and without a thought she pours the twenty-year-old whiskey, and I down both shots in quick succession.

It's 12:05 on January 1, 1986.

I am twenty-three years old.

"You're still hot." Michelle puts her hand to my forehead, the fever constant now. She holds a cold washcloth on my forehead and covers me with blankets.

"Here, take this."

I take a sip of water to wash down the Tylenol she hands me and throw them back up.

"I can't." I spit the words out with the puke, heaving over the edge of the bed into the bucket Michelle has set out.

"You should try to eat."

"I can't." I moan, spitting into the basket, a long string of spittle hanging from my lips.

She brushes away the drool and leaves me alone. The last time I stepped on a scale I weighed 115 pounds.

"My head hurts. It hurts bad."

Michelle sits next to me as I moan, brushing my greasy hair back. I squeeze my temples between my palms, trying to will myself not to move even an inch, every movement making me feel like I'm in a boat tossed on the waves, the room spinning, my head pounding and my stomach convulsing.

"You'll be okay," she promises. "Just rest."

I can't quiet my mind, even though no cogent thought is possible. If I sleep, it's only long enough to wake up in shock, afraid of something I've dreamed, or something I think I heard.

My stomach aches, deep down inside all the way to my backbone, and my ab muscles won't quit trembling, like a jackhammer idling in my gut, never stopping. My forearms hurt, too. I keep my hands curled up by my chest to keep them from shaking, but that doesn't stop the internal buzzing sensation, a tuning fork vibrating against my bones.

I'm used to food making me sick. For the past year or more, I've thrown up food, even small bites of cheeseburger, but usually it only takes a minute or two for the puking to pass. Now, I can't stop. It comes in waves at first, me hanging over the side of the bed while Michelle holds a plastic wastebasket under my chin, but soon escalates to an almost constant storm of dry heaves that only stop long enough for me to curl up and shiver for a minute or two, pouring sweat.

"My stomach hurts so much. It won't stop."

I'm not able to focus or see anything in the room. All I do is cry, but without tears. Michelle threatens to call an ambulance, and I snap a response, ready to kill her one minute then begging the next, holding in the pain and trying to smile.

"It'll pass, don't worry, it's just a bug, a twenty-four-hour bug or something."

The sickness only gets worse. Except for a few minutes snatched here and there, I haven't slept in two days. The next time I wake up, everything is dark, quiet and still, like the moment before morning breaks.

I sit up, and my feet hit the cold floor. "What time are we leaving?"

"Where?"

"We'll be late. I don't want to be late."

"It's too cold out," she says, urging my head back to the pillow.

"I hear waves." I look up at her weakly, confused.

"It's the wind outside. In the parking lot."

Michelle keeps the lights off during the day, only slightly cracking the window blinds. Even the weakest light makes my eyes water.

The next day the vomiting finally lets up and I sleep, in momentary fits at first, then ten or twenty minutes at a time. When I wake, it's sudden and angry, snarling at Michelle, fidgety, flopping back and forth on the mattress. The sleep isn't deep, but it adds up until after a few hours of these brief naps, I sit up on the floor with my back against the bed, next to the puke basket.

Michelle tries to soothe me, but I bark at her to leave me alone and sit with my head between my knees, breathing short shallow breaths, slow gasping inhales. I think I'm dying. Michelle stays away, cringing on the other side of the room, sitting on the floor with her back to the closet door, watching me. She has not left me alone since New Year's Eve.

After a week, I begin to sleep through the night. Michelle stirs all the bubbles out of a glass of ginger ale, just the way I tell her my mother did when I was sick, and I hold it down.

"Take a shower with me."

Her naked body feels hot next to mine. I'm so cold, my whole body shaking. Too weak to stand by myself, I sit on the edge of the tub, and Michelle gives me a sponge bath.

"You'll start feeling better now." Somehow, she makes the exhaustion in her voice sound like a smile. "You need to eat."

"I do? Okay. You're right. I think I'm better. It was just a nasty bug, right?"

"You'll feel better."

I want to believe I'm better, but still I feel sick inside my head. I smell the shit on the underwear she peeled off me, can feel her wiping the crust from between my ass cheeks, the warm water stinging, burning. I'm not a man.

After she bathes me, I sleep hard, exhausted, and wake up screaming and drenched in sweat. It's only eight at night, and I've only slept a few hours, but the fear is strong that I will never sleep again. Michelle holds me, wiping my face and the back of my neck with a wet washcloth.

"Shh." She rubs the cool cloth over my forehead and hair as I hyperventilate until I choke on my own spit, coughing until I lose my breath. "Shh. Just breathe. Can you try to eat a little?"

The food stays down, and I lie on the bed while Michelle cleans up around the house. I think I'll be okay now. It was just a bug. A bad, week-long bug.

My mind is floating from one half-thought to another as Michelle undresses and crawls in bed next to me, rubbing me through my clean underwear.

I know where we are, then my senses get confused, but quickly refocus as she mounts me.

My body is tired, my arms so limp and weak I can't even reach up to grab her waist or touch her breasts.

She begins to speak the words I taught her, the words she's practiced so many times. I know the story, where it always leads, where it ends, again and again, every time.

I want her, if only because she wants me to want her. She's nursed me, not left my side for over a week, and this is what she needs now. She needs to know that she can please me, too, that after all the sickness, I can still see her and want her.

I do want her. My body feels different, responds faster, more fully, but something is not right. The story sounds familiar, but the distance between the story and the present, that gap that always protects me, isn't there now, and I can feel the terror swelling up, spreading through me, as I lie there under Michelle with no way to escape, nowhere to go.

A flash, a giant shock blasts my eyes wide open, and I see all that I truly am, all that I've done and become. The visions seem murky and vague, yet I can see every detail. Heavy curtains that have shielded my mind for so long are thrown open all at once, and I see everything.

I freeze in the glare of my past, almost as if I'm dying, watching my life play out in front of me, tragic and horrific. Everything, from every year, and every day and night. I see cock after cock, sucking and fucking. Every dollar from my father's wallet, money from my mother's purse, my grandmother's purse, anyone's money. Every needle, every drink, every white line on a mirror, every puff of smoke.

It feels like a wave and, just when I think it's about to recede, it comes on full force. My face collapses into a slack-jawed, soundless scream. I go completely limp as my body caves and folds in on itself, into my chest and my gut, then exploding out again in a blast of pure pain.

An inhuman strength in me grabs Michelle and throws her off me, not with violence or anger, but with pure fear. She flies across the room, crashes into the closet doors, and lands with a heavy thud on the cold floor.

I know that I should die. I deserve to die. I have no value, nothing of worth to give, or say, or hope for. I have caused nothing but sadness and pain, have been fully evil, completely devoid of any good of any kind.

I don't deserve to be here. I should never have been born. I am, and always have been, a mistake.

The sickness of the past week is eclipsed by the sickness that I now recognize. I am without remedy. I should find a way to die. I'm not sick; I *am* the sickness.

An immediate and immense pain engulfs me, picks me up and smashes me back down, shatters my insides, racks my mind.

I crave relief. My mind and body ache for what I need, but I know I can never fill the void. I feel hungry, appetite raging in me, but I can't bring myself to eat or drink, can only cry, curled into a ball. I roll on my side, hug the blue and purple stuffed bears, moaning and soaking them with tears and drool.

Dreams won't let me sleep at all. Each time I wake with a confusing urge, a need I remember but cannot name. I drift in and out of sleep, the sounds and smells mingling what is real and what is a dream. I'm broken, and I feel nothing anymore.

"Maybe I need help. Maybe I need help."

I mumble the words for hours, crying, pausing when the fear and thoughts swell up inside me, only to fall back into my catatonic state again, repeating the only words I can find that seem to make sense.

"Maybe I need help. Maybe I need help."

Michelle sits across the room, her spent gaze on the floor. In the face of my desperate mantra, she has run out of words.

"Maybe I need help. Maybe I need help."

I rock back and forth, then I hear the only words she can find.

"Maybe you do."

Her voice slices through the room, words of frustration perhaps, or sarcasm, or a last-ditch remnant of hope. Wherever they come from, they shoot through the air and inject me with what I only vaguely sense is divine.

Maybe.

Everything in me stops at once. The days and nights of constant sickness have left my body weakened, but the absolute fear that has plagued me quiets, seemingly without cause, like a warm breeze that gently dissipates foul air.

I CAN'T KEEP the memories at bay, but I fight them off one minute at a time, moving forward or sideways, but at least I'm moving. I sleep longer, and the rest strengthens my body, but the dreams only get worse.

"You were screaming in your sleep." Michelle holds me as I shake, my whole body racked with fear.

"I can't take this." Each word is broken by a gasp as I suck in air, my throat raw.

"Do you remember the dream?"

"Not a dream." I shake my head. "It's not real, but it's so fucking hard."

"What?"

"My mother dies. She doesn't say anything, or look at me, she just dies. I stand there, and she's just dead."

I hardly get the words out. I fall into Michelle's lap, pull my arms around my ribs, clutch at my sides.

"But your father's the weak one."

"He's not there. Right before I wake up, I can tell he's not coming, he's not going to help, and I can't do anything, so I just stand there. My feet won't move, I can't even take one step forward to help her. I can't go to her. She's not lying down, or peaceful, or anything like that, she's standing up, far away, but just dead. Her eyes are closed. She doesn't move, doesn't breathe."

My head jerks left and right, like I'm looking for something I hear but can't find where the sound is coming from.

"It'll be okay."

I lie there as Michelle holds me, until I cry myself quiet.

"I can't take it anymore. I want it to stop."

"It will stop."

"When?"

16

EMERGING

*M*y mind wouldn't stop swirling on the plane ride home. I had prepared myself all summer for this time in the clouds, time to let all my thoughts filter through and arrange them-selves, for my body to be still so my emotions could find a place to swell and contract, to re-experience every moment. I had it all planned out.

Like most everything about my life, things didn't go as planned.

I had not lied to James, and I didn't mean to omit anything. I sat in my seat now looking out the window from high above my brothers and sister, above my mother's grave, higher than Pikes Peak, and I remem-bered my choice by the fire pit, my decision to wait. I told myself, if only we had more time, or on my next trip out, or when he comes someday to visit, then I'll tell him everything.

Now I was alone again, and all I wanted was to turn the plane around and sit again with my brother.

It was true that I was sad because I never knew our mom. I wasn't sad because she left; I had no anger or regret at all about that, but there was something else. Something much more permanent, primal.

All of my losses, starting with my mom but compounding over time, left me with a deep inner belief, my oldest truth: That nothing about me was worth anything, and that was why no one ever fought to keep me.

This was my enemy, and it is me still. Every day that I wake and take another breath I make the choice to strike out, to seek and fight the enemy, but the enemy is me.

The enemy, my worthless self, born and rejected, left and unwanted, adopted and abandoned, nothing more than meat for men and women to use and abuse and discard. Unworthy of the perfect passion of my marriage, the love of a daughter and son, the adoration of a mother, the strength of a father, deserving only of loss. Every razor cut to my wrist, every drug I put into my veins and drink I poured down my throat was meant not to escape, but to kill that unworthy self.

I wanted to stay here, away from that unworthiness, away from those who had hurt me, and from everyone I had ever hurt. I wanted this flight never to end. I wondered what would happen tomorrow. My new family, these broken, beautiful people, who had been so loved by our mother, had now chosen to love me, to welcome and accept me without question or qualification, as family. Would we stay this close, get closer, or would this feeling fade away? Would I ever again feel the way I felt sitting by the fire pit?

I wanted to stop time. I wanted to be home.

James had given me a book to read, and he promised it would be a real page-turner. I told him I didn't like science fiction and fantasy much, but that for him I'd give it a shot.

I pulled the book from my bag and felt infinitely closer to my brother. If I couldn't stop time, and couldn't turn the plane around, at least I could be close to him through a story that he loves.

The flight home seemed to take minutes. Though I had just met him, my brother knew me well.

"In the moment when I truly understand my enemy, understand him well enough to defeat him, then in that very moment I also love him. I think it's impossible to really understand somebody, what they want, what they believe, and not love them the way they love themselves."
—Orson Scott Card, *Ender's Game*

AGE TWENTY-THREE

"Jayne."

"Who?"

I hadn't realized I'd spoken. Michelle's sitting across the room, next to the closet, a spot close enough to keep an eye on me, but not so close as to spook me.

"Jayne McCarthy."

I clear my throat, sit up on the mattress with my back against the wall.

"Who's she?"

"She might help."

"You want to call her?"

"I don't know."

The panic rises up, as it does all day long. Every time I have a thought, I shut down from fear. Every indecision feels fatal.

"I will. I'll call her."

I've been at her home many times, back when Jayne was my counselor at WAITT House. They'd moved, but are still living in Rotterdam, about five miles from their old home. I haven't spoken to Jayne since the last time I was arrested. Before I would call my lawyer, or my parents, I'd call Jayne. Not that she could help. I just wanted to hear her voice.

I dial the number and recognize Jayne's voice right away.

"Jayne?"

"Is this you, Kevin?"

"Yes."

I can hear her husband, Emmett, in the background. "Who is it?"

"What do you want, Kevin?"

I feel like I'm going to throw up. Her voice doesn't sound the way I remember, or expect, or hope. I want to hang up.

"I need to talk to you."

"Are you in jail?"

I stumble, my tongue thick and unwieldly in my mouth. My mind is in a deep hole, sinking down fast. I try to get the words out before I can't speak anymore.

"I need help."

"Are you in jail?"

"No."

Thoughts swirl in my head, but I can't make sounds to match them.

"I don't have a drug problem." I'm shaking now, head to toe. I can't breathe right. "I quit those a few weeks ago." My vision blurs, and Michelle grabs me as I sink to the floor.

"I have a personality problem. I need you to help me put my personality back together."

My heart pounds, my head is ready to explode. I rub my forehead, trying to push down the pressure.

"You want to come to the house?"

"No!" I hear Emmett, his voice loud now, bellowing. "No! He's not coming here!"

I strain to hear Jayne over the ringing in my ears while she pauses. The wait feels like several lifetimes.

"Okay, Kevin. You can come on Tuesday. After work. After dinner, at seven o'clock."

WHEN I ARRIVE, Jayne lets me into the parlor through the front door, with the rest of the family closed off in the back of the house. I sit next to Jayne on the sofa. I'm shaking, beads of sweat pooling at my temples, collecting in my eyebrows.

"How can I help you, Kevin?"

"I felt sick. I was sick. I'm okay."

"Why were you sick?"

"I'm okay," I stutter. "I just need help."

"Why were you sick?"

"I had a fever. Hot."

"Okay. You're better now?" Her voice calms me, has always had that effect on me.

"Yes."

"But, Kevin, look at yourself."

I don't understand her words. My eyes flitting to her face, then around the room, then back to her. I lock my gaze on her, unable to respond, helpless to grasp what she wants me to see.

"Are you doing drugs?"

"No." I blurt out the words, repeating what I had said on the phone. "I quit. It's not that. I don't know what's wrong."

"You're shaking, Kevin."

She puts her hand on my arm, a feather touch.

"I'm better. Just the fever. Still cold. Feel cold."

"Kevin, look at how you're breathing."

I suck in air, blow it out hard, in again, out. My eyes go in and out of focus.

"Oh, that's because I quit . . ." gasp, "I quit smoking." My breaths are sharp, deep, held for a second, gasped in the next breath. "This is what happens . . ." gasp, "when you quit smoking . . ." gasp, "you need oxygen . . ." gasp, "more oxygen."

I can't speak, only gasp. I hold each breath, my eyes pleading, distended and staring.

"Kevin, this isn't what happens when you quit smoking."

"It's not?"

I shake my head back and forth, left and right.

"You're sweating."

I wipe my face on my shirt sleeve. "Then what is it?"

Jayne sits back, her hands folded in her lap.

"I don't know, Kevin, but you might be a drug addict and an alcoholic."

I hear the words. I'd heard them before, long before, maybe even from Jayne. Heard them from every social worker, every probation officer, every judge, Father Ralph, the U.S. Navy, my wife. Their words, like in a brownout, always came at a distance, telling me I had a problem, that I needed to stop. This is different. Jayne doesn't say I'm an addict, doesn't say I'm an alcoholic.

She says I might be.

Maybe.

I struggle to focus, my thoughts scattered. "If I am, what do I do?"

"You can go to twelve-step meetings. They have Alcoholics Anonymous meetings, and Narcotics Anonymous, that you could go to."

"Where?"

"I don't know, Kevin. Look it up." She waits while I wipe the sweat and tears from my eyes. She pauses just long enough to let me catch my breath. "If you go to a meeting, you can call me again."

She stands, holding my arm to steady me, and walks me to the door.

"Are the kids here? Can I say hi to Emmett?"

"No."

THERE'S NO LISTING for Narcotics Anonymous in the phone book. I look again, this time for Alcoholics Anonymous. Maybe they'll know where I can find NA. I don't know if I have a problem with drugs, but I know I love them. Drinking is normal, I think, and I never had a problem with that anyway. The Schenectady white pages have a listing for Alcoholics Anonymous.

An old, gruff voice answers on the other end of the line. "Hello."

"Hi. Do you know where Narcotics Anonymous is?"

"What?" The voice snaps back, confused and indignant at the same time.

"Narcotics Anonymous." I try to speak clearly, like talking to my *babcia*. It doesn't help. "Do you know where an NA meeting is?"

"NA? This is AA! We don't know nothing about NA here."

I sit in my bedroom, taking in the space around me that looks like someone else lives here. I feel awkward, like I should be looking for something to steal and leave in a hurry. Michelle has dusted and organized the room, put a small, potted lily on the hanging table I'd gotten in Korea. Everything is clean, and without all the pipes and scales and paraphernalia, there isn't much clutter.

My soul feels as empty and foreign as the room. The quiet surrounds me, makes me want to fill the silence with something, anything. Even screaming would have been better than the sound of that man's snarly voice echoing in my ears.

Giving up feels like an option. Jayne can't fault me. I tried. I did my best to "look it up," for fuck's sake. It isn't my fault the dickhead was an asshole. It isn't my fault NA isn't in the phone book.

Even as the "not my faults" ricochet around my brain, the new serenity of the room calms me, helps the faults fade in intensity, opening up space for other thoughts to sneak in.

The radio at work is always tuned to the classic rock station. Twice a year the station, PYX 106, has a radiothon for a place called Hope House in Albany, and it has something to do with drugs.

"Hope House, how can I help you?"

I feel myself cringe. If this doesn't go well, I'm done, and I know it.

"Hi." My voice weakens, trembles, and I hate myself for it. "Do you know where there's an NA meeting?"

"NA?" The voice sounds chipper, ready to laugh at me. I'm ready to bolt. "Sure! I've got a list here."

THE ONLY MEETING I can make is in Albany on Friday night after work. Anxiety is already building, my head swirling with a million small fragments of fear. The deep winter air is cold and wet, the temperature dropping by the minute. I wipe the sweat off my forehead with the back of my jacket sleeve as I park my car in front of a brick building with a small sign: "St. John's Project Lift."

I think the meeting starts at 7:00, so I walk up the dark steps and open the old wooden door at 7:15. Two guys in the first-floor room are setting out chairs and making coffee. I've written down the wrong start time and arrive at 7:15 for a 7:30 meeting.

Fifteen minutes early, and I'm already shaking, the sweat beading on my forehead, dripping down my back, chilling my skin to a shiver, as I hunch down in a folding chair. It seems like I'm in the center of the room and all the lights are glaring down. The men go about their business now without talking, adding chairs around me, and I can feel them watching me, feel a spotlight on me.

Every sound in the room scratches at my already-raw nerves. As people start to wander in, hugging and greeting each other, laughing and chatting, I can't look up to see the smiles on their faces, can't bear to stay in this place even one more second.

A hand on my shoulder makes me jump in my seat, nearly toppling over, and I look up and see a woman take a half step back and pull her hands away, not threatening. My eyes bulge out of my skull, panic and fear screaming, *RUN!* Somehow, her voice slices through my dread.

"Hi. I'm Janet. How are you?"

Adrenaline shoots through me, roars in my head. The noise in the room recedes. No one has asked me how I am in a long, long time.

"Jayne?!?" I swallow hard but spittle still sprays from my lips. The metal chair rat-tat-tats on the floor in time with my shivering.

"No, I'm Janet."

She reaches out again, slowly puts her hand on my shoulder to steady me.

"Janet." She speaks slowly, with kindness and understanding. "My name is Janet."

I can't comprehend anything, but her hand holds me in my chair. Over the next ninety minutes, my shaking subsides to exhaustion, leaving me too weak to run, too wrung out to think. I don't remember one word that's said.

As I leave the building the wind picks up, and I dash away from the crowd, down the steps to the car, and drive back to the apartment where Michelle meets me at the door. I'm tired, drained, but feel cleansed if not actually clean.

"How was it?" She looks up at me, her curly black hair framing her smile, her eyes pleading and hopeful.

I take a breath, let it out, long and slow. The words come easily, gently sounding out everything I feel inside.

"I think I'm going to be okay."

Michelle lights up like the tiny Christmas tree that's still in the room, dim but present, persistent.

I feed off of her light, find an extra spark of energy. "Let's go shopping."

"Shopping?"

I nod weakly and manage a smile. "I'm hungry."

I take the keys to her Chevette and turn down the long, dark road from our apartment complex. Snow is falling, beginning to stick to the road.

Michelle's animated, chatty, making a list of what we need, some snacks for the night, a late dinner. For the first time I can remember, my mind feels calm. I lean into the steering wheel, my body bouncing in time with the bumps in the road, fidgeting instead of shaking.

"You look happy." She watches me.

"I feel something."

"What?"

"I don't know. Like those people in the meeting."

Michelle waits while I drive slowly on the wet road.

"They were all smiling. Not bullshit smiling, but smiling like they meant it."

"You feel like that now?"

"I don't know what I feel."

"Are you going to go back?"

I nod as the car eases to a stop at a red light. "Michelle, if I could have just five percent of what those people have, I'd be happy for the rest of my life."

We both smile. The light changes to green. As I turn right and pull the car out, we're slammed from behind, snapping our heads back, bouncing the car on the road in front of us.

"Okay, it's okay." I grip the wheel, looking at Michelle. "We're okay now."

Another, bigger hit crashes into us from behind, then another, as a fully loaded eighteen-wheeler tractor trailer plows us down the road.

The driver couldn't stop in the snow and ran the red light, first hitting us square, crushing the hatchback, pushing the back seat forward up to the front seats. Subsequent hits finished off the right back corner, then left rear, as the Chevette spun off the side of the road, and the truck finally slid to a stop, fifty feet down the road.

When it's all over, we lock eyes. We're okay. In shock, but not a scratch.

The car is totaled. I step away from the car, Michelle crying, wiping her tears, talking to the trucker. In a dream I see the car, the truck, police arriving with their lights flashing, the passing drivers rubber-necking, red flares burning, shooting sparks in the snow.

I look up, out over the streetlights. The snowflakes are thick but not heavy, hovering, blowing in my face, making me squint. The snow tickles my eyelashes and my eyelids flutter, and I know that I'm not going to die today. I feel like giggling.

THE HOURS between the NA meetings are interminable. Every second not in a meeting is a moment of insane desperation that only a drink or drugs will relieve. Getting high screams in my head as the perfect, and final, solution.

I know I won't be able to carry my burdens much longer without getting high. To cope, I find my way to the Saturday service at Immaculate Conception Church, where Father Ralph had been the priest when I was at WAITT house. Compared to drinking and drugging, going to confession at the Catholic church seems the most sane thing to do.

I sit through mass, not hearing the sermon, the kneeling, sitting, standing, reciting prayers and responses by rote nudging me with memories, a salve on my mind if not my soul. The sermon is delivered by a visiting priest from Africa who is making his way across the U.S. church circuit. He's young, early thirties, and as we all file out, I slip in at the end of the line.

"Thank you, Father. I really enjoyed your sermon."

"Thank you, my son."

His accent is strong, but his articulation nearly perfect.

"What time is confession?"

"Ah." He looked at the church bulletin. "One o'clock tomorrow."

"One o'clock?" I can wait an hour.

"No, no, no. Tomorrow. Tomorrow at one o'clock."

"Tomorrow?"

He looks at me, sees hope drain from my face. "Why? You cannot wait?"

I shake my head, slowly, painfully. My knees are ready to buckle.

"Okay. Okay." He holds my shoulder, walks me to the doorway. "Wait here."

He steps back to shake the last of the hands, hurries them out the door, and returns to me.

"Come."

I follow him through the doorway, the room where the altar boys change, and close the door.

I know this room. When I was fourteen and living at WAITT House, Father Ralph grounded me, forced me to wait upstairs while the elders met in the basement. I had a girl meet me at the church, and we lay on the floor of this same room. Later that night, I lost my virginity to her in the church's bus parked across the street.

"Kneel here with me."

This is my confessional. No claustrophobic closet with a scrim between us. No hiding my shame in the darkness. I'm literally kneeling in the exact place where I had sinned. High noon with the sunlight streaming in through the curtainless window.

"In the name of the Father, and of the Son, and of the Holy Spirit. Amen."

I start, the words slow and halting at first, then emptying out as if pulled from within me, finding their way to a place where words like these go to die. I talk of drugs and drink and theft. I speak aloud of abortions. The words tumble out for him to hear, for me to hear, for God to hear. I had beaten my wife. I had abandoned my children. I had had sex with men for drugs and money.

The lid opens no more than a crack, but the little I let out spurs me on. As I look at this man's face, seeing only his listening eyes, the door behind me opens. A parishioner stands in the doorway, stopped in her tracks, frozen with wonder at the scene.

"Wait, wait," he says to me and looks up at her. "What is it? You have to use the bathroom?"

Still frozen, she nods.

"Okay, go, go."

He jerks his head toward the bathroom door behind him, off to his right.

"Quickly, now!"

She shuffles in and closes the door, as we kneel face-to-face, this man and I, and the sound of an elderly woman peeing filters through the old wooden door. I hear the flush and hold a smile inside, remembering watching *All in the Family* with my parents, my father's wheezy laugh, my mother scolding him with a smile, and Edith Bunker's cackle, "Archie will be right down."

My confession ends, as confession always does, with his absolution and my penance. As I finish, he pauses, longer than I expect.

"You . . ." he begins, hesitates. "You do not do these things anymore?"

"No, Father."

"Good. You must stop." His accent seems thicker now, his voice soft. He takes a breath, and another. "For your penance, you will go to church every day."

Every day seems completely reasonable to me.

"You will pray every day. Ask God for forgiveness. Tell him your troubles. Do you know how to pray your act of contrition?

"Yes, Father."

"Pray every day."

We pray the Lord's Prayer, and he rests his hand on my head to bless me. Together we walk out of the room; he stops and hugs me goodbye, and I thank him again.

As I leave the building, my feet never touch the steps.

I'VE FORGOTTEN how good it feels to not throw up my meals. My body slowly stabilizes, my weight inching up from 125 to 130, 135, 140. Obsession lessens day by day, but the compulsions, especially the physical cravings, only relinquish their grip on my body in manic ebbs and flows.

Food helps curb the insanity, sugar more than anything. My favorite is the cinnamon buns in the vending machine at work. The massive sugar and carb fix, combined with Mountain Dew, makes a fine afternoon-break snack.

The physical changes mask a mental dysphoria. Every free moment, however brief, fills with new fears and old memories long repressed. Constant diversion is the only way to keep them at bay.

A desire to look and sound more like the healthy people I now see leads me to an open registration day at Schenectady County Community College. The admissions officer is shocked when I shake and stutter at her suggestion of a three-credit course, but a look of kindness quickly replaces the concern. I opt for a non-credit writing skills class, primarily intended for those with English as a second language.

Gaining weight and being seen among respectable people forces me to buy new clothes, and I find myself in a foreign environment—for the first time in years, I go to the mall. A placard outside a storefront stops me in my tracks, advertising "Free Dental Exam and X-Ray." Another sign inside the door urges me forward for a "Free Orthodontic Consultation." It's weird but, with my entire life shifting and veering in new and unfamiliar directions, a dentist in a mall seems completely normal.

I freeze and stare at the signs, forgetting about my need for new jeans. My parents had tried to get me braces when I was fourteen, but I'd refused, and as a result I've rarely laughed or smiled in public without covering my mouth. I haven't brushed my teeth in years.

I HAVE SIXTEEN CAVITIES and cringe in shame while they review the results. The x-ray tech, maybe thinking he's being helpful, smiles and calls them canine teeth. I can't stop the tears and barely hear their recommended plan for fixing my mouth.

The dentist throws the tech out with a sour glance and speaks in supportive, gentle, short sentences. But it's his hygienist who mesmerizes me and brings me back to the chair week after week. Red hair, blue eyes, pale skin. She's the most beautiful girl I've ever been this close to.

Each week, after the shots of Novocain, she sits and talks with me, telling me about her day, what she had for lunch, what movies she wants to see. She asks about my work, my college class, how I like the school and the teacher. I slowly begin to forget the fear of pain. The dentist pulls four teeth as prep for the braces, taking care of five cavities, and drills and fills eleven more cavities. I have no idea I'm infatuated.

It takes weeks for my gums to stop bleeding every time I brush them. More than a month after I first walk into the mall, the braces go on, giving me a shiny new smile.

The cinnamon buns are both a short-term fix for my now gradually receding cravings, as well as a compelling reason to brush and floss. The many trips to the vending machine also weigh down my pockets with several dollars' worth of nickels, dimes, and quarters, which I dump onto my dresser every weeknight.

Work at the warehouse and NA meetings fill my nights, with school, church, and AA meetings structuring the weekdays. I find a part-time job on Saturday afternoons washing dishes at a local restaurant. With my dental work in progress, I need a new activity to fill my free time.

A rack in a gas station advertises classes and events in the area, titles like "Learn to Paint" and "Photography for Beginners." Nothing jumps out at me on first read-through, but I recognize that I don't need a hobby like "Learning to Knit." I need a reward to strive for, a pot of gold at the end of the rainbow.

One big-ticket item is priced at 250 dollars, buried on the last page. I flip through the brochure repeatedly, always coming back to that same page, and finally give in to the temptation. I circle the title, tear the page out, and prop it up on my dresser.

Life Is an Adventure
Learn to Skydive

"Have you jumped before?"

"No, first time."

"So you're the static line jumper?"

"Yes."

"You're on your own up there, you realize that?"

I nod.

"Okay. Let's do this!"

He takes me for a quick walk around the facility before we start our training in the barn. The instructions are serious and terse, always preceded by a demonstration, followed by hands-on practice.

"The chute is packed by me, not you, so you don't have to worry about it. The static line is what pulls your chute. You have an emergency chute, and if the main chute doesn't open, then you'll be on your own to pull the auxiliary chute. You don't open it, you die. Got it?"

"Yes, sir."

"Body position is important. You do it right, you'll be fine. You don't get it right, you could get hurt. You're not doing a freefall today, but if the static line doesn't open the chute, you'll be in a freefall, and body position will save you or kill you."

I lie down flat on my belly on a wood plank bolted to two posts.

"Point toes.

"Feet parallel.

"Thighs above your pelvis. Higher!

"Arms at your ears.

"Don't arch at all. Don't do it."

After lunch, I put on a jumpsuit, snug the straps tight to my groin, and slap the rig onto my back so I can get the feel of the weight. We walk to a plane parked in the barn, not the exact one we'll use, but close enough.

"This is the most important part to practice."

We crawl in and he kneels by the open door where I'll jump out of the plane.

"When we get up to 4,500 feet, I'll call you over." He stabs his finger toward my face. "You can't hesitate. You hesitate, you don't jump. You do exactly what I say, you jump. Got it?"

I nod and give him a thumbs-up.

"I'll call you over, 'Ready Barhydt!' You'll hear me say three things after I call you over, and it's all about timing: 'Feet out! Get out! Go!' Say it back to me."

"Feet out. Get out. Go."

"Right. When I say feet out, you grab this handle here, and put both feet on the step right outside the door."

He points to a handle attached to the outside of the plane, and the step that we used to get up inside. With my feet on the step, I'm sitting with my body in the plane, my legs and feet out.

"When I say get out, you keep your left foot on the step, hang on to the handle with your left hand, and reach out and grab the strut here with your right hand."

"My right leg just hangs free?"

"Right. You got it. Ready to practice?"

I slide back into the plane with a nod.

"Ready Barhydt!"

I crawl up next to him at the door opening.

"Feet out!"

I put both feet on the step and grab the handle.

"Get out!"

I balance on my left foot, reach out and grab the strut.

"Good. When you hear me say 'go,' you let go with your left hand, push off with your left foot and right hand, and don't look down."

"Why not?"

"When that chute opens, you're going to get whipped around. You need to have your head up," he poses with his head cocked back, looking upwards, "otherwise your head will snap back, and you'll get whiplash."

Still hanging out the door, I cock my head back.

"Right. Good. Now climb back in." I sit next to him in the plane. "When you're there, in that position, head back, I'll yell 'go,' and you push off and let go. We can't do it now on the ground, but you got it?"

"Yes."

"Good. Let's run it again."

We repeat each step until the process becomes muscle memory. He stands outside the plane, and I sit back on the edge of the plane, my feet hanging out.

"Once you're out of the plane and the chute opens, you're not on your own. You've got a radio in each arm." He shoves the small rectangular units into my shoulder pockets. "I'll be talking to you all the way down."

We spend the rest of the afternoon going over everything again. Then again, and again. We end the day sitting on a picnic table, watching the last of the tandem jumpers land, all of them executing the tuck and roll that I've learned.

"Tomorrow, when you arrive in the morning, you check in with me first. After you gear up and board the plane, it'll take about five or ten minutes for the plane to reach altitude for your jump, around 4,500 feet.

"When I call your name, you need to be ready. The door will be open, and we only have a minute to get you out and for your chute to open.

"After you're out, and your main canopy opens, it's up to you to navigate. I'll be in your ear the whole time on the radio, but I can't pull the toggles for you. If anything goes wrong, I can't pull the ripcord for you. You have to do it.

"Once you're on the ground we'll debrief, and you get your jump certificate, and you're done.

"Got it?"

I get it. I want to go up right now. I don't want to wait a day, or even an hour, but sleeping on it will make the jump that much sweeter. I reflect that waiting a day will also make for an interesting gravestone:

Kevin Barhydt
Born June 27, 1962
Died June 28, 1986

SATURDAY IS ANOTHER PERFECT, warm day, same easy morning breeze, same blue sky with hardly a puff of clouds, the air so crisp and clean you can see for miles. On the drive out, it feels like this all could have been my imagination, that yesterday never happened, was all in my head, as if I daydreamed the whole thing.

My instructor meets me at the barn.

"There might be some mild gusts, but the winds are looking to be around five miles per hour. Perfect."

I suit up and wait with the other jumpers. Most did their tandems yesterday and loved it so much they have come back for more of the same. I'm excited too.

My instructor takes me into the barn alone, and we run through the order of events, then sit together in the shade, drinking water and keeping cool in our gear.

When the call comes, he slaps me on the back and follows me to the plane. The engine is already running on the Cessna 182 when we climb in and move to the back and side of the plane. It has no seats, so I sit on the floor, leaning against the wall, my instructor crouching next to me.

"Enjoy the ride," he shouts as we take off. "We'll be ready in about five minutes. Hang on tight."

If I'd thought about what came next, if I'd had any idea how hard it would be to get sober, to see myself without the scrim of denial and self-hate, I'd never have had the courage to make that New Year's resolution. I've learned, at least, that to fearlessly look back I need to spend every shred of hope I can muster on keeping my mind, body, and soul in the very moment, every moment, that I find myself.

For six months, I haven't let one moment of doubt creep in. Every day I've focused on one more cinnamon bun, one more meeting, one more day out from the day before. I don't think about what might come next. It's all I can do to just hang on by my fingernails and not slide backward.

"Ready Barhydt!

"Feet out!

"Get out!

"Go!"

ACKNOWLEDGMENTS

Thank you, Mom. And thank you again, Mom. Without you both, this book, and I, would never have been possible. Kevin loves you. Stephen loves you. My gratitude is without parallel.

James, my brother, I am you, and you are me. I never knew when I cried as a child that I was longing to hear your voice saying "It's going to be okay, bro. I've got you. I'm here." If I had dreamt of a brother like you, I would never have wanted to wake.

Julie, my sister, without you there would be no memory of mom's love for me. Of the millions of memories you and I will make together, the perfect memory will always be of your voice screaming in my ear, "Oh my God! Are you my brother?!?" Yes. Yes, I am.

John, my brother, we two are the elders. Yet, each day I'm grateful for my place as simply one of four. We are family. You have accepted and loved me as only an elder brother would know. I have, and will continue, to learn from you, and with you.

Kyung, my sister, your sweet voice was the first I ever heard of our family. Your place in this story is important. Your place in my heart is vital, and permanent.

Jesse, Paige, Breandan, and Peggy, you are just spectacular. You have made me into Uncle Kevin. With you in my life I am more than I ever imagined.

Eri, to express my thanks for your support throughout this journey I would need to write another book. I am in awe of the vast love you have for our family; I am so proud that my most consistent title is "Eri's husband." You are my complete inspiration, my stunning soulmate, my forever partner in this world, and after.

Dawn, I've always known that my love for you is as perfect as I am imperfect. When you were born, I became a father. My only solace as your father is that you have always loved me for who I would become as a man.

Sera, we have a forever between us that time cannot erase, and no life storm can destroy. You're my JoJo, and I'm your BoBo. Nothing will ever change that.

Kentaro, I aspired as a man to be the best dad I could to you. Now that you are older you are a model of my aspirations for the man I want to become.

Tyler, I always knew as your father that you would only be guided by inspiration. You lifted me to be the most inspiring dad I could be, and now you have become my inspiration.

Richard, you are always right behind me and by my side. I know that you will always be right behind me and by my side. I thank God for you. We did this. We really did this.

Jim Hetland, there are few people that I trust as deeply as I have you, and even fewer men. I share no thanks here except to say, "Let us stay here together as long as we can, my friend, and let that be our eternal gift to one another." To you and Lea, however, I must convey directly, I would not be here at all had it not been for you. For that I, and my family, give you our profound gratitude.

To my Saint Anne Heffron, sister from before and forever, I cherish us, and I am in awe of our friendship and the road we travel together.

To Arlene Lev, my thanks to you is deserving of a full chapter. I thank you in the memory of the beautiful young man we loved so much. I am eternally grateful for your words, kindness, and full commitment to this lifelong mystery we call friendship.

To Omar Hassib, Liana Nunziato, Lai Wa Wong, Jahicol Baralt and Darnesjia Buford-Creighton. As students you were exceptional. As apprentices you are peerless. As my friend, I thank you from the absolute bottom of my soul. You have blessed me more than you will ever know.

To my courageous readers, you braved where many dare not go, and for that I will always count you as wonderful co-conspirators in this project of mine. A very special thanks to Chi-Ling Moy, John Birchler, Rob Austin, Julie Hetland, Martin Egan, Martha Bondinello, Michael Turner, Kewan Harrison, Hal Sossner, and Linda Franklin.

There are a few people that have left their mark on the production of this book. Thank you, Rachel Brune, for your guidance, organizational skills, and pure patience with me. As a writing coach, well, let's just say you killed it. Thank you, Ginny Ruths, my wonderful editor. It is impossible for me to ever believe that Betty Ann would not have loved, and have as much gratitude for you, as I do. Thank you, Susan VanOmmeren, my final-final proofreader extraordinaire. You are simply the best icing on the cake a writer like me could ask for. Thank you, Doug Bartow, my book cover designer, for making my dreams come true. Your magnificent creative talents accepted my artifacts, some old, dusty images, and created something new, yet immortal.

To my tribe: Vince Akins, Matt, Joe Wolfe, George Martin, Mike, Damien, Stephen Honicki, David, Tom, Jac, Pete, Jon, Tom Lukacs, Jermaine Wells, Dave (work wife) Sindoni, Ping, Shige and Mai, Bryant, Helen Lee, Bernie Gerstner, Jayne McCarthy, Connie Ostrowski, Christina Harrington Stutzman, and Stephen Adly Guurgis.

MORE FROM KEVIN BARHYDT

Visit Kevin at www.kevinbarhydt.com for:
- Free multimedia materials
- Blog posts
- Resources related to adoption, child sexual abuse, addiction and recovery
- Events schedule
- And more!

Follow Kevin on social media at:
YouTube: https://www.youtube.com/c/KevinBarhydt
Twitter: https://twitter.com/kevinbarhydt
Facebook: https://www.facebook.com/kevinbarhydtofficial
LinkedIn: https://www.linkedin.com/in/kevinbarhydtofficial/
Instagram: https://www.instagram.com/kevinbarhydt/

Thank you so much for going on this journey with me. I would love to know your thoughts. Reviews are always appreciated, on Goodreads and/or Amazon!

Made in the USA
Middletown, DE
14 July 2021